**HYWEL WILLIAMS** is a historian, journalist and broadcaster, author of the classic account of British politics in the 1990s, *Guilty Men: Conservative Decline and Fall, 1992–7* and *Cassell's Chronology of World History*, described by the *Guardian* as 'staggeringly clever' and praised by the *Times Literary Supplement* for its 'brilliance – confidence and elegance.' His history of modern Wales, *A Promised Land?* was broadcast on ITV Wales in 2004 and he has been elected an Honorary Fellow of the University of Wales, Bangor.

# BRITAIN'S POWER ELITES

The Rebirth of a Ruling Class

HYWEL WILLIAMS

CONSTABLE • LONDON

I'r Arglwydd Roberts o Gonwy

For Lord Roberts of Conwy

Constable & Robinson Ltd
3 The Lanchesters
162 Fulham Palace Road
London W6 9ER
www.constablerobinson.com

First published in the UK by Constable,
an imprint of Constable & Robinson Ltd, 2006

A copy of the British Library Cataloguing in Publication Data
is available from the British Library.

ISBN 13: 978-1-84529-169-3
ISBN 10: 1–84529–169–7

Printed and bound in the EU

1 3 5 7 9 10 8 6 4 2

# Contents

# Acknowledgements

Dan Hind, as editorial director of Constable and Robinson, suggested that I should write this book as an extended account of a topic discussed in some of my commentaries published in the *Guardian*. I am grateful to him not only for that suggestion but also for the insight and enthusiasm he brought to the work of commenting on the work's earlier drafts. Barbara Docherty, at a later stage, copy-edited the book with a knowledgeable and efficient panache. I am also grateful to Hannah Boursnell, Claudia Dyer and to all those at Constable and Robinson whose attention to the details of the text ensured the book's publication.

For clarification and advice on various particular questions of fact and of interpretation I am indebted to: John Adamson, Anne Applebaum, Tim Devlin, Clare Dyer, the late Paul Foot (especially for his work on the Private Finance Initiative), Richard Griffiths, Tony Howard, Robert Jackson, John Jungclaussen, Cristina Odone, Peter Oborne, James Vallance White, Andrew Roberts, Simon Sebag Montefiore, Robert Service, Guglielmo Verdirame, Alan Watkins and Francis Wheen. I am also grateful to the QC whom I interviewed and whose wish for anonymity I have respected.

David Ruffley MP guided me in my understanding of the role of the hedge funds in the modern British economy and the book in general owes much to the stimulation I have derived from our many conversations on the historical, political and cultural questions which are discussed in this work.

I owe a further debt of gratitude to Catherine Bailey, Robert Caskie, John Harrison, Alastair and Sue Hutchinson, Laura Sandys and John Underwood who all, in their various ways, encouraged me while writing this book.

# ACKNOWLEDGEMENTS

The dedication to Wyn Roberts records an affectionate regard for one who has retained his independence of mind while walking cautiously among the power elites. Lastly, this book could not have been written without the enthusiasm and advice both of my agent Georgina Capel and of my ever-supportive and tolerant family.

*At the centers of public decision there are powerful men who do not themselves suffer the violent results of their own decisions. In a world of big organizations the lines between powerful decision and grass-root democratic controls become blurred and tenuous, and seemingly irresponsible actions by individuals at the top are encouraged. The need for action prompts them to take decisions into their own hands, while the fact that they act as parts of large corporations or other organizations blurs the identification of personal responsibility. Their public views and political actions are, in this objective meaning of the word, irresponsible: the social corollary of their irresponsibility is the fact that others are dependent on them and must suffer the consequences of their ignorance and mistakes, their self-deceptions, and their biased motives . . .*

*Never before have so few men made such fateful decisions for so many people who themselves are helpless.*

C. Wright Mills, 'The Powerless People: The Role of the Intellectual in Society', *Politics*, 1(3), April 1944.

# Preface

This is a book without heroes for it deals with the degradation and subjection of a country. But behind it there stands a thinker of heroic stature. In his comparatively short life C. Wright Mills (1916–62) became celebrated as one of the most prophetic voices of his time among those who wished to understand the nature of modern life lived in western democracies and especially the forms of life evident in those societies' influential inhabitants – the politicians and administrators, lawyers and professionals, financiers and businessmen, trade unionists and generals, as well as the celebrities, broadcasters, commentators and writers of various hue who are thrown up by the demands of the times. Much of Mills' writing and investigation was about the nature of the power that was being exercised and the quality of the new kind of people who were predominant in the USA during the years after the Second World War. But the fact that the USA had by then become the prototypical modern democracy meant that his voice acquired a global resonance. His urgent conclusions are now more relevant than ever before when we consider the spectacle of British and European governments in the early twenty-first century – those systems of power in which the consent of the people is massaged, where the national will is little more than manipulated pseudo-morale and where government is something that happens by default in the absence of a populace which has grown indifferent. *Britain's Power Elites* is a book much influenced by Mills' masterpiece *The Power Elite* (New York: Oxford University Press, 1956), and it therefore seems appropriate to explain why that should be so.

A more conservative American writer on power, Edward Shils (1910–95), thought that Mills was 'a rough-tongued brawler', but it was that maverick status which gave this son of Texas his edge. He was born into a Catholic family and grew up in Sherman, Fort Worth and Dallas. The fact of being reared in a minority church in an overwhelmingly Protestant state may have been his first education in the experience of being the odd man out. But his own family history also taught Mills that something deep, strange and disturbing had happened to America in the twentieth century. His maternal grandfather, Braxton Bragg Wright, had been a Texan cattle-rancher and, after being killed in a gunfight on his ranch, had attained something of a mythic family status as the rugged loner making his way in the world and extracting meaning as well as a livelihood out of the native soil. The young Mills contrasted that glorious past with his own father's life and career as an insurance agent, and concluded that the generational shift of existence from the noble solitude of the farm to the enclosed coercion of the office was just one illustration of something that had happened on a more general scale in the recent history of the USA as well as in other advanced industrialized societies. Big government and big business – the monopolies of power operating in the corporations and the finance houses, in government bureaucracies and in political parties as well as in the professions and some forms of intellectual life – were crushing the American tradition of radical and nonconforming dissent. Mills' life work would be the examination of how and why this had happened, and he brought to it an entirely original flair as well as the ability to look far into the horizon of his subject in something of the spirit of a spectator of those vast expanses of the Texan landscape he had known so well as a child.

Anyone who disturbed quite as many people as Mills did must have been getting something right. Although most of his career was spent teaching at the University of Columbia in New York City he had a healthy contempt for metropolitan values, suspecting them of being merely shallow and self-interested while masquerading as sophistication and expertise. He was an atypical figure within the academic grove, disliking a sterile pride which turned its back on the world as well as being mistrustful of narrow professionalism in any area of life. His ambition instead, he said, was to be 'a good craftsman' and one who would 'avoid any rigid set of procedures' (*The Sociological Imagination*, New York: Oxford University Press, 1959, p. 224), while he set about the job of employing his mind and dirtying his hands in the awkward and necessary task of showing how the dominant ideas, people and institutions of his time operated at a practical level.

*The Power Elite* exhilarated because it was the first time any writer had shown how that elite had been allowed to establish its hegemony in the USA of the Eisenhower era. It was also offensive to the New Deal liberals since it considered F.D. Roosevelt's achievement to be little more than an entrenchment of corporate capitalism beneath the facade of a liberal grin. The book's most disturbing aspect was that it showed how the machinery of government had become geared to the waging of near-continuous war, either cold or hot, with business and government colluding to mutually assured benefit. This proved to be a lesson accepted in the highest and most surprising of quarters when President Eisenhower, in his farewell address to the American people on 17 January 1961, said: 'We must guard against the acquisition of unwarranted influence, whether sought or unsought, by the military-industrial complex. The potential for the disastrous rise of misplaced power exists and will persist' (Dwight D. Eisenhower, *Public Papers 1960–61*, Washington, DC: USGPO, 1961, pp. 657–8).

Mills the social craftsman thought therefore that something shoddy had happened in America and that the country's history had become a process which was going on behind the people's backs. It was his job to sound the alarm about how power had become something hidden, manipulative and anonymous, affecting the lives of the people in ways they neither knew nor understood. There was much romanticism in Mills' reversion to the position of the defiant Puritan idealist of an older American tradition, preaching the truth at a generation grown decadent, but at the basis of his analysis there were hard facts and cold observation. He showed how the members of the power elite, wherever they were to be found in their different jobs and offices, homes and clubs right across the USA, were increasingly similar to each other in their views and tastes, in their education, beliefs and aspirations. They lived the same kind of lives and they thought much the same kind of thoughts. And the result of their rule was that:

> Men of decision enforce their often crackpot decisions upon world reality. The second-rate mind is in command of the ponderously spoken platitude. In the liberal rhetoric, vagueness, and in the conservative mood, irrationality, are raised to principle. Public relations and the official secret, the trivializing campaign and the terrible fact clumsily accomplished, are replacing reasoned debate of political ideas in the privately incorporated economy, the military ascendancy, and the political vacuum of modern America (*The Power Elite*, pp. 360–1).

# PREFACE

In the pages that follow I have tried to show how Britain's power elites have in some cases merely survived, in other cases declined and in yet others advanced and consolidated their power within the political vacuum, the martial jostling for position and the privatized economy of modern Britain. I share Mills' dislike of a narrowly professional spirit which is a mere comfort zone for the unenquiring mind. I have therefore tried to emulate his practice of the good craftsman who can make the connections work and fit the elements together in the creation of an object – in this case, a book – which may be found useful. Consequently, I hope that *Britain's Power Elites* may open eyes and alert minds in its discussion of what has happened, and is continuing to take place, in our country. If, like Mills, I manage to cause offence right across the political spectrum of received opinion, then I will regard that as work well done. My book has more history in it than did Mills' because Britain is an old, complex and fundamentally mysterious place. The nature of elite power in such a society must therefore be traced back to its roots with eyes still firmly set on the contemporary scene in order to appreciate the astonishing nature of the revolution which has been accomplished and the depth of the chasm which now separates Britain from any period in its history. Mills was undoubtedly starry-eyed about America's past and provided too innocent a contrast between the individualism of the old land and the managerialism of the new. I do not offer any such consolations of an Arcadian escape route which might be taken into British history in order to avoid, and reproach, the present. I merely seek to show the scale of the difference between now and then. The theme is an epic one and I have tried to do it justice, but although there is much that is rapacious, cynical, murderous, nasty and brutal in the tale that follows, I hope that the abundance of satirical material which is basic to the story will also make its sardonic presence felt.

*Chapter 1*

# Elite Power: Idea and Reality

## Creation of an Elite Narrative

Both as an ideal and as a reality, elite power has a long, distinguished and combative history. The elite group of the chosen few, of those who are either born to rule or selected by themselves and by others for the purpose of administering and influencing the lives of the many, has inspired and infuriated in equal measure. Elite members have produced explanations that justify their existence as lives lived on the inside track of access and influence. And theorists of power, wishing to join the elite circle, have drawn on their knowledge of people and events in order to portray and dignify that same group. Meanwhile, on the imagined peripheries of power and far from the self-congratulatory delights of elite existence, there are those whose imaginations have been infuriated by resentment at the thought of an elite at work and at play. Radicals have decried the established elites' monopoly of power while conservatives relegated to the margins have been frustrated by the new elites whose avid pursuit of connection and influence, of money and power, overturns the once-settled conventions. For all the members of these groups the notion of an 'elite' is basic to their lives, careers and rhetoric. Whether by self-identification, by affirmation, or by alienation, they need the power elite to exist since it is that elite which supplies the standard by which success and failure, scandal and outrage, ambition and ideals are to be measured.[1]

Right across the western developed world in the early twenty-first century the language and the vocabulary of elites has replaced the language of class. The fall of the Berlin Wall in 1989 saw the end of Europe's 'short twentieth century', and it also meant the disappearance of old solidarities on both left and right. Both Marxism and capitalism had supplied their adherents and their adversaries alike

1

with a grand narrative, a purposive scheme which explained the past and gave a guide to the present. And, as is often the case with such overarching narratives, the aim was to console as well as to explain. Once provided with a structure to which they assented, the adherents of the two systems could relax safe in the knowledge that socio-economic function ruled the world. Like the readers absorbed in a great novel, or the theatre-goers taken over by the illusion of the stage, they themselves became the characters in the dramatic narrative which unfolded before them as they identified with either the claims of labour or those of capital.

This is why the twentieth century was the great age of collective solidarity and of the mass-consciousness which had succeeded the earlier nineteenth-century cult of liberal individualism. That preceding period had witnessed a great push for those reforms of the franchise systems which would extend the vote to the majority of the male populations in the new western democracies. Campaigns for a more equitable system of land distribution and ownership, for a reform of the tithe, and then the imposition of taxation on land-holdings, led to the break-up of great aristocratic estates. Meanwhile, in commercial life, the removal of old systems of protectionist economics in the name of 'free trade' promoted the exchange and distribution of manufactured goods and foodstuffs. It also advanced the interests of a commercial class impatient of the old aristocratic paternalism which had run the machinery of government and skewed the economic system in its own favour. The free traders and political reformers who agitated and won those battles certainly thought, acted and campaigned as groups who came together to campaign and agitate. But the rhetoric which brought them together was that of the individual who, once freed from the shackles of anti-competitive restraints, would then flourish and regenerate the social, economic and political world.

Behind all the campaigning, therefore, there was a high moral claim about the dignity of the individual, the worth of work and the ability of individual agents to redeem themselves by the light of their own energetic self-interest. Unsurprisingly, the intellectual scene posited a quite uncomplicated picture of how to change the world. The force for reform had seen what was wrong and, having shown the way to progress, it demanded the individual mind's enlightenment.[2] Mind and its thoughts, its agendas and purposes, its manifestos and language, was really its own place. And its power was meant to be such that it could transcend its own immediate environment, see further, dream a dream and then awake to the discovery that it could be realized.

But the political parties and the trade unions of the period which has just ended were the result of an entirely different kind of picture of how the world worked. Ushered in by the spread of heavy industrialization in the Europe of the 1880s – and then gaining in strength and popularity through the spread of industrial discontent and the strikes of organized labour – the new world picture showed how consciousness, far from shaping society, was actually the result of society and its workings. The old world view of nineteenth-century liberalism was stood on its head. And as a result thought, far from being free, was shown to be both the result and the reflection of how people lived their lives.

## Rise of the Corporation

The waning of nineteenth-century individualism was also evident in that key event in the history of twentieth-century business – the rise of the corporation. Cold War rhetoric inflamed minds and kindled debate by opposing collectivism to individualism. But all that noise obscured a deeper story of power – the steady economic and intellectual advance of the corporation to a point at which even the state itself could, in many of its workings, be seen as one of the corporation's many subaltern institutions. The history of the twentieth-century university, for example, has been largely a story of its increasing exposure to that same corporate power. Those who ran these corporate institutions, companies and businesses acquired authority, status and well-paid recognition. But these honours arrived at a certain cost. The corporate elites were not, and are not, a body of autonomous individuals who have substance in their own right, as one might find existing within an aristocratic system or a merely plutocratic one. High rank in a corporation certainly confers elite status, but most of the managers depend on that high rank in order to retain their elite membership cards. There has been, however, one highly significant British exception to this steady tidal drift, since individualism of a very high order is still found in the City of London. Here there are very large private fortunes, a significant number run their own companies and the balance of power between 'star' employees and the companies they work for differs from that which obtains within most corporations. These employees' independence is derived partly from the fact

3

that they have become rich in their own right. But their mobility is also an important fact in establishing and maintaining their individualism. They can conduct their business, however nefarious, anywhere that has a broadband connection.

## Group-Identification

Marxism was the most eminent intellectual subverter of the old liberal innocence that it was easy to change the world just by having a thought independent of circumstances and then implementing it.[3] But the new attention to the interest groups formed by income, class and function was not just a 'left-wing' phenomenon. The rise of European Catholic political parties and also of peasant parties in central Europe, of groupings which pursued the idea of a lay and anti-clerical state (especially in France), the popularity of fascist parties which idealized the notion of cultural roots and a sense of belonging – especially among the survivors of the trenches who hankered after the lost solidarities of army life: all show the popularity of that associative impulse which encouraged group-identification.[4]

The mass immigration of southern Europeans into the big cities of the USA also meant the importation of the old collectivist traditions of the village and the small town – traditions which were associated with dependence on the guidance of the priest. And this in turn encouraged the spread of a reaction – especially in New England where the old values of the introspectively individualist, Bible-guided, Protestant farmer were seen to be under threat. So was born the idea of the 'quiet American' and the packaging for political purposes of that myth of rural virtue which had once created a country, and which now considered itself imperilled.[5] That Arcadianism shaped the politics of the rural interest in the USA. But it also played a powerful role in the politics of what for many was still the mother country. In England the Conservative Party of the early twentieth-century found it difficult to break free from its protectionist past and engaged in a long and costly struggle[6] between those who were attached to the free trade truths of economic liberalism, and those who wanted to protect the landed interests of farmers not just at home but in the empire as well. Cheap food was the economic aim – but this Conservatism of nostalgia also encouraged a particular picture of what counted for English virtue: that ancestral wisdom which was bred out of the soil and was sustained by the rural life whose organic rhythms were the key to the mystery and the glory of the stubborn continuity of English institutions. Baldwin, the former iron-master, and Tolkien, the professor of Anglo-Saxon, were the two most influential rhetoricians of this school – the Prime Minister achieving for his Tory Party and the novelist achieving for his readers an effective packaging of mass-association dreams which deflected attention from the realities of economic dislocation and social crisis.[7]

## Elite Knowledge

All of these groups, social classes, unions, syndicalist organizations, churches, clubs, fabricators of literary myths, organizers of petitions, agitators, reformers, anarchists and politicians, produced their own elite organizations and elite members. The leaders proclaimed the virtue of a common solidarity and the need for mass-action in order to achieve the goals common to the self-interest of all group members. But the practicalities of power created groups who were propelled by their own energy and ambition, by luck and circumstances, beyond the immediate circumstances of the masses in whose name they acted, wrote and agitated. The twentieth-century's most famous example of this dynamic is Lenin and his Bolsheviks, who developed a particular theory of the leadership's advanced consciousness in the professed service of a mass-solidarity.[8] The Leninist model of the political party was avowedly elitist since it consisted only of those who were dedicated to full-time revolutionary action. Its novelty in secular politics lay in its opposition to the idea of a political group or party as a broad-based coalition whose members and leaders could drop in and out of phases of more or less enthused participation. That had been the pattern of political parties as they had evolved in Europe by the early twentieth century. The Bolshevik system, by contrast, coincided with and was itself part of an even wider development: the arrival of the full-time professional and salaried politician in industrialized societies. It was that development which led to the emergence of political elites in their managerial form. Such professionals would be the mainstay of the system of bureaucracies that evolved in the years after the end of the Second World War in order to run the new welfarist systems which attempted to create social consensus through a collectivist social security.

Addiction to bullets and a taste for conspiracies divided the Bolshevik mind from the desk-bound managerialist of the post-1945 settlement. Nonetheless, both shared a common dedication to the political organization in which they had risen and found an occupation as elite members. The esprit de corps of each elite was founded on the knowledge which was shared by that group. What espionage and the instruments of terror were to the Marxist–Leninist, form-filling and taxation were to the political managers. Both of these techniques provided the means by which each elite could discover what was going on in their own societies, proclaim an authoritative insight into what might be about to happen and so decide what should be done now. Knowledge, often regarded as 'scientific' and objective, was the key to the influence and prestige of the elites thrown up by the age of mass-engagement.

But the nature of elite knowledge went beyond intelligent measurement of the data. It also had an important psychological function to play in the formation of an elite self-confidence. Groups who exercise power and who wish to justify their privileged separation from the rest of society need to create an aura of invincibility to surround their every action. The mistakes that they necessarily make have to be explained away in the name of a purpose which is hidden to the uninitiated.

This is a persistent theme in the history of elites, of their grab for power and their success in holding on to it. It links the history of power elites with the history of elite activity in fashion, design and artistic styles. The history of taste is the history of various strategies in marketing and publicity as the vogue for one brand of taste supplants another before being in its turn replaced by another style which has more powerful adherents and supporters. To this extent the history of what counts as 'fashionable' and 'desirable' as a commodity is no different from the history of systems of power, along with all those different accounts which are written in order to justify the exercise of such power. Both these kinds of history reflect the desire to appear to be in the know as well as the aspiration to be a member of an avant-garde which has a privileged access to the Zeitgeist. Both are the product of that nexus of power and influence which varies with the shifting hegemonies of the times.

But power elites have more to prove than do the elites of fashion. They need to convince, against the odds and against the evidence of history, that their kind of knowledge really is reliable and designed to last. Plato's notion of the philosopher-king is western history's most rigorous elite theory and its intellectualist attractions recur in the course of that history. Platonic anger and passion opposed the messy

6

subjectivism and dishonesty of democratic power-politics and regarded it as a sordid game which appealed to cruel and debased
gut-instincts. Its own ideal was that of an objective truth whose beauty
compelled both the assent and the service of those trained to follow its
dictates. When elite justifications start to press into service the idea of
a meritocracy, of those who rule because they are cleverer, Plato's
anti-democratic shade is usually to be found hovering in the background. The meritocratic elite, whether found in civilian or in military
life, in the conduct of commercial business or of public policy, elevates
a certain idea of rationality and equates it with reason itself. Opposition to its rule and its particular idea of order then becomes tanta-
mount to a declaration of war against reason itself, after which the
insurrectionary threat of mob rule is supposed to lurk just round the
corner. The attraction of the meritocracy with a Platonic pedigree,
however, is that it promises to govern in the light of objective truths,
qualities which are thought to correspond to the very structure of the
universe itself. Modern democratic societies are therefore taught to
regard themselves as being intrinsically unstable. Consequently, they
are supposed to require the guiding hand of the enlightened and the
superior who can govern according to the dictates of a wisdom which
is genuinely disinterested – and the numbers who can grasp that
wisdom are limited. It is the secrecy of that wisdom, and the clandes-
tine nature of the groups who control it, which entice and guarantee
the self-confidence which is such a distinguishing public mark of elite
facades.

The fear and the control that motivates the elite hierarchy, and its
august guardianship of a secret wisdom, is older even than Plato's
fourth-century BC formulation. In one sense, the history of elites is the
history of civilization itself and starts with the invention of a scribal
authority in the civilizations of the Middle East in the Mesopotamia of
the third millennium BC.[9] Once settlement starts and nomadic existence yields to the civic existence of palaces and temples, records
begin to be kept – both secular and sacred. The world's first elites were
the scribes who guarded those records and who interpreted them in
order to keep order on behalf of the authority of a sacred kingship.
The rulers first of the Sumerian city states and then of the Babylonian
dynasties and empires which succeeded them claimed to be legitimate
because they had the gods of their time with them. Liver divination,
the details of astrological science, the details of temple worship were
all forms of a sacred knowledge, a theology to be proclaimed by the

few and on behalf of the many who were controlled by it. It was an essential part of this elite knowledge that it conflated the secular with the sacred, the process of tax-collection with the performance of liturgy. To question the order was to declare a heretical form of treason, a rejection of the gods as well as of the ruler who, through his scribal–priestly intermediaries, governed in the name of those gods.

## Sacred Elites

The persistence, until very recent times, of a religious elite in the history of the West is a dominating, and complicating, feature of elite activity and influence. The power of a sacred elite has often been coterminous with the power of the more secular elites on whose thrones of power it has sprinkled holy oil in order to justify their authority. But religious elites have sometimes kicked against the traces. The Gnostic sect of early Christianity maintained the idea of secrecy in order to reduce true religion into a cultic affair for certain, self-selecting, group members who followed the path of perfection. This spiritual elitism – or spiritual conceit – contrasted the true religion of the few with the more relaxed and accommodating attitudes of the emerging Church hierarchy which saw that perfection was not an attainable, or a desirable, goal for the vast majority of human beings. But the intensity of Gnosticism, like that of other early Christian heresies, was an implicit and sometimes a radically explicit rebuke to what it saw as the Church's accommodation with the world. That churchly ease with the realities of power-politics[10] came from the relaxed acknowledgement that life in this world needed an accommodating, interim, ethic while waiting for the true arrival of Christ's kingdom. But the history of the Church in the Latin West throughout the Middle Ages was interrupted by occasional waves of millenarian fever which often coincided with bouts of radically disruptive political rebellion. Behind many of these movements lay the original Gnostic idea of the spiritual elite, those who claimed that they understood the gospels more adequately than the official Church and who – in circumstances of tightly controlled communication – met together secretly so they could share their insights. This was a class of leaders who offered an alternative to the established order, rather than upholding it. The power and the appeal of these radical religious elites came from the fact that, although emphasizing initiation and secrecy, they could also disregard social origin in recruiting their neophytes and leaders. Like Lenin's Bolsheviks they were the shock troops of a future society who regarded themselves as seeing further than the masses and who saw their role as that of instructing the unenlightened in the vision that had inspired them. Whether we look at the followers of the Mani in ancient Iran, who divided the world into the light and the dark, seeing that world as a continuing contest between the good and an equally powerful evil, or at the explosion of radical and religious energy which came in the England of the 1640s with its movements of proto-communist Diggers, egalitarian Levellers and those millenarian visionaries the Fifth Monarchy Men, what we are looking at is an explosion of energy from below. The knowledge is then guarded and guided by the elite who have been, as it were, let into the secret and whose goal is a society which is more open to the gifts of the spirit. Elitist means are justified in the name of a brighter future. If this seems perilously close to the kind of utopianism which, in the twentieth century, has justified atrocity and totalitarianism, it has also, in its own time, been a means of questioning and subverting hierarchies of Church and state which had turned oppressive and stale.

## Elite Leadership

But the chief function of the established religious elites has been to emphasize their own authority and hierarchy in specialist and professionalizing terms. The idea of a radical religious elite is then anathematized as 'heretical' because it threatens the basis of order. Knowledge in this scheme of things has to be an affair of the written record rather than of the secretive whisper in the initiate's ear. With such an ordered knowledge arrives the idea of a systematic theology which classifies and controls, as well as the possibility of a career in the service of such an idea of knowledge. Sometimes this establishment religion blends in with the secular authority and sanctifies that system so that it becomes impossible to distinguish at all clearly between what is God's and what is Caesar's. There is a long history of this approach in the history of the Orthodox Churches of eastern Europe and its origins are found in the merged secular and spiritual duties of the late Roman emperors of Byzantium.[11] When the twentieth-century Kremlin found that it had a pliant assistant in the official Russian Orthodox Church, whose bishops it had a role in appointing, it was building on the legacy of the emperor Constantine who personally presided at councils of the

Church. But modern and western European history's most explicit example of an elite rule which straddled the secular–spiritual divide arrived in the mid-sixteenth-century Geneva of John Calvin.

The Calvinist order was built on an earlier political tradition – that of the city-state with its Athenian democratic roots and, in more recent history, that of the Italian Renaissance republics.[12] But it was Calvin's peculiar genius to infuse that tradition with a new purpose through his concept of the elect – those who were chosen by God to provide elite leadership. Before Leninism and its Bolsheviks, it was Calvin's doctrine of the elect which gave the European history of the elite group its most startlingly effective twist. He did so in a way that has shaped all subsequent elite activity, for the key to the Calvinist elite was the immense psychological comfort of knowing that history and the march of progress was on its side. Order and method was the clue to the ability to keep in step with that march, as well as the power of the group solidarity and the group thinking which kept the elect together. The conformity of dress, the use of certain key words, phrases and jargon, the possession of a similar gleam in the eye: all of these features of elite activity appear for the first time in their distinctively modern form in the group who governed Geneva, and who then, through an internationally organized solidarity, spread its message to similar organizations bent on realizing the rule of the elect right across the European world. And with that assurance came also a kind of creative uncertainty, for the elite of the elect could not be entirely sure, until the very end of human time, whether they were justified in regarding themselves as chosen by God. Their psychological confidence was balanced by an anxiety and a consequent need to prove to themselves, as well as to those they governed, that they were in the right. Both this confidence, and this anxiety, would recur in the future history of the more secular elites who would go on to govern the societies of the modern, post-religious, world of the West.

That world has prided itself on its democratic advances and regards its history as a story of increasing rights for individuals. It is unhappy with the idea of a self-consciously proclaimed, obvious elite and is more at ease with the idea of a meritocracy. Indeed, elites which are genuinely powerful in the modern West (as opposed to being merely fashionable and social) dislike being identified as such and shy away from investigation. A power elite, in order to be genuinely powerful, cannot afford to advertise its elitist nature. Promotion and self-promotion through open access to privilege and power are considered

10

more virtuous and more defensible in the public interest than the idea of an elite, which carries with it such strong connotations of an anti-democratic agenda.

This has been, and is, particularly true of Britain – a country which combines some strikingly undemocratic features of its daily life along with a strident rhetoric about the virtues of parliamentary democracy and of government based on a dominant culture of political parties. But democratic elites are very similar to the elites of the pre-democratic and the proto-democratic past. They, too, have to justify their monopoly of force, if they are part of the power elite of government, law and army, of bureaucracy and of business. And they share with the elites of the past certain behavioural features, tricks of thought and rhetorical gestures – traits which bind them together across the more obvious superficial divides of left and right. Democratic elites carry with them a very heavy burden indeed in terms of justification and propaganda, given the heady weight of expectation that is associated with the democratic hope that emerged first in the Paris of 1789 and which has shaped European history ever since. These elites govern in the name of that hope, but they also have to manage expectations, especially when such expectations might destabilize and threaten the existence of elite power. For an elite, when it is successful in a democracy, must always be aware of its own potential fragility, the precariousness of its hold on power and the delicacy it needs to display when it talks about what is good for a society. It governs and it influences by consent and by assent. It uses language and deploys ideas which may, very easily, lead to the loss of its own position, which is why the clannishness of the power elite is one of its most striking features.

## The Modern Law of Oligarchy

A successful member of the corporate and political elites is a natural courtier. Business and financial elites, by contrast, need not show an equivalent concern with the politics of manners – and their style of power shows how the ranks of the elites have always included barbarians as well as bureaucrats. Political, administrative and professional hierarchies, however, reward those who enjoy life at court with its eddying currents of influence and responsiveness to events, its gossip about who's in and who's out, its heightened susceptibility to the revolving turns of fortune – both good and bad – and the need to

11

hop on and off that wheel in order to curry favour and escape the disgrace of loss of face. Machiavelli's *The Prince* is the first handbook written for those who have to survive in such a world,[13] but it transcends the circumstances of its composition in the cut-throat world of Renaissance diplomacy and the kaleidoscope of alliances whose only constant goal was self-preservation. Behind the democratic facade of modern governments what remains striking is the continuance of princely politics and the habits of court life. The distribution of the spoils of power and the dispersal of patronage is the most important activity of government, and the habits of successful people who place themselves in the best position to receive those rewards are very similar whatever society's form. In Britain's highly centralized state, the court of power has long since moved from Windsor to Downing Street. But the strategies that once kept a sixteenth-century Groom of the Stool or a seventeenth-century Gentleman of the Bedchamber in a position of influence remain much the same. If landed estates are no longer at the disposal of a democratic prince and his immediate retinue, their modern equivalents – government contracts and positions of non-elected influence which then lead to boardroom rewards – are quite as desirable in the view of a society which has added other commodities to land as the source of wealth and as an element in investment portfolios.

Britain's power elites illustrate the extent to which modern democracies – when it comes to the practicality of power – are governed by an iron law of oligarchy. Whether the oligarchs use the language of liberal dignity, of conservative virtue, or of socialist equality, they are all driven towards similar techniques of government. As modern administrative systems become ever more diffuse and complicated it becomes more, rather than less, important that the members of a particular political elite grouping should have confidence in each other. They need not like or trust each other, but they do need to know and feel that they are the same kind of people if they are to keep the controlling show on the road and achieve their personal goals. Only on the basis of this kind of goal-determined confidence can they plan and plot, write manifestos, conduct press conferences, read briefings and frame legislation. It is on this basis that elites can then deal with members of the media class who, for all their prominence at the commentating and observational end of things, remain what they have always been – facilitators of the relationships and the transactions that take place between the power elites. The media mediates. It has grown in personnel and in the opportunities it offers the power elites to communicate with each other in print, on camera and on the airwaves. But it has, and can have, no independent voice and no critical mass influence because it lacks that powerful class-consciousness that keeps the elites together, which energizes them and focuses their interests.

It was Thomas Carlyle[14] who first noted the rise of a new class of opinion formers in mid-nineteenth-century Britain and who characterized this novel secular priesthood as sharing many of the features of the old religious priesthood that it was supplanting. As journalists and commentators, novelists with a social message, politicians with a talent for writing, this class ascended into the new pulpits of the age – the newspapers, journals and pamphlets of an expanded democracy. And, just like the old clergy, they preached to the masses in order to enlighten and control. This was the high noon of British liberalism with the extension of the franchise and the removal of tariffs promoting the idea of a democracy which would be commercially successful as well as virtuous in its promotion of the idea of a common good. But what is very striking about the liberalism of that age is how it was shaped by fear about the possible consequences of democracy. The priests of liberal opinion were clear that there was no alternative to democracy, and regarded aristocracy as not just the system of government of an age that was fading away but also as a morally inferior way of conducting human affairs. But they also thought that the democratic alternative was a gospel which had to be interpreted with care.

## Property and Liberty

Democracy arrived in Britain with a heavy weight of virtue draped around its shoulders and was part and parcel of the spirit of busy ethical improvement which shaped Victorian Britain. But it also arrived with a very heavy burden of fear shaped by recent history. All of nineteenth-century European politics was governed by the elite recollection of the Terror of 1793–4 and the example on the streets of Paris of what could happen to property and individual rights when the masses took democracy too literally. From then on it became the job of the leaders of democratic opinion everywhere, and especially in Britain, to manage democratic advance and make sure that it did not destabilize a society and degenerate into the street disorder

13

described with such salivating intensity in Thomas Carlyle's *The French Revolution, A History*. The conviction that democracy in its purest form was in fact another name for anarchy runs like a not-so-golden thread of argument and debate throughout the history of Britain's commentating elites from their first, Gladstonian, golden age right on to all the expanded job opportunities that arrived in the successive ages of radio and then television broadcasting. This notion of the essentially violent nature of democracy has been basic to elite careers because it justifies the need for sermons about order and control, as well as the continuance of the liberal elites' hierarchies of influence.[15] Behind all the sanctimony about democratic advance the reality is always that of the need to control democracy lest some British Robespierre arise to threaten order. The basic form that that order takes is property rights – the true fundamental value of British liberty and the reason for the historic constraints on any central power which might threaten those rights. The constitutional settlement of the late seventeenth century was arrived at in order to protect aristocratic and gentry estates against the centralizing power of princely government – with its pattern of wasteful spending and desire to raise money by central diktat. The persistent power of property rights on a more general scale has developed to a point at which it has now become an established feature of the British political system and it continues to impose its characteristic limitations on any display of centralizing pomp. It is the fundamental reason why a British Prime Minister does not have the monarchical helicopter on the lawn or the saluting presidential guard. Instead, he has to wander around in shirtsleeves holding a mug of tea.

The kind of liberty that took root in Britain was very different from that which emerged from the mainstream European continental tradition and the rhetoric of the post-1789 settlement about fundamental human rights. Parliament's existence and its constitutional position was linked indissolubly to the right to approve and raise taxation. And parliamentary consent was based on the rights of the propertied classes. When parliamentary reform was accepted in the nineteenth century it was part of a wider recognition that a restricted franchise was actually imperilling British order and property. The old order had become indefensible in the light of the new aspirations about the spread of popular rights. But the new order led to an even wider entrenchment of property as the basis of liberty, which is why Britain's politics to this day is dominated by discussions about home ownership – and by assumptions about the essentially virtuous quality of the mortgage with its capacity to root the British in an acceptance of the way they are governed. It has therefore been the function of Britain's commentating elites to preach an essentially pessimistic view of democracy – along with an assumption that democratic practices must be controlled and guided by the enlightened few.

It is a striking feature of British elites that they have been, and are, adept at concealing their own elitism – and, indeed, offer some strident condemnations of the very idea of 'elitist' power. In Britain, identification as a member of an elite grouping always means a significant threat to the continuation of one's covert authority. The success of these strategies of concealment owes much to the power of various deep collective myths that the British, and especially the English, have embraced as a satisfactory way of explaining themselves. Hostile to rationalism and prone to a rough and ready empiricism as the ultimate explanation of life's mysteries, the hardy island race is averse to theory. Even that founding element in national identity, the Reformation, seems to be English first and Protestant second, for it offers confirmation of the basic national temper of individualism and dislike of a caste of experts who decide what is good and bad in doctrine and belief. British politics, too, is supposed to offer a healthy confirmation of that same genial scepticism. Over the water – in continental Europe – there is supposed to be a 'classe politique', a group of policy professionals who are sadly detached from the vigorous grass roots which keep British democracy vital, and it is their mania for theory which is meant to explain their undemocratic attachment to grandiose governmental visions.

These exercises in self-gratification show the continuing power of the Whig mind in British public life – and its myth of a purposeful, progressive evolution which has guided Britain to its present happy state and away from mayhem. Right across the political parties and their elected representatives, in novels both popular and more arcane, in television and radio debates, in the assumptions of business and City elites and in a myriad newspaper articles there is a similar appeal to that final court of judgement – the genial commonsense of the British. It is a useful myth because it can be appealed to by all parties to suit their particular purposes – and to that extent it therefore shows the essentially vacuous quality of this propaganda exercise. The traditional right can of course use the myth in order to explain why Britain will always be an unEuropean country while hymning the glories of that mysterious growth – the British unwritten constitution, something which the British have somehow stumbled on without any forethought or planning. But elements of the radical left can also find the myth a consoling one for it also promotes the idea of the essential geniality of the British – their ability to cooperate and rub shoulders in a spirit of common purpose – while also fostering the illusion that class cooperation is a greater truth than class conflict in Britain. Orwell, that very elitist writer, is the great laureate of this leftward-leaning version of a common British conservatism.[16]

There may be some elite members who do actually believe this ideology which is common to their class. But if they do believe it then the circumstances of their lives and careers disprove their professed theory. For the aim of most preachers of the theory is to promote a useful myth – something which may or may not be true but which is pragmatically useful in promoting a certain picture of Britain and one which keeps the hierarchies in their place. Modern careers are managerial in their structure and the negotiation of career success involves the adroit use of management language. The invention of a political party which calls itself New Labour, and its consequent concern with the branding of a product in order to sustain the political cadre in office, stands out therefore as the apotheosis of all modern British politics – its essential and defining concern with the technocratic management of democratic expectations. Careers such as these do not emerge out of some benignly consensual insular fog. Rather are they the result of hard graft at exploiting a certain picture of Britain, one whose aim is to keep people in their place at both the level of elite careers and at the level of the lives that are governed by the elites.

## Behaviour and Custom

As we shall see, elite careers in law and in business, in the City, the professions and the universities, in the army and in media activity do all share with the elite political careers this carefully constructed and manipulative picture of what Britain is and is not, what its citizens should aspire to and what is out of bounds. Among the most significant achievements of the modern British elite is the promulgation of the essentially ideological idea that Britain is an anti-ideological place. Criticism of its fundamental features can therefore be dismissed as the ravings of the marginalized – those whose temperaments fail to show the kind of finesse required in order to understand Britain and the British – and who need not therefore be admitted into the contest and the debate. Anti-royalism stands out among such criticism, and its objection that what is attributed to the British mind as an acceptance of neutral fact is really the elevation of a certain constitutional theory, one which makes 'sovereignty' into an attribute of a legal personality – that of the sovereign-in-parliament – rather than the possession of a democratic national will. Royalism's seductive hold on the British imagination – and its maintenance there by the elite writers who have been the heirs of Bagehot – goes far beyond the domain of fashion elites and of Cartier-wearing observers of polo matches at Windsor. Royalism is part of the story of power elites because it promotes rank, birth and money over ability as a determinant of power, status and respect in modern Britain. The search for honour, that visible respect which may be accorded you in the eyes of others, is what motivates the ambitions of power elites in all societies. In Britain, that search is institutionalized to a unique degree in the notion and reality of the crown as the fount of honour. The survival of a royal–aristocratic elite is an astonishing British fact – one which seems natural only because of the deadening impact of pageantry and prerogative, ritual and pomp, on the national mind. As a result, that which should be national is subsumed within the details of dynastic and family life.

Royalism, however, is only one particular instance of a much wider power elite preoccupation in Britain – the expression of power and influence through certain learned habits of behaviour and of custom. The domestic arrangements of the house of Windsor – the rules governing the succession and the civil list but also those governing precedence and the protocol of presentation – cast what might otherwise be seen as a brutal fact of domination in a personal light. The intimacy is a sham, of course, but this family question of how to behave, of how to express gratitude and avoid rudeness, something that we all learn in early life, has been turned into a truth which justifies by analogy the domestication of power in a royal household. This was once part of the way in which royal power became a dynamic and, strangely enough, a modernizing doctrine of elite power in early modern Europe. Absolutist kingship was concerned with centralized, administrative streamlining and with the removal of ancient, parti-cular, liberties. But it did so by exploiting a patriarchal picture of the king as a father to his people – one whose direct familial linkage enabled him to govern in their best interests.[17] Modern British royalism, though no longer concerned with the crown as a direct

17

instrument of government, remains suffused by a similar sentiment about the naturalness of the connection between the crown and the people. It was by means of this sentiment that the British first became convinced of the naturalness of royal dynastic continuity and its influence in a democracy.

Knowing how to behave, what to say and how to say it forms part of the necessary rules of engagement if you wish to join an elite and keep yourself there. While the rhetoric of democratic openness, of meritocracy and social ascent becomes ever more urgent, so also the new elite members need to learn how to conform to the rules of the club they have joined. Britain's power elites therefore learn very quickly how to disparage the idea of 'elitism' as something which is fundamentally unfair and anachronistic.[18] They have also to stress the morally superior nature of power arrangements in Britain today compared to the country's past. What went before must, therefore, be dismissed as snobbish, hidebound and reactionary as well as cruel in its treatment of those who, for reasons of class, transgressive conduct, dissenting belief, or sexuality happened to fall outside the orthodoxies of the newly asserted hierarchies. But however insouciant their self-presentation, our modern elites are no less driven by the neurosis of success than were their pre-democratic and proto-democratic predecessors. Modern elites may be drawn from a greater diversity of origins than obtained in the past, but the rules which govern them are quite as rigid as the ones their predecessors had to observe. Being successful and looking successful are both demanding disciplines which consume most of the power elite's time and energy. The track record of the career has to be continuously encouraging and one's reputation needs to be upheld in the eyes of others while not causing undue offence to fellow competitors in the power stakes. Money, income and assets are the material signs of these achievements and their possession means that one is then treated as a person of consequence and substance.

## Wealth and Power

Elite status is connected with wealth and a certain level of material comfort. Degrees of wealth, of course, do not translate automatically into equivalent degrees of power. A common or garden bond trader, for example, is not necessarily more important than the Home Secretary. But all the elite groupings exist within a condition of life and experience and ease of material circumstances which separates

18

them from both the working classes and the remainder of the middle classes. Differentials of income have their own story to tell in this regard. But it is the wider question of the distribution of total marketable wealth which gives the more revealing picture of how the British power elites have been able to re-establish themselves in recent years. For most of the twentieth century wealth became ever more evenly distributed. In 1911 the richest 1 per cent held around 70 per cent of the UK's total marketable wealth and by 1986 this figure had dropped to a holding of just 18 per cent of a total figure for marketable wealth estimated in that year as being £955 billion. But by steady degrees this process was first stopped and then started to reverse during the following two decades. By 2002 the richest 1 per cent owned 23 per cent of the country's total marketable wealth. It had also managed this remarkable feat during a period when that total wealth had increased by more than three times to £3,464 billion. During the same period the richest 5 per cent saw their position strengthening as well. In 1986 they owned 36 per cent of the total marketable wealth and in 2002 they owned 43 per cent of it. With the wealthiest 50 per cent owning 94 per cent of the UK's total marketable wealth in 2002, the remaining half of the population were left behind to share out between them just 6 per cent of that wealth.[19]

If one excludes the value of housing as an asset from these estimates, the results become even more skewed in favour of the power elites. In 1986 the richest 1 per cent owned 25 per cent of the UK's marketable wealth (less the value of dwellings) and the richest 5 per cent owned 46 per cent of it. But by 2002 they could congratulate themselves on owning, respectively, 35 per cent and 62 per cent. These are the figures that provide the sardonic epilogue to Britain's century of supposed democratic advance and which threw that process into reverse gear in order to sustain the material comfort, the wellbeing and the career successes of the power elites.

## Education and Training

Lacking for the most part the background which rooted previous elites in the assumption of a rule which was somehow natural and ordained by birth, the modern elite has to work that much harder at its self-maintenance. But while it gets to work on this task, Britain's dominant contemporary elites show the persistence of some very old elite habits and tricks. After all, even the old elite members had to learn from their families and their instructors, in the nursery and on the playing fields, how to behave in a way which suited their status. Modern power elites undergo the same process but do so for the most part at a later stage in life and through the observed imitation of their bosses and peers. In Britain – where morality is mostly a matter of conduct and of good, or appropriate, behaviour – these questions of learned social conduct and their power to sustain elite membership have never really gone away.

It is in the British approach to education that we see most clearly the origins of the elite preoccupation with social training. A carefully managed national reputation for anti-intellectualism – another example of a manufactured mythology placed at the service of power – has coexisted with a respect for social adroitness as the best and most useful form of cleverness. Indeed, when we look at the history of education in Britain it often seems that what we are really looking at is the history of techniques of social understanding. Whether at the radical progressivist end of things or at the level of traditionalist conservatism, down the plate-glass corridor of the comprehensive school or within the ivy-covered public school quad, there has been a common and philistine prejudice in favour of character training as the true aim of British education. Schooling has been a synonym for socialization – whether through the goal of a united society which would remove some of the disparities of class through social cooperation or through an ethic of gentlemanly conduct which prizes the rounded individual who may not know much but who is excellent at getting on with others. In this respect, the comprehensive ideal of inclusivity has seen the application to a wider society of the original public school ethic, which prized the communal and cooperative virtues. The price to be paid in both instances has been a certain loss of individuality.

The exception to this duopoly in British education was the grammar school which, from its consolidation as a system in the early twentieth century, and more especially from its post-1945 expansion until its effective demise in the 1970s, did encourage the notion that education was a question of scholarship and of learning. And it is therefore unsurprising that that system did produce a highly distinctive period in British civilization along with its characteristically meritocratic and grammar school-educated elites who, unlike our modern power elites, were less prone to neurosis, guilt, evasion and manipulation in the deployment of elite status. D.H. Lawrence, F.R. Leavis and C.P. Snow were the voices of grammar school civilization in literature, criticism and science,[20] while Roy Jenkins, Harold Wilson, Denis Healey and Edward Heath were the apex of a whole class of grammar school-trained politicians. These were careers made by the power of intelligence alone and were quite strikingly detached from the ambiguities that plague our new power elites, who have to play the game of ostentatious anti-elitism in order to maintain, covertly, their elite power.

The grammar school elite, by its rather coat-trailing display of intellectuality as the qualification for access to power, formed a highly uncharacteristic interlude in the history of British elites. Its decision to preside over its own institutional destruction through the abolition of grammar schools remains a remarkable fact. It is as if, rather like the Roman dictator Sulla (in power from 82 BC to 79 BC) who rose through Roman republican politics but when in supreme authority sought to strengthen the power of the senatorial aristocracy, they were trying to make any future repetition of their own careers impossible. Perhaps, again like Sulla, who chose for himself the name of Felix during his dictatorship, they were struck by their own good luck and therefore wanted that joy to be a one-generation affair.

The impulses of the grammar school elite during its brief predominance shared some of the qualities of another post-1945 phenomenon – the French elite dominated by the *énarques*, the graduates of the École Nationale d'Administration who came as an elite grouping to dominate the worlds of business, politics and public administration as well as academic and cultural life. This powerful technocracy concentrated on knowledge as technique – a set of attitudes and methods which could in principle be applied to any area where a certain kind of clarity and rationalist order needed to be brought to bear. The group was an invention of the state and was intended to solve a particular problem of the state – the requirement that its authority be re-established after the collapse of 1940–4. Its moral and intellectual authority has come under sustained criticism, amid accusations that although individually clever this elite class is collectively stupid and prone to arrogant and impractical governmentalist solutions. These accusations have been particularly vocal in Britain as an aspect of British hostility to the European project, itself a fundamental part of the French elite's process of corporate self-identification since the 1950s.[21] The criticisms have focused not just on the occasional and spectacular examples of bribery and corruption – those systemic features of any system in which too many people in a narrow milieu

21

know each other too well. There has also been a concentration on those long-established cultural predispositions which explain the rule of the énarques and their appeal – features which long pre-date the 1940s which saw their birth. After all, the cultivation of a certain mystique of rationalism and of intellectual élan as a source of the public intellectual's authority – the justification for his role in human affairs as counsellor and disentangler of problems – was the product of two streams of thought. First came the French crown's elevation of its own authority in the seventeenth century as a classicizing and normative enforcer of order. That was followed by the eighteenth-century emergence of an intellectual class both within and beyond the court – propagandists who colonized the public space of commentary in books and pamphlets, and who established their authority as the excoriators of prejudice and the standard bearers of progressivism.[22] Merely to observe these defining characteristics is, it seems, to note also their absence from British culture and thereby to show that the *énarque* experience was culturally specific to the French and therefore non-transferable.

## The Hidden Nature of Intellectual Power

But acknowledging the gap is not the same thing as giving in to a self-congratulatory reflex. If individual cases of corruption reveal defects within a complacent French elite, the nature of the corruption within the varieties of British power elite activity, while not actually illegal, may be far more profound, less open to detection and, therefore, more harmful. The activities of the British elites discussed in this book are of this kind and, whether in politics, law or business, they affect the fundamental nature of Britain and its incapacity to operate as a democracy except at a formal level of institutional self-assessment.

That supposed, un-French, absence of a class of 'intellectuals' is an example of just such a mental corruption at work. Britain has in fact a highly successful, and self-congratulatory, class of networking intellectuals. They may not merit the term 'intelligentsia', because that is a term reserved strictly (in its original Polish and then Russian usage) to a class of outsiders who are the critics of the established order. What typifies the British intellectual class, by contrast, is its successful absorption within the power elites to a point at which its thoughts and stances are reified and appear to be simply the neutral observation of questions of fact.

This hidden nature of intellectual power is one aspect of the more generally concealed nature of the British power elites. Hidden beneath their rhetoric about Britain being unintellectual and anti-elitist, our power elites consider themselves to have cut a deal. The moment they are revealed for the elites they truly are their power will be taken away from them. But the notorious national hypocrisy (one myth which may actually be a truth) allows elite power to flourish as long as the elite members play the game of mouthing anti-elitist language. The longer this kind of corruption goes on, the greater the degree of distance between the genuine national life of the many and the power games of the few. The difference between the British and the French attitudes to power elites could therefore hardly be greater. The true difference is not between the pragmatic commonsensical British and the theory-driven French but between two different kinds of elites and what they are – or are not – allowed to get away with. The French elite is allowed to be obvious and can be publicly identified. It is granted its salaries and perks of office. There is no particular problem about its existence as an elite group. But the other side of the deal is that it is required to deliver and is undeniably part of the whole corporate business of being a citizen of the French state. This is an elite whose energies have to be directed towards making the structures of national existence efficient. Which is why, apart from the occasional futility of presidential monument-building, French public services in transport, education and health reach an excellence far ahead of their British equivalents.

## Offshore Attitudes

Britain's elites are at one and the same time both absorbed within the structures of power and also strangely detached from the practical consequences of its exercise – its capacity to make the details of ordinary life either more or less burdensome for the majority of the population. They are not identified publicly as the elites they truly are and are therefore not obliged to bear the burden of the consequences of failure, whether that happens in transport systems, corporate misgovernance, educational standards, or any of the myriad other areas of failure in what is quaintly termed 'British public policy'. One of the most significant developments of the 1990s was the emergence of a highly paid public sector management elite. Reorganization of the health and education services in particular has created a top layer of management whose salaries (on or about £100,000 a year) are a witness to their ability to use the right kind of language about targets and benchmarks of excellence and delivery but whose careers are strangely devoid of can-carrying responsibility. Here, as is so often the case in the elites' manipulation of reality and their management of expectations, the ability to handle language correctly is a key to their success. Elites use words differently, cynically and with a carefully calculated disregard for truth. Beliefs are indeed the currency of their conversation, for these people can argue and present ideas in a way which is plausible. The successful handling of ideas in a deceptive manner is indeed one of their core competences, and is basic to the successful management of their careers. But the beliefs are really strategies and positions to be staked out rather than contributions towards a picture of reality. In this respect journalistic and media commentary is entirely consonant with the elite view of how words can be used. In both cases the ideas advanced and the beliefs claimed by an individual can change, especially so in a media world where attentiveness is at a premium and today's outrage is tomorrow's forgotten fable. The genuinely powerful elites are the beneficiaries of that episodic attention span and can therefore build a pragmatic, or cynical, attitude towards truth into the very structure of their own careers.

By these means Britain, increasingly, has an elite whose attitudes are 'offshore' and disconnected from the business of being British. The public sector elite contributes towards the failure of public services because their career impulses exist in parallel to, but not as a part of, the services they are meant to run, while City, business and legal elites can become offshore financially and sometimes residentially as well as in their mentally disengaged attitudes. Britain is to them a country which may be a convenient place to live and work, but the success or failure of its public institutions is not really the preoccupation of their lives. The more successful they become the greater their degree of approximation to that ultimate model of such elite attitudes – 'Davos man', whose internationalist minded compassion is allowed to ex- ercise itself for a week's conferencing during which he can model and create a world in which all men of energy and good will can agree on what needs to be done.

Davos man represents the elite of elites and is quite self-consciously on holiday from the attitudes which have brought him to the apex he now enjoys, and to which he will return once the serious business of undercutting the competition resumes with his return to the desk. Once back and immersed in the mêlée of elite attitudes he can join the managing director and the cabinet minister, the successful silk, the fashionable general and the former of opinions in that struggle for position which is the unceasing preoccupation of the elite mind. These are people who, even when they do not know each other personally, can recognize each other for what they are, and understand the strategies deployed by all of them in the management of opinions. They can and do disagree with each other, representing as they do the superficially wide variety of opinions available to those who want to dominate public discourse and occupy an elite position in Britain. But beneath all the apparent disagreement there is a fundamental agreement, a common point of view whose existence allows for the divergences of opinion. For common to all elite chatter is the assumption of the impossibility of disinterestedness. Everybody in this world of the clash of opinion and the battle for position operates on the basis that everybody else is a chancer, too. This is the common ground on which all may join – and in which the struggle can be as fierce as the clash of egos can make it. It goes on for as long as the opponents can look each other in the eye and find therein the common comforting gleam of the solipsistic hunter and hear in each other's tones the insistent, undercutting assumption that public concerns and public statements can always be reduced to the urges and needs of the private life of the person who expresses that concern and makes those statements. This is the destructive consensus of the elite class. But if the rule of that engagement is broken, and if criticism is based on a genuine objectivity, a disregard of elite amour-propre and a detachment from its clashing subjectivities, then the consensus breaks down. In those circumstances, the power elites simply have no way of dealing with the critic who rejects their central assumption – the impossibility of disinterestedness.

But while it enjoys its dominance the power elite has drawn within its domain previous components of elite activity – such as the academic elite of university life – which might have stood out against its urgent mental totalitarianism. The end of the university as a source of independent-mindedness in the face of power has been both self-willed and enforced upon it. Individual members of an academic intelligentsia are drawn to the habits of power elites. The loss of individual mental independence is paralleled by the universities' own diminished institutional independence.

Emboldened and sustained by their shared assumptions, the power elites have established a Caesar-like mastery both over the give and take of manipulated opinion and over the jostling for position, status and power in Britain today. Augustus' genius was to preserve the outward institutional facade of the old Roman republic while subverting those spent structures in order to establish a personal autocracy. In a very similar way our power elites deploy the language of democratic engagement as a cover for their own advancement. They participate in the stale celebrations of a common history, such as the ritualized observance of the great democratic war (1939–45) which recurs so often, and so self-servingly, in their talk, writings and speeches. Occupying positions at the very apex of our society, they use the language of national interest, valour and endeavour in order to keep themselves in power. But by their very existence they have proved to be the destroyers of the democratic aspiration and effective debate which should lie at the heart of an open society.

*Chapter 2*

# The Political Elites: Strategies for Survival

## The Party Machines

The upper echelons of the party machines – especially those politicians who have been elected to represent parliamentary constituencies – constitute Britain's political elites. Taking into account politically active members of the House of Lords and party administrators as well as members of the Commons, we are dealing with a group of no more than about a thousand individuals. They maintain a certain distance from the councillors and officers of local authorities – a level of government which has suffered a continuous attrition of influence and status in the second half of the twentieth century. But the political elite has a close relationship with the higher reaches of the civil service. Britain's civil servants assert their political neutrality but the fact that they breathe the same air as those politicians who are in office means that they are often barely distinguishable from the political elite. This is partly a question of their fundamental mental similarity as management types. But the similarity is also a result of the officials' physical proximity to ministers when it comes to the daily details of administering a department of state. The civil servants who run the minister's office in Whitehall – those who counsel him, communicate his views and organize his life – are collectively known as 'the private office'.[1] That quality of an advertised, yet secluded, intimacy is reflected in British government as a whole, a system which exists to serve the public interest but which also values the kind of privacy which is synonymous with a debilitating secretiveness. The history of government structures, however, also reveals occasional spurts of real executive rigour – most obviously so in the degree of coordination that the British government was able to achieve in 1939–45.[2] Few active members of the political elite have by now any personal memory of the Second World War. But the transmitted recollection of that government élan by means of the testimony of those who were there, as well as through books, journalism, film and radio, means that the period has become a persistent and reproachful ghost within the administrative mechanisms manipulated by Britain's contemporary elite.

Political parties, like British government generally, illustrate the convergence of the different forms of elite power and that power's innate propensity towards oligarchy.[3] The underlying sentimental feel of the two main parties remains different and neither of these brands are entirely detached from their respective histories. But the personnel who sell and service these products exist within a largely visual dimension, and it is that reality which subsumes them within a common and unifying purpose. The Westminster elite, like that of Whitehall, exists in order to be seen, inspected and proclaimed as the embodiment of the nation's decision-making. Our political leaders are the heads of an imaginary body politic and are treated as such by those who are paid to comment on their activities. As a result the parliamentary classes, and their journalistic attendants, concentrate on the strenuous business of putting on a show which attempts to maintain the drama of high purpose and substantive debate. The emergence of the young-ish Tony Blair in the last decade of the twentieth century and of the equally young-ish David Cameron in the first decade of the twenty-first century shows how an entertaining production can be fabricated out of initially quite unpromising material on both the Labour and the Conservative benches.[4] Commentators in these circumstances will talk, in lofty constitutional terms, of the need to produce a 'credible opposition'. But that facade of Olympian disinterest masks a concern which is essentially dramatic and is comparable to the commercial impulses behind the management of a West End theatre which needs to pack the stalls with punters. Political and journalistic ingenuity in Britain is directed towards the conversion of molehills into mountains as interchangeable managers seek to seduce a few thousand floating voters with the cut of their jib, the sweetness of their smile and the persuasively soft drape of a tailored suit.

In the early-to-mid-twentieth century the narrative drama of the party political system was sustained and made comprehensible by differences both of class and of social and economic interest. This represented the impact of an outside force, that of the conflict between labour and capital, on the politics of Westminster cabals.[5] But the peculiarity of the present political scene is that it represents a collapse into a much older kind of politics. Britain's eighteenth-century parliaments were dominated less by the contest of party than by the hunt for office and by the search for governmental patronage which, directed back to the local member's constituency, would then secure his re-election.[6] The successor elites that sat in the nineteenth-century parliaments were tormented by the question of how to control the new democratic beast and the volatilities of mass-opinion.[7] In the early twenty-first century the two great parties continue to sit opposite each other in that frozen architectural condition of the House of Commons which seeks to systematize the respective functions of government and opposition. But post-Cold War politics, as well as post-Thatcher politics, has deprived the parties of their previous socio-economic roles. The very completeness of the triumph of market economics, combined with the collapse of organized socialist politics in the face of market consumerism, has narrowed down the differences between the parties to a very fine shade – one which is represented by the difference between a couple of percentage points in public expenditure as a proportion of GDP.

## House of Commons Man

Looking at the modern membership of the Commons and its means of subsistence involves inspection of a group of people who have far more in common with each other than they do with the lives lived, the careers pursued and the ideals advanced outside that foetid existence. The stage dramas of ritualized debates and oppositional tactics do, of course, continue along with the signing of early-day motions, the grave enunciation by ministers of their statements to the house along with the questions posed to them and the answers they give. With all of that apparent heat – along with the generation of occasional light – there is also the urgent appeal to ideas of the public interest and to an imagined public opinion. There is no limit to the ideas that can be attributed to the British public by the parliamentary class as it searches for self-definition and tries to keep itself in office. One of the chief features of political rhetoric in Britain over the past decade – a period when Euro-scepticism has tightened its grip – has been the invocation of sterling British worth and a heightened suspicion of continental entanglements to the east. Parliament as an institution has been basic to that rhetoric since it is the institution whose longevity and character is meant to define Britain to itself. The red and green leather padded-ness of the place offers, through its neo-Gothic grandeur, a fake architectural claim to mediaeval antiquity and is meant to lend dignity to the occupants,[8] while the creature comforts of smoking rooms, restaurants, tea-rooms, libraries and drinks on the terrace both feed and water parliamentary man and woman's inner being. The Palace of Westminster is at the heart of the socialized understanding of power in Britain: something which has to be learned by practice and by adaptation before it can then be negotiated and enjoyed by initiates. It retains a certain ornamental significance but now corresponds to Bagehot's dignified element within the British constitution, leaving Downing Street as the centre of that constitution's effective element.

The House of Commons man (a being who is – invariably – a masculine construct), close cousin to the club bore, is a figure who rises above party in his attachment to the spirit of place. Whether he is a Tony Benn, an Enoch Powell, or a Tam Dalyell,[9] that character is a safely decorative institutional adornment and in his speeches he can make the kind of jokes which, accorded a hilarious reception in the chamber, fall flat outside: perhaps one needed to be there at the time in order to get it. But the point about the Commons is that you need to be there practically all the time – in spirit and in attitude if not in physical fact – in order to get the point of its power elite games, which is why Westminster lobby correspondents become quite as steeped in palace mystique as the parliamentarians themselves – and end up constructing press rituals which mimic the hierarchies that they report. Journalists therefore hunt for the leak which, precisely calculated, can be helpful to power as well as boost their careers. They chat informally on the phone with ministers and their shadows, maintain contact with friendly cabinet advisers and then settle down to have lunch with power. Within his own domain the senior member of the lobby is almost as august a figure as a cabinet minister – and the regard of the cub parliamentary correspondent looking up at his chief is similar to that of a junior minister in search of a powerful patron. Worker bees, if fed on royal jelly, may become queen bees,[10] and so the point of this journalistic class is not so much to expose as to honour the greater power it observes and tries to decipher.

## Feeding the Lobby

Lobby deference has been around for a very long time and it parallels a well established feature of camp and prison life. Guards and warders

30

may sometimes become unduly attached to their prisoners since a long period of close contact means that the two, supposedly separate, groups get to know each other well. Hostages report similar experiences with their abductors the longer their period of captivity. As a result of this closeness, those in authority may connive at occasional special favours for the people they are employed to observe in the prison or the camp, such as the importation of unusual drugs for a special festal occasion, an indulgent attitude towards bullying, or the toleration of male rape. But the deference of the lobby is now systemic rather than occasional and the jokes which punctuate the copy illustrate the easy and casual collusion between the lobby and the political elite. Even when the humour is at the politician's expense the point of the joke is that it should demonstrate the journalist's ease and confidence in the presence of the political elite. He has, as it were, been licensed to amuse and is therefore a beneficiary of that press obsessiveness which marks both main political parties. New Labour's version of that condition marks a high-water-mark in a development which started under the Tories in the 1980s and which has accelerated the post-1945 deformation of all political parties.[11]

The restaurant to which the politician is taken for lunch is a reliable indication of status and that meal remains a major activity between 12 and 3 in SW1 and its adjacent areas. The nouvelle cuisine of the 1980s – along with the lunch-averse austerity of early New Labour – has come and gone, leaving behind it a substantial body of those who are capaciously and regularly out to lunch. Once this was a rite for the select, really powerful, few who enjoyed true access to power and secrets. Significant journalistic lunchers such as the late Peter Jenkins[12] of the *Sunday Times* would frame his weekly column around the views of the latest cabinet minister or permanent secretary to have been entertained. But the demands of the political elite both high and low – who have come to regard the lunch with the journalist as part of the perks of political status – have now replaced what was once a privilege for the few. After all, the lobby with its expense accounts has itself grown in numbers, and the demands of the political stomach have kept pace with this new source of supply.

Tories at the top of their form still like to be taken to Wilton's in Jermyn Street where the black and white photographs of 1950s Britain on the wall evoke memories of an England governed by Churchill and Macmillan – a time when Tory men wore Homburg hats and the female of the species rarely moved out of doors without a pair of white

31

gloves. Further down in St James' the designer chic of the Avenue attracts the smoothly metropolitan end of New Labour and the restaurant's oil-drizzled sun-dried tomato replaces Wilton's pungent game. It's best – if the politician is really important – to lunch discreetly since you do not want to be overheard. But discretion is not the same thing as invisibility, for the political lunch is an institution which exists to be seen, as well as being a product to be consumed. It is a demonstration of power and access – for both the politician and the journalist. Which is why the Savoy Grill still has a role to play at political lunchtime. The restaurant where Noël Coward once held court now puts on such shows of the altered times as a former member of the Communist Party, the Labour cabinet minister John Reid, and a lapsed Young Communist, Charlie Whelan, Gordon Brown's former adviser (and continuing conduit), being expansive on separate tables at 1.30.

It is a reasonable rule of thumb that the grander the lunch, the further away it will be from Westminster itself – an area of few, and indifferent, restaurants. The humbler political luncher will have to be content with Shepherd's in Marsham Street and, perhaps most melancholy of all within that third division for the breaking of bread, the Footstool restaurant in the crypt of St John's church in Smith Square. The restaurant at the Tate with its extensive wine list is one Westminster local which can *vaut le détour* for the oenophile member. But a real knowledge of wine – like a taste for Francophilia – is a dangerous admission for the political elite, which needs to keep some things well under wraps. Elite sensuality is a powerful instinct – and the political elite in particular likes its creature comforts – but these characteristics need to be discreetly managed if significant ambitions are entertained. Roy Jenkins'[13] reputation never really recovered from his claret-drinking swank despite the seriously driven nature of his ambitions. Alan Clark[14] with his knowledge of *premiers crus* is dead and has no political successor in the stakes which are constituted by the first, second and third growths. But a judiciously advertised demotic acquaintance with other kinds of alcohol does no harm to a political reputation. The beer at the Red Lion pub in Whitehall has swirled its way around many an indiscretion and Kenneth Clarke's[15] fondness for Campari – although placing him firmly in that 1960s world which shaped his views as well as his tastes – constitutes no threat to his political position.

The list of second-division restaurants beyond Westminster is long

32

enough to accommodate most day-to-day needs within the game of journalistic–political contact. Residual Old Labour still hankers after the Gay Hussar in Soho with its heavy Hungarian cuisine and deep-red velvet-covered banquettes to which the capacious behinds of Labour bosses long since dead still seem to cling. Just round the corner that Greek old stager Beotty's still has its supporters since a certain traditional continental heaviness is still in demand at this middling level of the political lunch where ambitions are either being watched on the way up or being inspected for a possible downward slide.

## The Body Politic

The health of MPs has improved in recent years, which may be why there are now so few by-elections as a result of those heart attacks and strokes which used to seize the arteries, puncture the parliamentary timetable and threaten governmental majorities. But the way of life – shared by both the lobby correspondent and the MP – is still exercise-averse and the House of Commons gym is an institution which is visited less often than any of Westminster's bars. While smoking is now frowned on in most areas of Parliament, there are still corners where the few can congregate and puff away on a cross-party basis. The library of the House of Lords, for example, presided over by a nicotine-friendly librarian, is one such area where, at certain times of day, the Tory peer and the ennobled trade unionist can meet in the furtive amity created by a common craving. It is therefore unsurprising that the parliamentary body can experience hygiene problems – and especially so in the summer months. Cabinet ministers are not unique among their Westminster colleagues in having occasional problems with stale and smelly breath. With so much talking to be done – and especially after some lunchtime drinking – there is a price to be paid by the sweatily productive glands and the overworked larynx. There are areas of Parliament, most notably in the bars but sometimes in the committee rooms too, where the aroma of stale and mostly male odour wafts into the nostrils and brings to mind a comparison with the enclosed air of the prison cell and of the boarding school dormitory. But after a few weeks' induction few of the inhabitants seem to notice – which is why a ready tolerance is extended to all those grunts and wheezes, to the coughs, rumbles, burps and farting which constitute the background dissonances and leitmotifs to the swelling sound of the political elites at work. The easy tolerance of physical malfunction has always typified the courts of the powerful despite their surface panoply of power's pomp. It's true of Westminster, too – another court in which men and women jostle in each other's company and have to learn to tolerate the body's adventitious rebellions.

## The Process of Power

Parliament is a place of procedural debate in which process is all,[16] while consequences and results are comparatively less important. Just turning up and being there is the member's most important business of the day, for within that small and enclosed world there is a daily battle in order to get noticed. Which is why – along with the White Rabbit busyness of the place – its other chief characteristic is a certain listlessness associated with the endless wait for the next vote, the hanging around in bars, as well as the insistently maintained preparedness to bow to destiny before being wafted into high office. Despite all the patter of the parliamentary tread there is an undoubted inertness in the parliamentary air and a quality of passivity in the face of events. While waiting for that heavenly breeze to raise the career, however, there is plenty of opportunity to practise that distinctive parliamentary walk – half swagger and half waddle, as shoulders and chest lurch dramatically from side to side. White papers and copies of *Hansard* reports, demonstrating a grasp of affairs of state, are clutched dramatically in the hands as bodies sway their way to galleon-like effect down those endless corridors.

The love of procedural debate, the infatuation with the very process of power, is a testimony to the fact that Parliament is also a court of law. Its authority as a maker of laws that have restrained the executive from Charles I to Tony Blair has been basic to its position in the pantheon of British liberties. But its present role is chiefly that of career opportunity for those members of the power elite who feel at home with a career in politics. Politics is a subject in which they have interested themselves and in which they have made a certain investment of time and of hope. They have therefore become professionals in a subject which provides precious little in the way of a body of knowledge – but which does provide the opportunity of a pretty easy dominance. Most, if they really want it, have a very good chance of being a minister of the crown at some stage in their careers. A political party needs some 300 MPs in order to become the party of government – and, with about 100 ministerial posts to fill, the competition for those jobs is therefore not that tough. No other profession or business provides so many elite jobs within so shallow and circumscribed a pool of talent. There is every justification for the reasonable ambition that one can make it to No. 2 in a department as minister of state, and that therefore the knighthood, which is often handed out on retirement from that office, is a plausible aspiration.

## Tribe and Party

Although so devoid of meaning when it comes to political agendas and beliefs, Britain's political parties remain internally robust. As political issues have become detached from the parties, and as those parties have been threatened by the exposure of their own hollowness, so they have become ever more preoccupied with form for form's sake, with loyalty and reward, news manipulation and media strategies. With less and less to distinguish the parties from each other, it becomes ever more important, internally, to demonstrate that a difference really does exist and that it endows a life and a career with meaning. But what 'difference' really amounts to here is tribalism – another example of how the Commons of the late-modern age has reverted to the condition of the Commons of the eighteenth-century regime. It is remarkable how many politicians, when pressed to explain their allegiance or behaviour, will revert to the justification that the party of choice is their 'tribe' and that politics is a 'tribal affair'. This, again, is one of those bits of parliamentary lore which fail to travel well much beyond SW1. After all, the tribe is a primitive grouping whose activities are dominated by group thinking and unquestioning acceptance of a higher authority. Application of tribal lore to an early twenty-first-century British career seems strangely irrelevant, as well as being a reminder of how far removed party political structures have become from the daily career lives of most professional people.

Other organizations in the professions and in business do of course have their career structures and hierarchies, as well as their creeps and toadies. But an organization which chose to define itself exclusively in these terms, with the elevation of obedience to the leadership as the highest form of virtue while regarding all internal criticism as the dissent of refuseniks, would rapidly implode due to its own paranoia and failure to manage talent. But the modern political party is an authentic Cold War survivor which, organizationally speaking, seems to have strayed from behind the old Iron Curtain and established itself on the conquerors' soil. Which is why the political party, just like those who choose to join it, is now seen as weird, secretive and dictatorial. The Tory and the New Labour political professionals are offered a Faustian pact which entails subservience to empty purposes and the promise that the supplicant will somehow be looked after. At the same time, the party's defenders are reduced to offering lukewarm justifications which explain that while party is horrible, the alternative is worse. Party politics is – on this analysis – a nauseating but essential feature of parliamentary democracy and is the only thing that stands between us and the dictator. These justifications would appear less specious if they were not used to justify some gleefully arm-twisting exploits of thought-controlling behaviour from the whips' offices. There has never been a time when the prestige, within the parties, of the whips' offices has been higher (or, at any rate, been more self-regarding) and there has also never been a time – since the 1867 Reform Act – when Parliament has seemed so odd and removed a place and institution. It has always been a place for conspiracies and plots – but now the party-sponsored stratagems within the parliamentary walls seem to be mere group exercise in self-assertion rather than the service of a greater purpose.

## Politics in Britain

The disenchantment with our political elites has many roots. There is, of course, a deep-seated British suspicion of politics itself and of politicians in general. In this respect, Britain is still living through the consequences of 1660 and the cynicism of Restoration politics about the rule of the saints that preceded it.[17] The Interregnum gave politics a bad name in England, associating as it did political upheaval and reform with theological chicanery, bloody violence and extra-parliamentary rule.[18] The modern British sense that politics is an affair of courtiers whispering behind the throne is a popular piece of disillusioned wisdom which is designed to keep politicians in their place. It is a way of avoiding and defeating the politics of expectation. But, by the same token, it allows courtier-politics to continue, and may even license them.

'Politics' in Britain – so far as the commentariat is concerned – is equivalent to 'what happens in the House of Commons and in No. 10'. That is also precisely the view of politics which encourages most members of the political elite to enter the trade in the first place. Political journalism in Britain is an extended commentary on this view of who's in and who's out. Cabinet government – that elevation of domestic seating arrangements into a central myth of government – is designed quite explicitly to feed this frenzy. The central drama of fluctuating relations between Chancellor and Prime Minister – along with the ancilliary speculative game of which cabinet member sides with which of the two gladiators – is one of the constant plots of British politics and, like all good plots in the history of narrative, it recurs with different actors occupying the same roles. The physical, emotional and mental qualities required of the successful politician, and often the unsuccessful one as well, also persist through the ages. Politics is a good profession for people who are mentally agile, intellectually incurious and physically robust. The political elites' conformist agreement that it is the drama of personal jealousy which explains the very foundation of politics is a conventional judgement which suits all those personal traits. You need a kind of clever agility to understand the personal dynamics of power-pursuit while being prepared to sit up all night negotiating your own advance through the shallows, peaks and troughs of a political career. Meanwhile, it is possible to avoid any real thinking about the business of government since 'policy' is really just another term for 'initiative' – a view which is echoed by the journalistic elite. The cynicism of the political elite about 'political thought' in this sense echoes the cynicism of the British public about what it considers to be an oxymoronic subject. The shamelessness with which an initiative is announced before then being forgotten the following week does not only happen because government is without shame. It happens because in Britain there is now a tacit acceptance that this is what politics is and that is what politicians do. After the great event or the momentous crisis the assumption of decisive action is followed by the illusion, which follows closely on the heels of the readily assembled public sector task force, that action this day is for the here and now. All of this is then forgotten in the noise and stir of the next announcement. If our political elite is thereby debased, if it seems callow, self-serving and trivial, then that is a result which rather suits modern British defeatism. The spectacle affords us the luxury of a self-confirming hypothesis.

## The Politics of Withdrawal

But there is a further reason for the modern grim cynicism about the political elites. For most of the 1980s the Conservative Party – followed then by the Labour Party in the 1990s – devoted much of their energies to the task of persuading the electorate that there were fewer and fewer activities in which government had a role to play. This was most obviously the case in economics where the privatization agenda – which returned nationalized industries to the private sector – was justified on the hypothesis of a greater consumer choice. This was partly true (in the case of telecoms) but mostly fraudulent (as in the case of water supply and most of the other utilities). In the process, members of the old political elite were granted a new lease of career opportunity as cabinet ministers went off to run the companies privatized under the legislation prepared by their own departments. More generally, there was a loss of confidence in the whole idea of central economic planning and a return to the notion that the inherently unpredictable market, with its buying and selling frenzies, its susceptibility to rumour, speculation, fear and mass-irrationality, was the only possible guide to economic understanding.[19] The invention of New Labour from 1994 onwards followed this new orthodoxy, along with a few sops to residual figleaf conscience such as the introduction of the minimum wage. Even in health and education – previously core competencies of the modern state – there would be less and less for government to do as private money came in to fill the gap created by the demolition of the former underachieving sectors.

'Millionaires to the rescue' has been one of the great themes of the New Labour government – as seen in its campaign to get 200 millionaires partially to finance the 200 city academies which are meant to transform British education. For a donation of £2 or £3 million, each millionaire is promised a personal involvement in the future of a chosen academy after a private lunch or dinner with the Prime Minister. In its by-passing of the traditional structures, its concentration of money power at the centre and the gratification that power and money can mutually bestow on each other, the spearheading of the city academies is a powerful illustration of how the power elites operate in Britain today. But if government can lend its lustre to the social ambitions of millionaires, it declares itself impotent or innocent in wider questions of economic strategy – except when it still suits its purposes to intervene. The withdrawal from economic planning has always been more apparent than real since energy policy continues to be fundamental to the business of government and extensive subsidies are distributed among the industries that really matter – such as the arms business and the pharmaceutical trade. A good deal of energy is spent on that other form of subsidy – the maintenance of European trade barriers against Third World economies. It was the faith in planning the details of heavy, old and dirty industries manned by recalcitrant workers which was abandoned after the deep socio-economic crisis of the 1970s – the period which dictated the present official, hypocritical, pessimism about governmental capacity. Having advertised their withdrawal from some carefully selected areas of activity, governments have encouraged the view that politics is a limited domain and one which, rather like badminton or chess, should be left to those enthusiasts who wish to specialize in an activity governed by arcane rules. Yet the consequences of inactivity and of withdrawal are no less profound than those which flow from activism and engagement. The passivity which is encouraged by our political professionals has certain power consequences – most obviously in the case of the management-driven state over which they preside. The consequences of delegating political power – and of the accountability which is meant to define such a power – to agencies and to trusts, to partnerships, associations and companies in fact suits the interests of the political elite. That elite's career existence may be strikingly different from those of the business and professional elites, but its interests increasingly coincide with those groupings.

## The Conduits of Power

Although they therefore have less to do in terms of the direct control of financial and economic power structures, our political elites do remain hugely influential. Their core capacity of knowing who to talk to, along with an expertise in knowing how and where that talking should be done, has always characterized them. That facilitating ability means that they can enjoy an important, residual, significance. Political elites have become the providers of those conduits which run between, and may at times connect, the various ranks of the other modern power elites, and the numbers of those who wish to join their ranks shows no signs of diminishing. Indeed, one of the deep truths of the British political system is the intensity of the elite desire to share a common life and to be encased within the institutional charms of the House of Commons. No other political elite in the world has quite this same degree of glue-like attachment to the patina of Parliament and to the rituals which can soothe and comfort, however fevered the debate. Whether in its unreformed, pre-democratic state or in its modern form, when it has been elected on a universal adult franchise, Parliament has always induced in its members the desire and capacity for convergence and congregation. Here, for example, is the future Prime Minister, George Canning,[20] recalling his emotions when he took his seat for the first time in January 1794:

> I cannot describe you with what emotions I felt myself walking about the floor which I had so often contemplated in my youth from the gallery . . . I sat down too upon the Treasury Bench, just to see how it felt . . . and from that situation met the grinning countenance of half my acquaintance who were in the gallery . . . I was all in a flutter. [Belonging to the Commons was to Canning] one of the highest entertainments that can be conceived. I had no notion that there had been such a difference, as I find there is, in the interest, with which one hears a debate, when merely a spectator in the gallery, and that which one feels, as a member, with the consciousness of having a right to join in.[21]

What is recounted here is a genuinely elite moment, a rite of passage which is also the gratification of a mental craving for the recognition which comes with performance. The fact that Canning was taking his seat in the unreformed Parliament explains the innocent frankness with which he describes his pleasure. He does not have to explain and justify himself in terms of democratic representation, of human betterment or national progress as MPs of all parties have been forced to do subsequently. But beneath all that later democratic rhetoric the modern parliamentarian is impelled by the same quality of ambition and the same desire for high-definition entertainment which drove Canning over two centuries ago.

## Quality, Ability and Class

The question of the quality and ability of those who now join in the game has been a point of discussion ever since the introduction in 1911 of a salary for MPs. That reform of Asquith's Liberal govern-

40

ment created a salaried professional middle class, a political elite who could – for the first time – entertain the ambition of a full-time parliamentary career regardless of their social origins, and the debate about whether the professional political class is more or less remote from the people as a result of that change has been more or less continuous ever since. Some observers of the political elite, struck by the difference between the first and the second half of the twentieth century, romanticize a past when the Commons contained parliamentarians with a genuine independence of mind. The history of political elites is often also the history of such golden age mythologies which ignore how the political elites have always contained a combination of the preening with the fawning and characteristic spectacles of self-esteem engaging in intermittent battle with insecurity. That elite's social origins may have changed with the broad mass of bourgeois manners replacing membership of White's club and of the National Union of Mineworkers (NUM). But Britain's political power elite knows that certain psychological types and forms of mentality tend to recur behind the surface story which chronicles the sociological changes. Even the history of the 'new man' who comes in from the outside has been a pretty continuous one in the history of the political elite in Britain – as the careers of Thomas à Beckett, Thomas Cromwell and John Prescott[22] in their different ways all show.

Nonetheless, the influence of the trade union elites, of philanthropists and of Fabian reformers on the early Labour Party did not just result in a wider composition of the political elite – it also encouraged a genuine debate of ideas within it. At the same time, the private incomes of some Tory shire knights possessed of broad acres meant that they could sometimes be detached from party conformism. The two ministers who resigned from the Conservative government over the Suez invasion in 1956 – Sir Anthony Nutting and Sir Edward Boyle – were both baronets.[23] Some Tory liberal 'wets' – detached from the Tory governments of the 1980s – claimed that lineage of dissenting grandeur even when it took a sacking (as in Ian Gilmour's case)[24] to ensure the detachment. It is also true that the immediate post-Second-World-War parliaments included men whose military service as young officers had broadened their horizons and sometimes enlarged their sympathies so that their perspectives were not just those of the political party in which they happened to find themselves. But even successful young soldiers turned politicians – such as Heath[25] and Healey[26] – had to be trained in the arts of political party hackery in order to establish their elite status. And that new, and very post-1945, political elite qualification – the Oxford PPE degree – became the badge of a new Westminster tribe trained at university level in both the theory and the practice of political hack life.[27] The experience of 1939–45 also proved to be an important element in the creation of a new sub-division within the political elite – the 'European' one which thought that Britain's future would be as part of a greater European unity. That wider loyalty which was formed in the immediate post-war world would, in time, become one of the most potent threats to the solidarity of the traditional British political party, since 'Europe' cut across party lines while engendering splits and rancour.

The notion of its own classlessness has been eagerly embraced by the contemporary political elite and the precise function of that idea is a rhetorical one: it has enabled that elite to redefine and consolidate itself, to increase its numbers while having significantly less to do than its predecessors. Here the contrast with the politicians and the administrators of Britain's past imperial elite is a painfully instructive one. The Parliament which debated and decided the affairs of the late Victorian empire discharged responsibilities which dwarf those of modern British government. The various offices of state – the Foreign Office as well as the Colonial and the India Offices – which administered that empire contained a fraction of the administrators who now try to administer a country of just 60 million people. Just 1,800 members of the Indian Civil Service ran the sub-continent and officials such as Macaulay[28] and Mill[29] were substantial intellects dealing with major questions of colonial administration. The scope of empire also lent a dignity of function to the Victorian political elite as well as providing them with an appropriate intellectual challenge. Their modern successors struggle instead with the consequences of computer-generated maladministration. The progress of our political elites is trailed therefore by clouds of diminished glory and their workrate displays the reality of modest mental ambition while nonetheless maintaining pretensions to grandeur. Perhaps Gordon Brown[30] is the only major British politician left who enjoys an engagement with issues on the traditional, grand scale. All other areas of political elite activity are framed by that generalized sense of disappointment which is Britain's post-imperial condition, its feeling of not yet having quite got past 1945 and all that. Health and education, those elements of the 1945 settlement which came to be justified retrospectively as new ethical boosts to the British enterprise, continue to underperform. As a result the question of what on earth British government is for – that Pandora's box opened by Margaret Thatcher – continues to plague the elite and its activities. Part of the appeal of the war on terror is that it offers a new and convenient justification for governmental activity, a novel access of dignity and purpose to an enterprise which has been running out of ethical steam. In this respect, the Blairite brand of liberal imperialism which pre-dated that war had already prepared the ground with its rhetoric about democratic rights which had to be imposed on the Third World as part of an Anglo-American condominium.

## The Burden of Office

The political elite, of course, complains about the burden of office and especially about what it calls the demands of a '24-hour news culture'. Exposure to observation, if not to real scrutiny, has certainly changed the elite's way of life and its privacy. Television especially has promoted the illusion of access to some political personalities who have been adept at using the medium in order to present their public selves in a winning way. That most formal and constrained of all art forms imposes its own rigid code on what can be said and how it should be said, even while presenting the illusion of uncoerced spontaneity. The political elite have therefore had to conform to the rules of televised debate, which promote a certain blandness of tone and uniformity of thought. The spectacle offers an occasional pantomine in which cages are rattled and broadcasting lions roar on both television and radio. On such occasions, 'media power' is accused of being too confrontational and aggressive. But the ruffling of feathers all round suits both parties to this contrived debate. The political elite is flattered by the thought that its high-minded devotion to the common good is being undermined by media injustice and by the vulgarity of personality-driven commentary, while media workers can get their frisson in two ways. First, there is the delight of the adolescent intuition that their immense courage is the spontaneous overflow of powerful emotion which, however, they really should control in the name of responsibility. Second, they can rejoice in the idea that all the squealing shows that they are broadcasting truth to power. Happily, therefore, the needs of both classes are gratified by these occasional bouts of bogus adversarialism. The public quarrel suits another purpose as well, for it deflects attention from the fact that the media elite spends most of its time observing obedience to the strategic needs of the political elite. The public tiff is a necessary but short-lived drama, and business on the usual terms and conditions is soon resumed. The reconciliation which is achieved by the media's mediation service then allows blandness to resume its sway over the political land. And since the blandness of tone required by television is also part of the new corporate style of our political elite, these rules of uniformity present neither a practical challenge nor a moral difficulty. Within that terrain of common greyness the needs of a '24-hour rolling news agenda' are mostly easily satisfied. It is only the truly dim politician who is discomfited by it and allows the requirement to become the master. Even a modestly competent minister knows how to craft the statement which then, with an economy of energy, can be communicated to the media functionaries by that army of advisers whose new arrival in government is itself an important part of the elite story. It is simply a question of knowing how the system works and then using it to your advantage – something that all elites tend to be good at.

It was the Labour government of 1974–9 which decided that it needed a new cadre of political advisers, paid for by the Treasury, but owing allegiance to the government of the day – and, especially, to the cabinet minister to whom they were attached. With that fondness for French parallels which used to characterize many a British elite mind, it was supposed that British cabinet ministers needed a chef de cabinet and a secretariat designed along the lines of the Fifth Republic's arrangements. What happened instead was Jack Straw.[31] The present Foreign Secretary, along with a number of other ex-student union politicians, found themselves in Whitehall with jobs which helped them in their search for a parliamentary seat. There were a few genuine policy advisers, such as Bernard Donoughue,[32] but most were policy hacks. The years of New Labour from 1997 saw a great expansion in the number of such staffers whose true job was, and is, similar to that of the old clerical grade of the civil service. They were in effect photocopyists to begin with in the early years of IT expansion and they graduated thereafter to being senders of e-mails and ministerial gatekeepers. But their profusion, despite bearing witness to the more superficial aspects of modern government, also shows how British elite politics is an incorrigibly domestic affair and does not take kindly to the rationalist spirit of French administration.

Government in Britain started as an affair of the royal household, and much of that intimate, improvisational, even conspiratorial nature survives in its modern arrangements. This is why the special adviser as an elite member in training works more as an equerry than as a real policy specialist trained in the art of administration. Loyalty here is a question of individual patronage conferred and personal fealty returned. This is another example of that stream of power in Britain which is a question of process rather than of explicit rules. The expansion of the adviser–minister special relationship in all its modern prodigality shows, certainly, the role played by the press and by media awareness in the development of a political elite career. Most advisers spend their time advancing their boss's cause by selective briefing of individual journalists. But the more important aspect of the adviser role is its demonstration of the ministerial elite's sense of self-hood, of what counts as display and importance, which is why the existence of a very grand adviser such as Lord Levy[33] – the Prime Minister's special envoy to the Middle East – personalizes the majesty of the elevating power. It may be impossible to explain what objective good he has done in the Middle East – but that is not the point. Here, being is everything and doing is nowhere. The adviser therefore forms part of the elite's prodigality, its capacity for the conspicuous consumption of resources way beyond its own needs in terms of administrative efficiency and media responsiveness. The point of his being is to show how the ministerial existence and office flows out into the world and changes that world by its touch and by its importance. That is the journey of the ambitious elite self on which the adviser has embarked and, having helped to realize his superior's ambition, he will then wish to imitate it in his own life and career.

## The Order at the Heart of Government

The comparative informality of British government has long since been presented as part of its virtuous flexibility and provisionality, that supposed ease with which it has been able to adapt and evolve without revolutionary upheaval. The idea of the informal – even haphazard – nature of British government has been confirmed when the veil has been lifted on the mechanisms of government in the age of crisis caused by the decision to invade Iraq. Cabinet government and cabinet discussion matter far less than individual discussions involving ministers, the Prime Minister, the cabinet secretary and permanent secretaries. Meetings are convened, the participants exchange thoughts on the sofa and officials are not always present to take the minutes that record the discussions. But it is wrong to treat this as a recent degradation from a lofty and pure earlier practice. The Suez adventure[34] – a combination of Anglo-French collusion in the Middle East with prime ministerial deception and general cabinet evasiveness – shows that same shifty informality at work. 'Cabinet government' has always been something that has loomed larger in academic treatises by professors of politics than it does in the rushed reality of day-to-day government.[35] It suits the innocence of the outsider's eye, as it tries to bring some kind of rational order to the subject, to suppose that government corresponds to the corporate management of a large public company with its shareholders, board of directors and an MD at the helm. It also suits the political elite to conspire in this picture of public policy because it reassures the public, whether it agrees with the governmental programmes or not, that there is order and purpose at the heart of the nation's affairs. This is why books and articles designed to answer the question 'Who governs Britain?' are so popular.[36] For the most part, those writings feed the public super-stition or the public hope that there is a single key which may unlock the secret and disclose the order which lies at the heart of government. But the reality, which would be disturbing if too many people started to believe it, is that British government is not just informal and haphazard but even more prone to chaos and misdirection, destructive bitchiness at both a high and low level, stubbornness and ignorance, than most other large-scale businesses. It survives by luck and flies by the seat of its pants. It is naturally obsessed by the potential for things to go wrong and, as a result, survival and holding the line constitutes a major victory and more than enough work for one day. But through-out all the daily dramas there is one central salvationist myth which must be upheld: government is the unmoved mover behind all events and everything that happens in government is explicable in terms of the initiative of the Prime Minister and his immediate circle.

Sprawling and informal systems of government are difficult to reform from within – but also difficult to attack from outside. That is the reason why the Austro-Hungarian empire survived into the early twentieth century but the more tightly structured French monarchy collapsed so quickly.[37] The one could survive administrative chaos and political failure because those were episodic features of its existence – recurring at different times in different places within the ragged empire but never all at once and at the same time. But the

French crown, having a centralized command structure, needed only to be attacked once and at the right spot for it to collapse completely. Of these two kinds of government, Britain's political elite operates within a situation which is much more Austro-Hungarian than French, and that is why the structure survives. Every generation throws up its wide-eyed reformers, those who would bring order, light and reason to the dark places. The first such modern foray was that of the Northcote–Trevelyan report of 1854 which abolished the sale of civil service jobs and established the principle of open examination as a method of civil service entry. The last successful reform was that presided over by Lloyd George as Prime Minister (1916–22)[38] when he abolished some ministries, established others, instituted the practice of political appointments to the civil service and brought in a whole raft of technocratic-minded individuals into government. Perhaps a world war makes it easier to reform on that scale but subsequent reform attempts have been very limited. Heathish managerialism led to the establishment of a Prime Minister's policy unit in No. 10 and much talk about the need to establish a Prime Minister's Department. Political elite ruminations revert regularly to this kind of elevated, but empty, chatter which misses the point. Such a unit and such a department, just by being so explicitly institutional, contradict that informality which is at the heart of the power of the prime ministerial circle in British politics. Once formalized, that circle's power would be diminished – which is why the reform is never implemented. That is not just an incidental truth of mid-to-late-period Blairism. Protean adaptability along with a cunning insidiousness have always characterized the running of the prime ministerial office, which has to adapt to daily events and hold the ring between the claims and the ambitions of different cabinet ministers. More recent reforms have concentrated on questions less of structure than of money and of numbers, and are broadly content to reduce the rate of planned expansion in bureaucratic numbers rather than achieve absolute reductions. The history of all recent attempts at government cutbacks since the 1980s shows that the attempt at reduction in government activity means that the numbers reduced in one direction are then redirected elsewhere. Quangos – that other invention of the Labour government of 1974–9 – have been major job opportunities for these deflected forms of civil service power while also offering the political elite the possibility of exercising new forms of patronage.

## Role Players

The British elite therefore operates a structure of government which is osmotic in its power to embrace the forces of change. It is also resourceful in its inert capacity to turn those forces to its own advantage while it sets about neutralizing the impact of the original complaint. In this, it has been aided by the mandarinate which, while remaining a powerful force, has seen a quite striking reduction in intelligent capacity. In that 'illusion and reality' manner which so typifies Britain's elite operations, a liturgical litany has been observed for some quarter of a century about the need to establish open competition to permanent secretary appointments, and the incantation has accompanied the maintenance of the traditional internal hierarchies. Even the critical voices are cadenced in that tone of gentle self-reproach which is consistent with the self-satisfaction of the civil service mind. The debilitating irony of *Yes Minister* appealed to the mandarin pieties and to the political elite's self-image in equal measure, since its critique was really a concealed form of flattery.

The reduction of political elite activity to a wry and resigned comedy is one form of the fatalism which is actively encouraged by the political elite and its media hangers-on. The knowing laughter at the Westminster press awards lunch where the journalist and the politician meet in collusive congratulation is a very public example of that love of a political process which is its own justification. This is a political comedy which never ends but always resumes its antic dance with certain set characters who are accorded their honoured role in the process which flows onward like the stream of time itself and never stops to question. The awkward backbench 'rebel' – such as the Labour MPs Bob Marshall-Andrews[39] and Diane Abbott[40] or the Euro-sceptic phalanx of Tory MPs – become eventually much-loved figures in this constitutional show since in fact they conform to a stereotype which is as conventional as that of the lovably naughty schoolboy. There are other role players as well: the stubbornly effective member of a select committee (who is seen as pertinacious if male and as a battle-axe if female), the member with a bee in his bonnet, the former cabinet minister making a decent fist of it on the backbenches and that jeune premier, the new member treading the boards for the first time. Certain forms of behaviour are required of all these archetypes, who then deliver their predictable lines on cue.

The human beings who play these roles vary from Parliament to

Parliament but the roles themselves never change, being as basic to this fake, Gilbert and Sullivanish constitutionalism as the overdecorative Pugin wallpaper which dominates one's visual senses at Westminster. Rebellion therefore itself becomes a form of ritual play among the political elite. It has its own forms of protest and is as hallowed by time's consecration as that ark of the covenant, the sovereignty of crown-in-parliament. Speeches are made in the chamber, concessions are demanded, and sometimes accorded. A few gratifying references to the doughty rebel in a lobby journalist's parliamentary sketch may be noted for recycling at future opportunities for publicity. Respect is then accorded the dissident by his peers and opponents – on both sides of the chamber. It is by following these well-trodden paths of ap-proved 'rebellion' that a Westminster reputation can often be made. Meanwhile, behind such well-advertised, and self-advertised, feats lie the great mass of the inert backbenches. Whether seen as loyalists or as toadies, these members of the lower ranks of the elite are a constant feature of the Westminster scene. They also serve since they are those who stand and wait and vote. Contrary to the prevalent myth, and insistent criticism, their numbers have not expanded very greatly in recent years. Most MPs have always been of this group. Neither heroic nor venal, they are merely the beasts of burden which enable Parlia-ment to be itself – a chamber of reflected reputations and of gossip about character and ambition, an institution where hope – if unrea-lized in the here and now – can always be endlessly deferred. If Churchill finally made it to No. 10 at sixty-five, then there's always hope for the rest who, all greased-up, can slide their way up and down the back passages of elite ambition while waiting for recognition to wind its way towards them.

## Lives Lived at the Centre

Given this inordinate interest in character and type – within certain rigidly defined limits – it is unsurprising that biography, autobiogra-phy, diaries and journals loom large among the interests of the political elite. From John Morley's *Life of Gladstone* to Roy Jenkins on Asquith, Churchill and himself, from Chips Channon's diaries to those of Alan Clark[41] and then in a welter of self-justifying auto-biographies[42] there are, apparently, lessons to be drawn from lives lived at the centre when Whitehall warriors decide it is time to declare. No other publishing industry in the world is quite so indulgent as the

British trade is towards the biography, and its comforting illusion that character is all we know and all we need to know when it comes to understanding politics. But the comforts of the biographical form are both escapist and fatalistic, encouraging as they do the elite belief that what matters is being on the inside track with people like yourself. The political past therefore becomes an inspiration or a guide to the political present – and it does so because nothing, it seems, ever really changes in British politics which then becomes a study of constant, ever-recurring political types. The kind of political history which is written under these circumstances is comforting to the elites because it shows that change and leadership can only ever come from the top, from the political leaders who allow change to happen rather than having to respond to demands from below. In this reworking of the 'great men of history' school of thought, it is the leaders who dominate and conspire by virtue of their strength of character and the fabric of their personalities. The biographical approach has been so basic to most of the recent elite plotting of British history that it takes some effort of the imagination to realize that this is not history at all. Rather, like the view that politics is 'what happens in parliament', this kind of elite history fails to explain the historical event, which is always a social fact composed of the decisions and failures of a multitude of historical figures all interacting with each other. But real history, being less easily malleable to elite purposes, seems best avoided and we have instead the narrative thrust of dominant personalities as the reworked story of Britain – a narrative which has been invented for the elite and is used by it in order to support its cabal-like dominance. But the example of recent British history's most dominant personality, Margaret Thatcher, shows – in both her rise and her fall – that the myth of a fabulous dominance is a fable designed to encourage rather than explain. A small group of financiers including Edward du Cann[43] and of businessmen such as Sir John Hoskyns[44] were important in propelling her to power and her fall was the result of the poll tax riots: both are examples of decisive change imposed on Westminster by extra-party political forces.

The collusive dominance of the political elite in recent years has also been aided by the fact that the clever minds who in the first half of the twentieth century were drawn to the permanent civil service have for the most part now disappeared, intelligence of that practical kind now being drawn to the law and the City. The self-confidence of figures such as Edward Bridges, Burke Trend and William Armstrong[45] has been replaced by Robin Butler[46] and his convenient doctrine of collective culpability – a belief which, applied to the 2002 failure to assess intelligence properly when deciding to embark on war, absolves any individual from blame. But despite the flight of talent the civil service, at its very highest level, is still rewarded with salaries and benefits which have to be hard earned in the private sector. Meanwhile, management theories and fanciful management systems have grown in authority and appeal, along with the superstitious veneration of management gurus, and have found a natural home in the civil service. Talk of management of change and of 'line managers' has been a refuge for the creation of new hierarchies in which mediocrity can shelter. Management chatter has therefore been a substitute for the reality of change – and can of course coexist not just with a lack of creative thought but also with confusion, mistakes, error and waste in government.

## Engaging with the People

Insulated within the sprawling centres of British government the political elites resemble a quarrelsome, noisy and very extended family. There are debates between the different generations of the family about the extent to which the older voices of experience should give way to the clamant urges of the rising and younger elites. Modernizers complain about traditionalists while also lamenting the difficulty of reforming party structures and changing party attitudes in order to woo the disillusioned many. All agree that party membership is on a downward spiral but disagree on why that should be so, and what the remedies might be. Might a political party be 'branded' and the attractions of its leading lights be sold by means of advertising accounts? There is a never-ending hunt for the slogan that encapsulates the message and for the manifesto that might connect the elite few with the many they wish to consider themselves as representing. Behind all those frequent calls for a national debate or a 'big conversation' about this or that matter of public debate there lies a real hollowness. For the elite anxiety about cynicism and 'disengagement' from the public sphere, although genuine enough, is also genuinely self-interested. Constant innovation in the matter of branding covers not only the conviction that serious change is impossible but also the determination to keep things that way.

That anxiety can exist as a form of intellectual preciousness. Onora

O'Neill's Reith Lectures on 'Trust',[47] for example, indicated a certain self-pity among the elites who long for the days when they spoke for a public or an interest group that was both trusting and well disciplined. But the graver forms of fear arise among the political elites themselves and their dread of popular insurgency. Their anxiety about their own isolation means that they have to resort, desperately, to techniques borrowed from marketing in order to attempt to engage with the public. It is the same anxious fear which lies behind New Labour's adoption of increasingly urgent, populist and anti-elitist rhetoric as a form of self-defence. Rather than creating movements and, thereby, elevating the elites that represented those movements with varying degrees of adequacy, the masses have become an increasingly elusive target that pollsters and public relations specialists spend their working lives trying to understand and influence. This elusiveness accounts for the almost frantic nature of New Labour language as it tries to convince itself that it is leading a mass-movement for change rather than one faction within a technocratic consensus. Thatcherism, its chosen model for imitation, did at least have a popular appeal beyond the ranks of the political party which spawned it. It threatened indeed at one stage to become a mass-movement, which is why the Tory political elite, although benefiting from Thatcherism, also came to fear its propensity to subvert party structures. But New Labour – knowing that it has little of that appeal – is reduced to looking at Britain with a barely concealed terror. Nonetheless, there are good careers to be made as suppliers of support services to all of these neurotic and edgy elites, plagued as they are by the knowledge that they must always be treading on thin ice when they try to talk to, or about, 'the people'.

The tracking of public opinion started in 1935 when George Gallup of Iowa established his American Institute of Public Opinion. His initial aim was to assess and monitor readers' responses to newspaper articles, and what has followed from that original Gallup poll and spread to all its later British imitators has been a similar exercise in credulity and expense accounts. Like magicians, con-men and fraud-sters down the ages, the pollster can recognize and exploit fear to his own advantage. Although hints and messages do get delivered to the political elite from the outside world that they seek to govern, they remain for the most part overwhelmingly, and necessarily, ignorant of what popular opinion really thinks. All the elite, or anyone, can ever know is that the public mind of Britain is a vast and formless mass of views, consisting as it does of fears, prejudices and hatreds as well as of hopes, ambitions and gut-instincts about what is good and bad, right and wrong. That mass-opinion is always fluid and never achieves a steady, settled form. Even to suppose that there is such a thing as 'public opinion', a settled disposition which is discoverable by analysis and by faithful reportage, is to encourage an illusion. For that notion of public opinion is always an abstraction, something extracted from a whole range of evidence and data and which is then moulded in order to arrive at some kind of specious objectivity. Polling aspires to the condition of science but in reality it is superstitious magic – and, like magic, its manipulations are designed to soothe away worries and allay fears.

The pollster's arts are a useful lie. They are useful in so far as they help to convince the elite that their hunches and intuitions about what might or might not work in government have some kind of basis in the reality of opinion. But they are also a lie in the spurious precision of their carefully index-pointed calibration of 'what is really going on'. Behind all the noise of elite chatter is a suspicion of the mostly quiet and undemonstrative British electorate, which is only given one opportunity every four or five years to really express its opinion. All of political elite life is directed towards that one general election day decision and during the intervening period the members of that elite have to survive and operate on the basis of hints, suspicions and uncertainty about something which is inherently unknowable – the public mind of Britain. All it knows, and fears, is that that mind is fickle and liable to transfer its enthusiasms with an equal passion from one belief to its very opposite – a belief illustrated in the political plays of Shakespeare, the man who illustrated and exploited to artistic effect the elite neuroses about the fragility of power. The fact, however, that public opinion does not really exist is no reason to stop a mountain of commentary being raised on its basis. This is, after all, part of the data which enables the political elites to continue talking to each other in television and radio programmes, in various forms of public debate and through newspaper articles and speeches, while all the time pretending to be addressing what it calls 'the public'. This raw material of public opinion supposedly collected from the front line is – like some forms of security intelligence – far too precious to be genuinely questioned. Instead, it has to be used urgently and turned into the basis of policy pronouncements, of rhetoric and indignation, of acclamation, newspaper headlines and parliamentary questions.

## The Centralizing Tendency

These are the strategies of survival that keep the political elite of Britain occupied and busy. And for all the quarrels within the family, the breaches of confidence, the noise and the rancour, the conflict between generations of experience and ones of hope, it is bound together by certain familial traits, habits of conduct and shared loyalties. Chief among these sentiments is an attachment to the 'orb and sceptre' aspects of House of Commons life. It is very easy to feel very important when walking down the parliamentary corridors while engaged in the search for that fugitive, ever-receding, commodity, the genuine transformative power which is the Holy Grail of many a political pilgrimage. Very few members of the political elite share Tony Blair's explicit impatience with parliamentary life and its crab-like proceduralism. Most find it a soothing reassurance. Many have chosen this second career having experienced mixed fortunes in their first and are genuinely gratified to be there. What obscure sense of inadequacy impels them to search for that recognition in the first place is perhaps an unanswerable question. But there is more to the adjective in the phrase 'honourable member' than mere convention, for Parliament is a place where one can gain honour through the recognition of others. Having arrived there the sheer oddity of the conditions of life and of work, whose hours are long but also somehow strangely empty, also combines to keep the political operatives bound together in a common and cohesive, if numbing, form of existence which transcends the particular details of party division.

This unity of the political elite – both intellectually and socially as well as in its shared conditions of life, its tastes and interests from preferences in suits and leisure wear to its choices in light entertainment and interest in IT – has been around for a very long time. But in the past twenty-five years, and especially since the governments of the 1980s reformed and so enfeebled local government, the institutions of the British state – as well as their personnel – have become more obviously consolidated around the centre. Britain's quango state has conceded an apparent independence to the 'quasi-autonomous nongovernmental' bodies, while making sure that ministers of the crown have the last word. Inadequacy of local government personnel was the justification given by central government for the creation of the quangos – agencies which took over many of the functions of the old local authorities. But that inadequacy was the consequence of a disregard and a stripping of powers which had already undermined and demoralized Britain's local government. Linguistically, too, the quango world of the agency and the regulator has been a powerful presence in the culture of the corporate glossy magazine and within the luxuriant growth of management jargon – mastery of whose obfuscating vocabulary is an important qualification for elite roles. Rate-capping of local authorities, together with the removal of many of their previous functions in running schools and hospitals, has substantially increased the powers of the Whitehall satrapy and extended the patronage it can bestow through appointments to the agencies that now run these services. Enjoyment of this centralizing role has been quite compatible with the superficial encouragement of local autonomy by those who are most hell-bent on government as a force for rational, streamlined modernity. Michael Heseltine's[48] belief in locally elected mayors and John Prescott's[49] campaign for elected regional assemblies are two such examples of superficial regional enthusiasm. But these measures presuppose that power is conceded from the top and the centre both downwards and outwards, rather than growing upwards from its roots in popular opinion. It is a bogus kind of enlightened wisdom – shared, quite appropriately, right across a political divide which is only superficially wide. For the power elite's common assumption is that power is something shared between them and then conceded to others in stage-managed form.

Those who are struck by this accretion in power at the centre contrast this decadent impulse with the earlier vitality of a world of provincial elites at a time when Manchester produced Cobden, Bright and Free Trade while Birmingham provided the stage both for the Chamberlain dynasty in politics and for the Cadburys, whose ex-ercises in philanthropic reform were designed to ensure that their workforce remained quiescent. Victorian municipal architecture in the age of Alfred Waterhouse, whose cragged Gothic style expressed the local pomp, encourages the idea that these localized elites were indeed proudly independent spirits, standing in some kind of line of direct lineage from the local burgesses who first wound their way to England's mediaeval parliaments in order to express their umbilical link with their locality.[50]

A little reflection should dispose of this sentimentality about the ruggedly virtuous local elite, powerful though it has been in terms of popular history from John Seeley[51] and G.M. Trevelyan[52] to Arthur Bryant,[53] and within the higher journalism as well. It has been an

aspect of that myth-making about English origins and English continuities which the political and public elites have always been very
good at producing. Sometimes they do genuinely believe these stories
and see them as part of that John of Gaunt romance of England as a
demi-Eden set in a silvery sea. More often it's just been a good line to
shoot as a method of defending that isolationist England which has
been the setting for their careers. Whichever of these two possible
motivations may apply, these mostly twentieth-century views of an
England composed of autonomous localities and liberties have been as
influential as their precursor, the mostly late-nineteenth-century literary invention of a mediaeval Merrie England which was a home to
the arts and crafts as well as being infused with a natural and organic
solidarity between the people and their masters. But the provincial
dynamism only ever really applied to Manchester and Birmingham
and, even there, it lasted only for the two generations or so that
straddle the turn of the nineteenth century. Thereafter, as Britain's
manufacturing economy went into long-term decline so did the
political importance of the localized elites. It may very well have been
the takeover of the local elites by the metropolis which contributed to
that decline.

## The Metropolitan Centre

The politics of culture in England reflects this same truth. The English
regional novel, having started with a work of genius in George Eliot's
*Middlemarch* (1871–2), starts to dwindle away almost as soon as that
book was published and then ends in the very minor talent of Arnold
Bennett[54] in late nineteenth-century Staffordshire. That author's removal to London, where he supplied the head chef of the Savoy with
the inspiration for an eponymous omelette, marks an appropriate end
to a chapter in English letters. Contemporary English literature – and
especially the novel – is quite insistently metropolitan, being largely
confined in its setting and its mental attitudes to an area somewhere
between Highgate in the north and Kennington in the south, and
between Hoxton in the east and Barnes in the west. At the same time,
there has been a striking decline in the political novel. Political figures
occur incidentally, and in a largely clichéd form, in some serious
fiction such as Alan Hollinghurst's *The Line of Beauty*. But the
attempt of an earlier generation such as C.P. Snow[55] and Maurice
Edelman[56] to give a rounded and human dimension to political actors

and their beliefs has now largely vanished. The London theatre records some attempts, notably by David Hare, to create a fiction on stage which takes as its subject matter the drama of politics. But the impression of an oligarchy talking to itself is an overwhelming one, and the artist who tries to breathe life into these dry bones is inevitably undermined by the desiccated quality of the subject matter. Even when the issues are genuinely ones of consequence, it is the manner and style of the political power elites which deprives them of a felt life and a human engagement.

The dominance of London as a metropolitan centre has always been the dominant fact in the making of England's political elites. Even at the height of their influence the provincial political elites always knew that it was Westminster which would supply them with the stage and the attention that they craved. Stanley Baldwin,[57] a Midlands iron-master, despite his affectation of the pipe-sucking Worcestershire squire, and Neville Chamberlain,[58] whose family fortune in screws propelled him to be Lord Mayor of Birmingham, were both West-minster slow starters because of their initial provincial focus, but were under no illusions about their ultimate destination.

## Context, Gesture and Accent

Here again, it is the fact of royal power which sets the pattern for all later political elites. Government in England grew out of the royal household and was conducted wherever the sovereign happened to be, since it was concentrated around his person. This was true of Alfred the Great, England's first, and arguably only, intellectual king,[59] whose seat of power witnessed the rise of ninth-century Wessex as the eventual winner in establishing predominance over the other early mediaeval English kingdoms. From 1529 onwards, the centre of the court life in London was the vast and rambling Whitehall Palace, which the crown had seized after the fall of Cardinal Wolsey.[60] That establishment of the court in the palace by the Thames would also establish the London-centric habits of the British political elites. These implicit and explicit truths of life in the royal household have survived into the operative ambience of modern Whitehall and Westminster. This is a cross-party consensus, which is as evident in such natural New Labour courtiers as Peter Mandelson and Charlie Falconer as it was in those natural Tory courtiers Cecil Parkinson and John Major.[61] Power is as much caught as it is taught, being a question of looks and asides, of the interpretation of a phrase and the use of the correct intonation and inflexion in the tone of voice and the delivery of an opinion. These are the subtle and quasi-Masonic means of communication and assertion which enable one elite member to recognize another at work and at play. Political elites need therefore to be alert to context and to be expert in the interpretation of gestures as well as of voices.[62] Since elite accents have now become more varied, these skills of detection have become more important than ever before. The British elite does not proclaim its presence with the same clipped linguistic register that characterized its predecessors and the reality of its power is therefore successfully concealed behind the variously accented sounds of modern Britain. Political elite accents can vary dramatically: Alan Milburn[63] does a mixed effect of Geordie with a distant Midlands twang in the same way that Peter Hain[64] mingles a Home Counties drawl with a recollection of South Africa; Margaret Beckett[65] maintains elocution-lesson perfection and Alan Johnson[66] gets away with a passable imitation of a London wide-boy; John Prescott combines Hull with Deeside (itself an amalgam of Scouse with North Walian) and Charlie Falconer is posh Scot. But if the linguistic register can vary, the political elites' methodology and views observe a smooth and courtly unanimity.

## The National Project

The constitutional crisis of the seventeenth century established that power would flow from courtly elites to parliamentary ones, but it never really changed the peculiarly personal way in which the British power elites operate their political styles. The first-stage losers in that contest were the Puritan and Congregationalist elites who opted for emigration and decided that New England was a more fertile ground for their democratic principles of government in both Church and state. Theirs was an authentically stubborn English voice of conscience and it encouraged a suspicious view of the professionals, whether they were princes, or prelates, or priests. Transplanted from England, that tradition became the most important element in the principles of the colonies that later became the USA.[67] Despite all the post-war talk of a fundamental identity of interest between these two English-speaking peoples, their political systems still distinguish the one country from the other. The senatorial and gubernatorial aristocracy which draws its strength from local roots is, and always has been, a fact of

American political life. The age of Bush is an additional reminder of how those provincial roots can sustain the dynastic principle in American politics. C. Wright Mills pointed out as early as 1956[68] that the war and the subsequent settlement had raised the military–industrial elite groups centred in Washington to an eminence unsurpassed in the country's history. But those globally minded elites in the capital still operate in a system where the localities retain both their meaningful government and their assertive elites. A myriad of different state elections show the democratic principle being followed to an extent unimaginable now in Britain whose soil, so ironically, provided the roots of that principle. The result is that the British political version of democratic order has been permanently skewed in favour of executive centralism.

This question of the unity of what was first England and then became Britain is basic to the propagandist business of establishing a national project. The power elites in politics have been adept at inventing a whole series of such narratives as a way of explaining the British to themselves – and, more importantly, as a way of getting popular endorsement and support for the elite-led project. If England's first unity was centred on the mediaeval royal court, it also received a striking, and more psychological, deepening with the creation of the Reformation state of the sixteenth century.[69] National purpose now became Protestant and anti-Catholic as the new narrative gave added strength to the idea, first established by Bede in his eighth-century history, that the English were a chosen people and the subject of God's special guidance. This meant that local rebellions could be crushed all the more effectively since the new rigour of power at the centre could summon up morality and theology as well as legislative power in order to make its case. From that point on, the unifying process has been remorseless, though it has adopted different justifications for its extension. Britain's Hanoverian elites in the eighteenth century saw the emergence of a more secular politics founded on the dominance of the newly established Bank of England as the guarantor of the state's creditworthiness which in turn financed colonial expansion, armed hostility to French hegemony on the European continent and then a panicky rejection of French Republicanism. Gladstonian elites in the late nineteenth century, though something of a one-man band, added morality to money as a source of power and established the vocabulary of ethical purpose as part of the justification for British power.[70] Exactly a century after the end of Gladstone's last ministry in 1894, the election of Tony Blair as Labour leader saw the beginning of the re-emergence of that same Gladstonian language of national virtue which equated progress and order with elite self-interest.

The twentieth-century national project brought to us by the modern elites has been mostly about modernity and technocracy, with the significant exception of the romantic Churchillianism which was important politically from May 1940 until the US entry into the war (December 1941) and intermittently significant culturally from then until today.[71] The streamlined state was meant to be both more efficient and more fair than any of its predecessors which had relied on aristocratic power and extended a paternalist protection to special interest groups such as farmers and Anglicans. This aspiration of a liberal state encouraged the idea of equal access and the rise of careers open to the talented and the energetic. As a form of state propaganda it has been used to justify the various forms of power elite activity: state-friendly new Liberals[72] in the early twentieth century, the neo-socialist governments of the mid-twentieth century and progressive Conservatism as it darts in and out of the narrative. Socialism in office turned out to be a question, first, of an English national sense of fair play applied to relations between the classes before then turning into the business of organizing a bureaucratically managed state, at which point the Labour elite had to disguise from its members the party's progressive integration into the national elite. Post-1945, the story was merely one of competition between the two parties in the race to get their hands on the Keynesian money pump. By this point Labour seemed to be managing Great Britain Ltd[73] and was therefore vulnerable to being subsumed by that 1950s managerialist declivity – one-nation Toryism – which prevailed before the Thatcher combination of nationalism with tax cuts arrived first to undermine a divided opposition on the left and then to sow the seeds of its own destruction as the 1980s economy went into first overdrive and then recession.

All of these have been power elite projects about the imagined national identity of Britain and have involved speculations or guesses about what might work as a line to take on that identity, necessarily a furtive and back-garden entity. That is why propaganda about the inherent sportsmanship of the national temperament and its fondness especially for team games acquired such a vogue during the first half of the twentieth century, as it became obvious that Britain was losing out in the game of global power and imperial influence.[74] Sporting tours of the Caribbean, of Australia and New Zealand, of India and

Pakistan became important, if increasingly desperate, assertions of Britain's continuing world role. Partial and editorialized views of the national character have been turned into apparent deep truths, but their real purpose has been to anchor the elites and protect their position. From the first, legislatively imposed, views of the Protestant elites right through to the Tory proclamations of buccaneering capitalism in the 1980s, there have been two basic truths at work. First, the legislative programmes gave the elite leaders substantial material rewards, whether in the form of sixteenth-century confiscated Church property which then became the political elites' new country houses or in the late-twentieth-century form of share options and company directorships. Second, this elite proselytizing and nest-feathering aroused comment but no real outrage leading to activist dissidence. Such political passivity has surely been the most important fact in the making of modern England. *Pace* Disraeli, England is not so much a difficult country to change as it is to convince, most of its people viewing its political elites with a cynicism which rivals that of their leaders.

In modern times, the outbreak of syndicalism and of organized labour which created the Labour Party[75] was entirely exceptional and, as a truly popular movement, it was also very short-lived. In its heyday it was a moral force infused with many of the enthused and visionary qualities of a religious movement, and it therefore proved vulnerable to the managerialist tone and methods of the men of 1945. After that election victory the Labour Party settled down to the serious business of discipline enforcement – something which is necessary if any political party is to provide reliable career structures for its elites. Both Old and New Labour, although recognizably different phases in the party's history, have been concerned with centralized authority and career-producing mechanisms. Herbert Morrison[76] and Aneurin Bevan[77] were to the right and the left, respectively, of Old Labour but both stood for the authority of party as a base for careers. The factionalism of Militant was a reaction against the increasingly remote quality of that authority, and meant an authoritarian response at a localized level against the authoritarianism of the centre: the Levellers who emerged from the radical army in the 1640s had been a similar local reaction against a centrist and reactionary elite. The emergence of New Labour simply did with pagers what Old Labour had done by speeches, it restored a rather monarchic cult of the leader along with respect for those who ran the administrative apparatus. But the difference is that New Labour has been prepared to live and prosper in the world created by 1980s Conservatism. Like previous Labour elites it is devoted to career-building, but it does so within a settlement that Old Labour would not have accepted.

## The Lineage of Connection

Beneath all the sentiment about what used to be referred to as 'this great movement of ours', there are some strikingly continuous facts of patronage and family connection which make New Labour the heir to the Hanoverian–Whiggish elites of the eighteenth century who also ran Britain through the mechanisms of family and patronage. Roy Jenkins had a significant career start as the son of Arthur Jenkins, a Labour MP, who was close to Clement Attlee. Peter Mandelson's grandfather was Herbert Morrison – a dominating party manager of post-war Labour London and a looming figure of consequence within the post-war Labour cabinet. Estelle Morris,[78] the former Education Secretary, is the daughter of a former Deputy Chief Whip[79] as well as the niece of Alf Morris,[80] a life peer and former minister whom she has now joined in the House of Lords. Hilary Armstrong is not just the Chief Whip[81] but is also the daughter of a long-serving Labour MP[82] who also served in the Whips' Office. Charles Clarke shows a political–administrative continuity at work, being the son of Otto Clarke, a permanent secretary with an invincible confidence in the rectitude of his own judgement.[83] When Bob Cryer died it seemed only natural that his widow[84] should take his seat in the House of Commons, where her son also sat as a member until 2005.[85] Hilary Benn,[86] the Overseas Development Secretary, is the son of Tony Benn and Gwyneth Dunwoody's[87] career starts with the fact that her father was Morgan Phillips, general secretary of the Labour Party (1944–62), while David Miliband, Minister for Communities and Local Government is an august member of the Labour aristocracy, being the son of Ralph Miliband, one of the main intellectual influences in shaping the party's identity as well as the brother of Ed Miliband who in 2005 was elected the Labour MP for Doncaster North. The career of Llinos Golding (Baroness Golding of Newcastle-under-Lyme) is a fine paradigm of familial politics since she is the daughter of Ness Edwards, the Labour MP for Caerphilly (1939–68), and succeeded her husband, John Golding, as the member for Newcastle-under-Lyme (1986–2001) having previously been his aide.

The fact of a Welsh connection in many of these examples shows the ease with which Labour, within a generation of the foundation of the ILP, moved from being a popular movement into solidifying itself as a local elite power structure whose establishment values ensured that it blended naturally with the power at the centre. The industrialized areas of England, Wales and Scotland have been easily mythologized by historians of organized labour into fulcrums of genuine political consciousness – a fact which is supposed to distinguish them from the more general history of the passive British masses. But even before the subtopia of decaying council estates and of mass-unemployment kicked in during the 1970s what really typified these localities in the 1950s and 1960s was their Labour-leaning political apathy – a condition which paralleled the Tory-leaning political apathy of the village, the country town and, finally, that of the suburb whose values would rise to eclipse those of the industrial British regions from the mid-twentieth century onwards. Within those areas of its greatest initial support Labour had created a structure which guaranteed a good turn-out at election and which helped people get jobs, especially the sons of the old working class who became teachers and administrators. But in making a non-Labour world seem unthinkable, in making Labour such a natural aspect of the landscape, the party leaders had also depoliticized their own movement to a point at which the highly unusual political activism of the pioneering generation died out with that generation.[88]

Family connection is therefore one of the useful habits of highly effective Labour people whose movement, like any successful political party, has some analogies to an extended family with all those hatreds and rivalries overlaid with sentiment that can typify such relationships. And, as in any family, the question of the leadership of any political clan determines the shifting patterns of political elite activity. Elites, having separated themselves from the rest of society, do nonetheless like the security of being themselves led. They know very well that in a democratic society their positions are inherently precarious and that they are vulnerable to attack – on the grounds of the envy of others as well as on account of the incompetence, venality and remoteness which are intermittently characteristic of the elite members. This is why the British political elites have to spend so much time seeking to cultivate a faux populist familiarity with popular culture as they learn to say 'cheers' to modern Britain. That same insecurity which leads them to look warily at the base of power also inclines them to look upwards, for the political elite will acclaim an effective and purposeful leadership as an effective strengthening of its own position almost regardless of the kind of positions and beliefs adopted by that leadership. Reservations are set aside, at least in public, and dissent goes underground. The disadvantage, however, for that section of the political elite which has decided to bow the knee to the dominant politician of the passing day is that it often disintegrates after the disappearance of such a leader.

## Strength in Leadership

Robert Peel's[89] creation, the modern Conservative Party, succumbed to factionalism after his early death. He had invented a new kind of party, one which was committed to free trade and which rejected the agricultural subsidies of protectionist economics. This revolution from the top transformed a ragged coalition of aristocratic and landed interests and turned it into a more urban, mercantile and middle-class affair. But Peel had treated his party very roughly indeed in order to achieve that end. He had used the executive power of the prime ministerial office in order to beat sense into his party, after which experience it lacked powers of recovery. This spectacle of the very high view of the executive, however, impressed Peel's young follower, W.E. Gladstone. Like all the modern elite prime ministers who have truly dominated their parties, he was both strongly driven temperamentally towards such an assertion of dominance and also capable of equating this psychological self-interest with high moral purpose. Having transferred from the Peelite Tories to the nascently modern Liberal Party, he then in effect equated that party with Gladstonianism, a blend of sanctimony with acute responsiveness to those shifting sands of popular opinion which might then be exploited to maintain his dominance. Lloyd George's premiership in both peace and war as well as Margaret Thatcher's period in office,[90] a peace-time premiership whose sinews were war-like, are the two pre-eminent twentieth-century examples of high executive assertion at the expense of their parties. Both premiers were strikingly creative in establishing new patterns and opportunities for political elite activity. Lloyd George's effective invention – the modern mechanisms of Whitehall government – included the bringing of 'new men' into office as both ministers and as political appointments to the civil service. The Thatcher government, though superficially pledged to the rhetoric of reducing the role of government, actually extended executive power in the areas that excited its interests and imagination, such as defence procurement as well as the intelligence and security services, while also presiding over greatly inflated budgets in benefits and social security. This last of the Cold War British governments also saw a major recreation and extension of that military–industrial complex which was such a feature of the internal politics of all the Cold War states on either side of the Iron Curtain. That extension was the opportunity for some members of the British political elite to merge its interests with those of a business elite, especially in the arms industry.

The dominance enjoyed by British prime ministers who have asserted themselves and recast their political parties has proved a pyrrhic kind of victory. Peel, Gladstone, Lloyd George and Thatcher all reinvented their parties. Those same parties then fell apart after their own time and were condemned to long years of rancorous opposition and internal factionalism. The British electoral system tends to approve of these periods of 'strong' executive-led leadership as the political elites are reshaped and refashioned by leaders who are harder with their own parties than they are with the opposition. What little we know of genuine democratic opinion suggests that it has a tolerance born of indifference when it looks at the necessary hypocrisies and cravenness of party as a power-seeking mechanism. But at times that tolerance veers towards contempt, as has happened recently. Party membership statistics continue to decline and are now a mere hangover from the earlier periods of mass-engagement and of the class-determined activism which once anchored the elites in the language and the reality of communal purpose. Now, political elites stand isolated on a peninsula of self-regard which encourages a disabused view of their activities. What, therefore, at one level could be more sadistically agreeable than the sight of a party being abused by its own leader – and then being forced to endorse him? There is also a quixotic element within the pathology of the political elites which enjoys all that beating-up. Increased majorities at the poll provide an initial sense of security. The intoxicant of being in on something fresh and new leads the political elite to march along with the necessity of an evident destiny and also to accept the rewards of patronage which are the most important means by which a Prime Minister can extend his system of clientage and of obligation. The masterful leader can thereby gratify the political elites' search for honour while also relying on their propensity to put self-respect on the back burner. But the longer the dominance continues, the deeper the subterranean fissures. 'Strength'

in leadership discourages the idea of a 'natural' successor and therefore increases the risk of mere anarchy being unleashed once the leader
disappears. The political elite's precariousness and its nervous sense of
its own mortality – though partly assuaged by the reassurance of life
lived under a dominant leader – can never be entirely removed.

## Party Solidarity

The Tory parliamentary decision to remove Margaret Thatcher from
office was the result of a collective seizure. Being the result of man-
oeuvrings within the parliamentary party rather than among the
constituency associations themselves, it was quite specifically an elite
affair and one which resulted in the elevation of a member of that same
elite, John Major. It issued from one of those collective failures of nerve
which occasionally afflict all political elites when they consider themselves to be in a condition of clear and present danger. The elite-led
appeasement polices of the 1930s enjoyed a broad coalition of cross-
party support because of similar reasons of self-interest. It was an
internal Tory elite which tried to get Churchill deselected as an MP in
the 1930s and another one which fomented the discontent behind the
proposal of a Commons motion of censure on his conduct of military
policy in 1942.[91] At such moments the constant impulses of self-
protection within the political elites vie with the occasionally self-
destructive ones and combine to create a collective neurosis when they
know that they do not know what 'the people' may be thinking, but
fear the worst. The collapse of the Tory elite from 1990 onwards shows
how long-lived the consequences of an elite failure may be for a political
party. The collapse of the Liberal Party elite in the 1920s was objectively determined by the rise of a new class-determined politics, that of
the Labour Party. In that sense, there was nothing strange about the
death of Liberal England at all. It was simply the working out of a
necessary pattern as a political ethic of collective solidarity replaced that
of political career individualism since the Liberal Party had degenerated
into a mechanism for the personal advancement of barristers–MPs on
the make. In the case of the Tory collapse there were two aspects. The
internal neuroses, plotting and counter-plotting were the symptoms of a
party which had lost its grip. But they were produced by something far
deeper, for the Tory Party had sacrificed itself in order to remake
Britain into a capitalist country. It was blamed for the recession and
collapse in house prices of the late 1980s and early 1990s and was

therefore vulnerable to a challenge from a Labour Party which was willing to accept the broadly capitalist outlines of the Tory picture of Britain. By an uncanny symmetry this accommodation echoes the way the Tories in the 1950s had accepted the broad outlines of Labour's 1945 picture, while not having to associate themselves with the strikes and the rationing which accounted for the generally glum condition of Britain in 1951 after six years of Labour government.

The Conservative political elites no longer contain the family connections which once helped to give them some kind of collective identity. Gene pool solidarity had once helped the Tory patriciate to stiffen its nerve in the face of traditional Labour's trade union cabal. But the age of Old Etonian cousins, nephews and uncles, of fathers and sons succeeding each other in Parliament and in ministerial office, ended with the premiership of Harold Macmillan. Those forms of familial and tribal loyalism had made the old Tory Party a subject for easy mockery but they have not been succeeded by any alternative means of establishing internal elite coherence within the Conservative Party. Consequently the effective New Labour cabal does not have to confront an equally effective Tory cabal. Perhaps the Tory elite of the 1990s swallowed the leadership line on the virtues of individualism so completely that they decided to apply it to their own party as well. But the whole point of being an elite member is that you often have to swallow the rather Hobbesian line that collective action is the best way of securing your own self-interest. Individualist methods, consistently applied, can mean a collective demise.

Among past and present members of the opposition front bench, Nicholas Soames[92] and Dominic Grieve[93] are very rare examples of significant Conservative politicians who have been reared from Tory political families. That should make them rather more coherent elite operators, but objective circumstances and altered times objectively change the requirements for elite success and, being somewhat pastiche examples of the stiffly pin-striped Tory, both Soames and Grieve end up demonstrating the gap between the Conservative elite and a wider democratic world. Some of that distance is also accurately measured by the occasionally self-destructive quality of the political elite when it reaches greedily for honour and gratification, as happened in the fin-de-siècle age of Tory sleaze. But despite the atomistic behaviour and the frustrations which typify all party elites at various times the elites themselves know that the party they have chosen is the one they are stuck with for the rest of their careers.

Defection from one party to another is not really allowed for in the collective consciousness of the political elites. Views, opinions and careers can evolve, change and develop in other areas of modern British life, and are allowed for as signs of creativity, renewal and adaptability in the evolutionary cycle. But, uniquely, this is only rarely permitted among the party political elites. The parties may indeed have become increasingly close to each other in views and parliamentarians practically interchangeable. But those very facts mean that it is important to maintain the charade of difference which conceals the reality of convergence. True odium is therefore reserved not for the opposition but for the turncoat as tears are disingenuously shed on behalf of all of those 'who worked so hard' to get the member elected and who have now been abandoned by the defector. It is doubtful if the electorate shares this lachrymose article of faith, being mostly convinced that local party activists are rather sad hackish types with nothing better to do than hang around on street corners handing out unreadable pamphlets.

The MP who has exchanged one solidarity for another soon discovers the melancholy truth that he is equally resented by both parties, however vigorous the protestations of conversion and despite the initial, formal, joy at the sight of a repentant sinner. There are two possible lines of explanation that may be adopted to justify both the disillusion and the abandonment. The convert may either say that he has himself changed or that his party has changed. Saying that he himself has changed is dangerously disruptive of the constant-as-the-northern-star stance deemed necessary for most political reputations despite the wildly varying 'lines to take' pursued by the political actors themselves. It seems therefore on the whole best to claim that the party itself has changed and left the original adherent anchorless. This has been a popular position and one adopted both by pro-European Union Conservatives in recent years and, before them, by the socially democratically inclined Labour MPs who left their party in the 1980s. The problem – for those sedulous of a reputation for sincerity – is that that position is adopted only when the political party being abandoned is already in a state of disarray. The argument therefore leaves the convert exposed to the charge of being heartlessly 'opportunistic'. These, however, are accusations which are strictly reserved for the internal debate between and within the parties themselves, and at no stage do they appear to attract the interest of a wider electorate. The future career of, say, a Shaun Woodward[94] – Witney's Conservative

MP who then became St Helens South's Labour MP, but had to wait six years before gaining ministerial office – is hardly high politics. The same is true of John Horam's[95] career which has included periods as a Labour MP and then an SDP one before coming to rest on the Conservative benches as the member for Orpington. But such examples do attract a quite disproportionate degree of interest within the political elites themselves, for they know very well how difficult it is to justify the transfer of allegiances in an age when the political parties have so much in common. The interparty transfer's real effect is to dispel the illusion of a chasm and so to reveal the common ground on which the party political elites stand. That is its true danger – a fact which accounts for the opprobrium heaped upon the hapless wanderer's head.

If, however, you can keep your head – as well as your seat – then there is really very little need to change party affiliation, however dramatic the change of views. The careers of Jack Straw, Peter Hain and Charles Clarke[96] have all shown a common pattern as radical and disruptive (if carefully career-managed) activism in youth gives way over the years to the party subservience which rewards them with office. The political elite has risen through party and can justify its changes as an accommodation to the higher purpose and necessity of party. Views may change, vary or evolve but at every stage it is the fact of loyalty to the office-producing mechanism of party which supplies the deepest continuity beneath the apparent contradiction.

## Intellectuals, Advisers and Think Tanks

By the beginning of the twenty-first century the British political elites have attempted so many different kinds of justification for their election, their elevation and their continuation that there are distinct signs of fatigue, both among themselves and within the various audiences they have addressed over the past century of democratic life. Recent examples of an attempt to discover a common plot to being British have included the idea of a European Britain, an independent and sovereign Britain, a stakeholding democracy and then a property-owning one marching in the vanguard of market capitalism – a direction which makes Britain into an aspect of the USA. The search for a theme that would redeem and explain modern Britain started with the early twentieth-century attacks on Church establishment, aristocratic monopolies and the House of Lords. Some of that

initial campaigning was advanced on behalf of working-class consciousness and solidarity. But it was also the first shot in the campaign
by the members of a liberal and urban middle class who were anxious
to secure a new power base for their political careers. It therefore led to
those who would have been power-hungry Liberal Party careerists
becoming equally career-minded operators within the Labour Party.
The professional existences of Harold Wilson and Anthony Crosland,
of Dick Crossman, Hugh Gaitskell, Roy Jenkins and Denis Healey[97]
would – a generation or two before their actual date of birth – have
been happily pursued on Asquithean or Gladstonian terms, had it not
been for the awkward fact of the demise of the party of Gladstone and
of Asquith. There is a similar truth at work in the careers of R.A.
Butler, Harold Macmillan, Edward Heath, John Major, Douglas
Hurd, Kenneth Clarke and Chris Patten[98] within a Conservative
Party whose merit in their eyes was that it was not a socialist
organization and could perhaps be turned into a vehicle which would
accommodate their own ambitions. Clarke, indeed, rather glories in
his story of how he applied to join both the main parties and ended up
with the Tories only because they were more prompt in replying. And
it is his sense that one group of political elites is really much like
another which explains his appeal to an electorate which is rather
wider than that of his own party. All of these political elite careers
have been lived out on terms which have been established by the fact
of the end of the Liberal Party as a party of government and the
consequent need to make sense of the available alternatives.

The banners unfurled have been many and various, and some have
inspired even when they led to failure. The post-1945 elite adopted
technocratic centralism as a way of justifying its existence. This had
been the rhetorical and practical mode of operation for the continental
European governing elites in one way or other ever since the Napoleonic invention of the modern machinery of government as so many
spokes on a wheel with a governing intelligence at its centre. But the
experience was an original episode in the history of the British elites,
whose previous experiences of large-scale governmental activism had
been confined to the pursuit of war and peace, the financing of the
armed forces and the assertion of national self-interest through
diplomacy. The readiness and the confidence required to undertake
a large-scale reconstruction of the British economy amounted to the
biggest change since the Reformation.[99] It was different not just in
scale but also in kind from every previous governmental programme

70

in British history. Just like the legislative details of the Reformation state drafted by Thomas Cromwell, this complete break with the past at both a mental and a governmental level involved the energies of a new elite, that of the intellectuals who wished to be associated with the political elite.

Cromwell's jurists, clerks, policemen and propagandist writers were harnessed to a new vision of an independent country, one in which sovereignty was vested in the authority of the institution of the king-in-parliament. This was 'humanism' with a purpose – the use of the authority of scholarship in order to achieve the renewal of England. In one respect, it was a continuation of the similar energies of the mediaeval clerks. But Cromwell's scholarly elites had an added edge – these were power-hungry intellectuals who were eager for position and personal fame. When the most important of the pamphleteering propagandists used by Cromwell, Thomas Starkey, rushed back to London in late 1534 from Padua where he had been studying Roman Law he did so because the king seemed 'set to the restitution of the true common weal' – a policy which would give him an opportunity to apply his learning 'to some use and profit of my country'.[100] Once Starkey got his government commissions his pen got going with attacks on common law practitioners, proposals to reduce the laws of England to a knowable code and advocacy of primitive Keynesian-ism so that government money could be spent on projects designed for 'the comfort of . . . profitable citizens living in some honest exercise in [the] commonalty', a real necessity since 'penury ever breedeth sedi-tion'. From Starkey onwards the intellectual armed with a fluent pen and endowed with a capacity for ingratiation has been an established adjunct to the operations of the British political elite.

In the world made by 1945 the political–intellectual elite were still operating at a time when the idea of the public intellectual counted for something real and independently authoritative, rather than being an unintentionally hilarious series of lists drawn up by – and containing – commentators boastful of a governmental association. 'What harm have I ever done the Labour movement?' was the reaction of the historian R.H. Tawney[101] on being offered a peerage. That tone of speaking some kind of independent truth to power was echoed not only in such figures of the left as Harold Laski[102] and H.G. Wells[103] but also, later, in some Conservative thinkers such as Michael Oake-shott[104] and Friedrich von Hayek.[105] Yet, even in that generation there were plenty of intellectuals who fulfilled the lapdog role. Isaiah

71

Berlin's[106] constant and boring paeans of praise for the quality of English freedom seem now to have been so many forms dutifully completed in order to qualify for the honours that were showered on him in his lifetime. Harold Macmillan's nomination of Hugh Trevor-Roper as Regius Professor of Modern History at Oxford (a crown appointment) secured a Tory–Whig voice in university affairs. These influential figures in the history of public–intellectual opinion have had plenty of successors, ranging from John Gray's[107] adventurousness in ideas, the fruit of a shift from disillusioned right to equally melancholy left, to Paul Johnson's[108] narrative histories written in the course of his journey from left to right. What is constant in the history of such figures is their desire to be taken seriously by the political elites, their rather needy search for attention and consequent readiness to produce the goods that gratify.

## The Third Way

Who now remembers, cares for, or believes in, the third way? Anthony Giddens' description[109] of a system of socially concerned, managed, capitalism was the vogue of the mid-1990s. It showed how the opportunism of the intellectuals is no less than that of the politicians, especially when the two worlds coincide and power seeks a convenient truth. Although packaged with the full panoply of Cambridge sociology, the third way was the reflection of the moment rather than an independent, ideological, shaper of it. The end of the Conservative dominance coincided with one of those occasional pan-European pattern of coincidences – such as the liberal–nationalist revolutions of 1848 – which suggest to the shape-detecting mind a deeper pattern at work. But, just like 1848, the third way regimes of the 1990s fizzled out. Germany's Social Democrats under Gerhard Schröder proved unable to reform their country's economy. France's socialists were voted out of office having displayed a combination of arrogance, pretension and obscurantism typical of their party. Silvio Berlusconi's Forza Italia was a reminder that the third way of state-managed capitalism was highly compatible with the lineage of Italian fascism.

As a confection of heated-up Keynesianism there was nothing in the third way which had not already been said, written and done in the 1950s and 1960s experience of economic councils and of development corporations, of all those government initiatives begun in the hope of demonstrating both social concern and a grasp of economic policy but ending in a series of opportunities for the self-promotion of business-men with a public image to burnish. But all the third way conferences and colloquiums, with their earnest lectures and speeches, did serve a purpose: they showed the ease with which the British intelligentsia could be rented out in order to lend a little added mental lustre to power. Tony Blair's interpretation of third way politics – a reading in any event shrouded in mystery – would be elbowed aside by his eagerness to trump the Tories on Atlanticism and his ready acceptance of American power as the major influence on British foreign policy.

At the same time, 'progressivism' in neo-Labour governmental circles was being reinterpreted to mean citizen choice. This consu-merist model for public services was the extension of market-Thatch-erism by other party means. It also borrowed heavily on some of the ideas current among American Democrats who had served in the Clinton presidency and been influenced by that presidency's mid-term abandonment of any radical welfare reforms which might alleviate the condition of the poor. *The Next Deal*, written by one such former Clinton official – Andrei Cherny – showed how it was possible to plunder the political vocabulary of the past and then exploit it to a manipulative effect.[110] His was just one of a whole crop of books which were popular at the turn of the millennium and were devoted to the subject of 'reinventing government' while also 'renewing' and 'redefining' it. But the true redefinition, renewal and reinvention was that of the elites of the political centre-left who needed a new justification for their existence and therefore turned to market man-tras on both sides of the Atlantic. Indeed, many of the Labour phrases about the need to have a country 'run by the many not the few; one ruled by the people, not an elite; one governed from the bottom up, not the top down'[111] were directly lifted from Cherny's book. Shop-ping where no real choice exists, introducing markets which were really varieties of local monopolies and averting their eyes from the classic Labour themes of poverty and inequality: these would be the next collective gasps of a government which was bent on consecrating the convergence of interest between Britain's political elites and the country's business elites. The tired clichés about the need for Britain to become Great Britain plc and for the country to be run by 'hands-on' management types had been around since the 1960s. The CBI and the IoD, aided by the Duke of Edinburgh, had been much given to the exhalation of sighs about Britain's backwardness in this regard and its urge to 'shoot itself in the foot' by ignoring the imperatives of business advance. But now that corporate dream – the incorporation of the political world within the business one – was at last being realized.

The danger for the thinker on the make, however, is that political elites are notoriously fickle and happy to move on when the thinker of the day has served his purpose. Will Hutton's *The State We're In*[112] was a famously third-wayish-leaning tract with its prescription of state-led investment in the capital projects deemed necessary to renew Britain's infrastructure. Hutton was the thinker of the moment in the early New Labour years until time moved on and his advice came into conflict with those late Tory Treasury guidelines on spending and borrowing so eagerly signed up to by Gordon Brown. There was always doubt about what the Chancellor (among so many others) meant by the 'third way' or whether he saw himself as travelling down those avenues of broad intent. But at least mental firepower seemed in evidence and commentators regurgitated reverential stories of the Chancellor reading into the early hours those first editions of the Scottish enlightenment classics of political economy that he had discovered in the Treasury library. A reputation for intellectuality can therefore, if handled properly, inspire awe and respect among the political elites, and it can be easy to pass yourself off as an intellectual in the generally unintellectual world of those elites. But the politician with a weakness for ideas can inspire a classic English mistrust of the intellectual if that figure appears either vulnerable or threatening. John Biffen's[113] resigned Tory stoicism detached him from the thrusting Toryism of the 1980s while Keith Joseph,[114] although a more influential politician, was also a nervously quirky one whose manner confirmed the national suspicion that the intellectual was an unreliable being. While William Waldegrave,[115] who adapted, perhaps too quickly, from a Heathite past to being a Thatcher regime server, confirmed another suspicion – that intellectual elites are clever at disguising their own self-interest through the deployment of abstract principle. Political elites, being so ready themselves to turn with the prevailing wind, recognize that very same quality in the intellectuals who seek to serve them but if they become too sardonic at the expense of those mental toilers there can be awkward consequences. Nigel Lawson, the most effective member of the intelligentsia–political elite of the 1980s, had a finely dismissive attitude towards the craven journalistic elites, the neo-intellectual ones as well as the lower reaches of the political elites within his own party. But those attitudes compounded his difficulties when the British economy ground into recession towards the end of his time as Chancellor, and he discovered that he had no sustaining circle to argue his case.

Gordon Brown – the Chancellor least tested by economic adversity of all the British post-war holders of the office – used his reputation to build up the Treasury as the undisputed source and controller of political and economic policy in Britain. He therefore centralized government decision-making in a classic Labour governmental manner. This was a properly synoptic approach – and one which was in the tradition of those other Labour elite political–intellectuals, Dick Crossman and Anthony Crosland. Once Brown had moved on from third way language it became obvious that his view of government was that of an eighteenth-century rationalist, and so perhaps those long evenings in the Treasury library really did bear some fruit. The Brown view of government is that it is a mechanism containing levers and pulleys, inputs and outputs, incentives and penalties which can then be used, pushed and pulled in order to achieve certain desired outcomes of human behaviour. And – in the manner of a political elitist with some mental ambitions – the policy cake that he baked in his best of all Panglossian worlds was one designed for both investment and for consumption. The aim of Brownism was an economy which was American in its expansionist and entrepreneurial energies but also European in its welfare-provisionist compassion. Like Tony Blair in foreign policy, he simply did not see the need to choose between the USA and Europe. In this view, he could rely upon a salon of thinkers, and in pushing the message out he could rely on Charlie Whelan, a press counsellor and adviser who was wide-eyed in his admiration.

The kind of intellectuals used by the political elite for purposes of public display reveal the elite as they would wish to be seen – thoughtful, measured, figures who have risen through the political party but are nonetheless sagely disinterested in their pursuit of the 'national interest'. But the kind of person with whom they actually choose to spend most of the day as their intimate advisers – Whelan in the case of Brown, Alastair Campbell in the case of Blair – shows the human type they most enjoy, figures who use robust language about the crap and bollocks talked by others and who offer a daily devotion to the patron. These men are a reminder that the political elite needs its bad as well as its good angel, for the maintenance costs of all that public virtue and all that earnest talk about identifying with 'Britain at its best' are high indeed. Hidden away therefore in the private office with chums the political elites can allow the unregenerate psyche to have its day and come out and play in the company of the, very few, chosen initiates before the dullness of a hypocritical decency resumes its sway.

Margaret Thatcher was an instinctive politician but one who had the provincial nonconformist's respect for intellect as the path to power. Thatcher's 1980s like Blair's 1990s spawned in their wake a host of politico-intellectual elites who scrambled for attention. The views they embraced diverged, but what was more important was the similarity of methods employed. Chief among these was the think tank which might call itself a centre, an institute, or a foundation but whose function was always the same: they existed in order to enable supposedly independent truth tellers gain access to power. The admired model to be followed was that of the Washington think tanks, places of genuine strength of purpose, as has been shown by their influence on the Bush administration. But for all the gaily contentious lunches, the noise of the seminars and the pleasure in announcing the conference to be attended by a cabinet minister, it is hard to credit the London think tanks with any genuine influence on government thinking and action in the sense of formulating measures that would not otherwise have seen the light of day. The comparison with Washington, DC shows the extent of the differences between the power bases in the two cities. The executive officers of the President are only rarely senators or congressmen. And so, when a party loses office, those officers flock to the Washington think tanks where they can congregate and regroup to form a government in exile or a government in waiting. The presidency of G.W. Bush therefore contains many power brokers who were biding their time working in such bodies as the American Enterprise Institute and the Heritage Foundation during the years of the Democratic presidency. But Britain can offer no equivalent to this experience. Its political opposition is parliamentary and is constrained by the fact that it has to work out of the House of Commons, which is why there is no British version of a sharpshooting and rough-tongued John Bolton and Richard Perle or an implacably lucid Paul Wolfowitz, all of whom have had a think tank immersion.[116]

Britain's most important think tanks, on the Conservative side, have been the Centre for Policy Studies (CPS) and, on the Labour side, the Institute for Public Policy Research (IPPR). The titles are grand but 'policy' here really means access and the promise of proximity to power which is offered to those who wish to give the money that keeps the doors open. More minor think tanks may also gratify an owner's possessiveness and nestle in his stable – a function which Politeia fulfils for its chief supporter, the Marquess of Salisbury. But in all cases the think tanks' true function is architectural – they are antechambers to the power elites. The think tank patron who is a millionaire on the make and wants 'to give something back' will be admitted to that antechamber and in his presence conversations will take place which suggest the reality of a policy to be changed or initiated. Since power elites always delight in the appearance of their significance and its reflection in the eyes of others there is never any problem in attracting the ministerial presence. Genuinely large public meetings which once gave the power elites the chance to display their grandeur are now few and far between. And the television appearance, though possibly beamed to millions, is a strangely unsatisfying and rather lonely affair because it fails to give that buzz of engagement which comes from seeing how others react to the fact of your power when you arrive and also when alas, and regrettably early due to pressure of business, you leave.

Where power elites are concerned think tanks are really therefore a source of pleasure as well as a place in which to extend the clientage systems among supporters who can both assist the further rise and inform on opponents. Aspiring political elite members can also use think tanks as a springboard, as David Willetts MP[117] did while director of the CPS and as Matthew Taylor did at the IPPR before being recruited to No. 10. The Low Pay Unit run by Chris Pond[118] was an unusual exception in its genuine and effective focus on a single issue, but its significance disappeared once its Director was absorbed within the Commons as an MP. The Institute for Fiscal Studies (IFS)[119] has enjoyed a similar success and a reputation for serious-mindedness among the political elites but that is a consequence of the fact that it deals with comparatively neutral issues of fact. The only possible candidate for the role of a think tank which has decisively altered government policy is the Institute of Economic Affairs (IEA), whose championing of free market economics accompanied the privatization policies of the 1980s. But even here this was more of a matter of reflecting what had become a very general current of opinion. The details of government policy remained, as they always had been, a question of internal power elite politicking within the private offices of cabinet ministers and in the policy unit of No. 10.

## Integrating Society and Setting Goals

Nothing is more destructive for the elites' reputation in general than the appearance of factionalism. Their power and appeal comes from the ability to set collective goals for a whole community, and then they have to show how those goals may be achieved by both themselves and by those whom they govern. The elites everywhere are primarily concerned with the question of their own survival, but they also have to persuade the governed that their collective survival is bound up with the continuing existence of the elites. They therefore need continually to discover new sources of power and new ploys which can be deployed as part of their strategy for survival. A readiness to appear ridiculous and to 'take a joke' plays an important role in these games which exist in an arena far wider than that of the Commons chamber and are directed to a wider audience than the one which may be amused by the parliamentary witticism. Such drollery dictates that John Prescott, a highly effective member of the cabinet elite, should accept the jokes directed at both his accent and his syntax. Much of the comedy broadcast on British television after all, from *Monty Python* to *The Royle Family* and *Little Britain*, consists of middle-class people finding the working classes excruciatingly funny. The more fundamental savagery, however, is that these portrayals of working-class lives as brutal, prejudiced and governed by appetite are written, performed and directed by middle-class professionals. But as long as the class base is not too obvious, then the working-class politician such as Prescott can accept the jibes secure in the knowledge that the jokes are a price to be paid for elite acceptance. Alan Johnson's use of cockney charm and a ready tongue can exploit self-deprecation to enhance the status which has been bestowed on him after his progress along that now very well-trodden path which leads from being an elite trade union leader to being an elite politician. The popularity of that journey shows how trade union careers are no longer autonomous but rather seen as a professional preparation for a parliamentary career. In British politics, the end of working-class consciousness and of aristocratic consciousness have marched hand in hand and led to the creation of a common managerial group.

When it comes to setting goals and integrating a society the political elite needs its wits about it. It can appear ridiculous when it parades too obviously its connectedness with modernity, as Tony Blair did with successive forays into cool Britannia, rock music (armed with an embarrassing guitar) and then sporting success. But the readiness to be mocked for the attempt is often a price worth paying, and all elite leaders in politics have to be prepared to be considered ridiculous since the jokes will eventually wear off while the chance of an impression, or an illusion, of connectedness may remain. The Blair–Oasis connection was in the same lineage of prime ministerial displays which gave us the spectacle of Ted Heath sailing, of Harold Wilson holidaying in his bungalow on the Scillies and then John Major's sepia-toned speeches on an England of mists and beer. All were ways of using an available and plausible cultural resource in order to bolster political power through a facade of connectedness. These exercises in light entertainment carry fewer risks of absurdity than the political elite's occasional use of books in order to bolster their authority. Thatcher's use of quotations from Dostoevsky[120] (selected for her) in order to illustrate Britain's loss of moral compass was both implausible and heavy-handed. Sometimes the cynicism can peep through and self-destruct, as in Macmillan's affectation of Jane Austen-reading languor and his pose with Livy for special occasions, displays which made him appear to be a more tweedy kind of Tory than he really was. But, whether light or heavy, these are the cultural hoops that, right at the top and some way down too, the political elites are obliged to leap through in order to show the personal responsiveness and sincerity which, they assure us, lurk beneath the mask of office.

Setting communal goals does of course go some way beyond being prepared to look silly and/or serious in the name of a higher purpose. The readiness to push for an integrated society, on terms set by the elite's self-interest, is a strenuous one, involving quite a lot of ethical uplift as well as the exercise of patronage which compels as many as possible to come in and join the enterprise. This is why government committees of enquiry, royal commissions and reports on various aspects of the nation's affairs are an important source of power, despite the frequency with which those reports fall dead from the printing presses doomed never to be implemented. But the fact that they have no consequences is nowhere near as important as the fact that they so often enable the political elite of one dominant party to reach out to the elite of another, as seen in the appointment of Roy Jenkins to produce a report on proportional representation and of Chris Patten to investigate policing in Northern Ireland. Sometimes the job can also be one of full-time honour, as in the case of Alastair Goodlad,[121] a former Tory Chief Whip, who was appointed by the

New Labour government to be High Commissioner of Australia. A period in which the political elite has fewer and fewer opportunities to move on to non-political elite jobs poses its own problems. City and business elites are now quite intolerant of the long-serving Westminster career as a qualification for the boardroom. John Nott's[122] chairmanship of Lazard's (1985–90) was a fine example of how things used to operate, but the independent British merchant bank, along with its agreeable habit of insider appointments, has been something of a post-Baring casualty. Appointments of Tory cabinet ministers to the boards of companies they had helped to privatize killed off, through the impression of sleaze, quite a few golden-egg-laying geese.

There are now 646 members of the House of Commons and the register of members' interests published in February 2005 shows that among those elected at the general election of 2001 there were fifty-eight with significant business interests. These members of the political elite linked up with the financial and business elite holding as they did a range of directorships, either non-executive or executive.[123] This number excludes those whose extra-parliamentary incomes were restricted to their registrable shareholdings, defined as being more than 15 per cent of the issued share capital or as having a value in excess of £59,000 (the current parliamentary salary). These rentiers were few in number and included Fiona Mactaggart (Slough), Richard Shepherd (Aldridge–Brownhills) and George Osborne (Tatton). Such shareholdings were of course a significant source of extra income for many of the fifty-eight MPs who were the members of the directorate class. The fifty-eight also excluded the twenty-one MPs who were remunerated as practising members of the professional classes.[124] This group included eight barristers, six solicitors, two solicitors' consultants, a member of the Edinburgh Faculty of Advocates, a dentist, a surgeon, a general practitioner and a chartered surveyor. There were also ten MPs[125] with incomes derived from ownership of land and property on a significant scale. Their seigneurial status gave them some affinities with the directorate. Three MPs[126] still had a connection with Lloyds, having survived in one way or another the insurance disasters of the late 1980s. The collapse of that underwriting institution as a source of easy income was a significant parliamentary event since it forced many members to realize that if they wanted a business income they would have to go out and earn it, rather than relying on an annual cheque from a business which was becoming risky in the age of accelerated environmental risks and increased natural disasters. Lastly, although there were many MPs who could rely on the odd bonus payment from newspapers and television work, there were just seven[127] who had built up a useful portfolio in that sector. In some cases their incomes from these sources greatly exceeded their parliamentary salary. George Galloway's regular column in the *Mail on Sunday*, for example, earned him between £85,000 and £90,000. But in all these instances the work which is offered is a tribute to celebrity status and therefore vulnerable to the dictates of fashion.

The register's publication has now itself become yet another ritual of parliamentary life, mingling as it does the comic and the banal with the significant. Alan Simpson (Nottingham South) felt obliged to declare that he was a guest at Wimbledon in his capacity as 'tennis adviser to the Minister for Sport' while Malcolm Bruce (Gordon) described eagerly his upgrade from World Traveller Plus to Business Class on his British Airways flights to and from India on 1 and 7 March 2004. Sir Patrick Cormack (South Staffordshire) informed the world that he had 'been presented with a watch by *First Magazine* in recognition of the fact that for five years I have chaired the annual award ceremony at which the First Award for Responsible Capitalism is presented'. The Caravan Club required the services of two parliamentary advisers: David Amess (Southend West) and Eric Illsley (Barnsley Central). But the introduction of the trivial has nonetheless an important role to play, since its amusements deflect journalistic attention from the salient facts.

Of the fifty-eight that mattered, only eight were Labour MPs. Two were Liberal Democrats including John Thurso (Caithness, Sutherland and Easter Ross) – a hereditary peer deprived of his seat in the House of Lords by the reform of the upper chamber. Two were Ulster Unionists. The remainder were all Conservatives, a fact which is a testimony to the influence of the years of opposition on a previous governing party. Deprived of the prospect of governmental power, these individuals settled for a different kind of elite influence. Eight of the Tory members of the directorate were former cabinet ministers and of this group the most significantly active were Stephen Dorrell (Charnwood), Kenneth Clarke (Rushcliffe) and Peter Lilley (Hitchin & Harpenden). But the group which had settled down most vigorously to being money men were those Tory MPs who had been junior ministers and had now probably missed out on the chance of future ministerial preferment since the years of opposition were ticking away.

Tim Yeo (Suffolk South) therefore decided to get into private nursing homes and Michael Fallon (Sevenoaks) into children's day nurseries, both boom businesses in ageing and dual-incomed professional Britain. The business interests of David Heathcoat-Amory (Wells) included that other major British obsession, property management. John Maples (Stratford-on-Avon) had become a cutting-edge directorial presence in companies developing shopping centres, producing software and operating cash machines. Of this group of former ministers who were on the way up until felled by the electorate Andrew Mitchell (Sutton Coldfield) came closest to the grandeur of old-style Tory banking with his directorships of Lazard Brothers and Co. Limited, of Lazard India (Private) Limited, of Lazard Asia Limited and of Lazard Asia (Hong Kong).

Labour members of the directorate could not rival these marks of opulence but Jack Cunningham (formerly the member for Copeland and now a member of the House of Lords) had a go, since he became a director and a partner of two political and public policy consultancies and a non-executive director of a management skills company. Dr Lewis Moonie (Kirkcaldy) was an associate director of a company which offered 'strategic advice' as well as being a non-executive director of AEA Technology plc (earning as a result between £25,001 and £30,000) and of Mining (Scotland) Ltd. But these are the exceptions to what has now become a melancholy rule for Britain's governing party. There are no corporate rewards for the footsoldiers despite their complicity in the abasement of the leadership to the demands of the business and financial elites.

The centralization of political power to the executive along with the centralization of corporate power in business life, the puckish candour of the former Labour cabinet advisor Derek Draper that 'there are 17 people in Britain that matter', the globalization of Britain's financial services: all attest to that paradoxical situation in which governments do all they can for business but the number of politicians rewarded directly by business falls. This has been especially and savagely true of New Labour for despite the thirty pieces of silver so gladly received there have been no more substantial emoluments. For New Labour MPs, if judged by their own career guidelines, this has been a spectacularly bad deal. Business money flows to those with access to the Prime Minister's court and, where propriety allows, to the senior courtiers. And, from a business point of view, why should it go anywhere else? For it is in those circles that especially useful policies originate such as no taxation on shopping centres' car parks[128] and support for nuclear power. There really is no need any more to look after anyone beyond those circles and the inert bulk of both parties, so helplessly convinced that their business-friendly reputation is vital to electoral success, can therefore be ignored.

The lack of any really lush business interests for the great majority of parliamentarians has one important consequence. Now, more than ever, official committees of enquiry, governmental reports and royal commissions need to survive. They may not offer any money but they are an important source of reputation-feeding honour at a time when the extra-political world is less inclined to hand out rewards to the political elite despite, or perhaps because of, the fact that that elite has become so amenable to its purposes. The appointments to these bodies cement a broad alliance among the political elites; and the comfort zone of occasional government appointments beyond the party of the governing class shows that life will be agreeable and that elite integration is possible whoever is in office in Britain.

## Scottish and Welsh Power

Establishing the unity of Britain has been a question of establishing the unity of the political elites. Both in Scotland and in Wales the powerful assimilationist tendencies of the local elites have, at different historical stages, ensured the brokering of a whole series of power deals and the incorporation of the national regions within the various myths of national purpose.[129] Ireland was the significant exception and the only real failure in this project. The Scots and the Welsh elites, like those they governed, complied both with the legislative measures necessary to secure elite dominance and also with the Anglo-centric invention of national identities that could be attributed to the new British regions. Thus the Welsh could be seen as charming, garrulous but devious while the Scots were grasping, mean but vigorous. In Ireland, these subtle forms of racism were also available as a cultural caricature designed to enfeeble. Portraying the Irish as fey and away with the fairies in an enveloping mist of Celticity was an essential part of the centralizing elite project. When it came to the question of confirming the authority of the Protestant elites in the seventeenth century there were even some backhanded compliments to be paid to Celtic culture which was seen as a genuine early form of Britishness. And so the Reformation break with Rome could be presented not as the novelty it really was but as the recovery of something older, the original Celtic Church which in some sense had never left the British Isles, had only been overlaid by the Catholicism of Rome and was now being reclaimed as the source of the newly recovered authority. Although a bit of bogus history, this was immensely gratifying to the local elites in Church and state, and was another way of tying them into the central elite. But the constant irruption of a very explicit racism in the English view of the Irish, something which has both elite and popular roots, was a major destabilizer of the more subtle strategies used so successfully in Wales and Scotland. Animal imagery has been a constant theme in the English view of the Irish ever since Edmund Spenser first started using it in his *A View of the Present State of Ireland* (1595–6). The portrayal of the Irish as inhuman, as dogs, curs and wolves has frustrated the process of accommodation, and the explicit racism, accompanied by anti-Catholicism, ensured that there was no popular consensus behind the idea of a British Ireland.

But in the North of Ireland the politics of the elite who were allowed to run their own statelet has been and is more akin to the story of the Welsh and the Scottish elites. From 1922 onwards the interests of the gentry and of the Protestant working class coincided to ensure their incorporation within a wider pattern which was at first an imperial one and then a British national one. In Wales, the continuities from the age of the Tudor gentry to that of Aneurin Bevan have been striking because they have always revolved around the job-hunting nature of the Welsh elite. The acts of union between England and Wales represented a deal between the English crown and the Welsh gentry class who were guaranteed their role as the local officeholders. The passivity of the population – its acquiescence in that assimilation – showed the effective success of the deal. The rise of Labour in Welsh politics represented a continuation of the same centralist and assimilationist impulse. Where once it was the English crown which represented power at the centre and endorsed the rule of lord lieutenants and magistrates, the equally centralizing Labour Party of 1945 onwards could offer its own endorsement of an office holding class. Although the officeholders changed, the conditions on which they were given power were the same: the maintenance of the thrust towards assimilation and of the hierarchies which kept the localities quiet and supine. The arrival of a series of English MPs as Secretaries of State for Wales during the Tory years in office was an inconvenience because it showed all too clearly the logic of assimilation. But

84

although a Tory embarrassment, English ministers running Wales only clarified and revealed what had always been the case – the absorption of the local elites within the greater power structure. Therefore in so far as local officeholders were concerned business continued as usual with Tory governments distributing jobs among the accommodating local Welsh elites.

In Scotland, the process was a more dynastic one, but followed the same path and used the same means. The union of the two crowns of Scotland and of England (1603) and the Act of Union (1707) created a much more explicit culture of 'unionism' than ever existed in Wales, along with a more obvious rejection of unionism as well. Jacobitism – as the only serious sustained threat to the unity of modern Britain – was a Scottish military export to English soil. In both Wales and Scotland,[130] just as in England, the working-class political syndicalism of the early twentieth century did represent a real outbreak of authentic and autonomous democracy. But for most of the twentieth century it was the power of elite politics which was the dominant fact at every level of government in both countries along with its extensive networks of clientage and patronage. Mastery of the language of party and subservience to its methods of control marched hand in hand in order to promote careers, and the idea of a distinctive Scottish and Welsh representation in Westminster was, until recently, enough to appease any lingering sense of national identity.

The arrival of a Scottish Parliament and of a Welsh Assembly has changed appearances while hardly affecting the substance of a con-solidated political elite. These were measures largely imposed on the local elites of both major parties who were initially, especially in Wales, unenthused and concerned about their exclusion from the wider political stage and its patronage opportunities. But the measures also recognized that the kind of unionism preached and used by the Conservative Party had self-destructed since it was too obviously Anglo-centric. Much of the old rhetoric has changed, albeit along the distinctly Whiggish–British line which maintains that the state which wishes to survive has to adapt, otherwise it will be broken. But what was sold to the local elites was similar to past Unionist legislative package deals, namely the guarantee that jobs and influence would be available as part of the new dispensation. The result has been the restructuring of the local oligarchies which are tied into the central elite – tightly in the case of Wales, more loosely so in Scotland.

Structures of Scottish and Welsh power are now more subject to formal debate, but their political power elites remain well in place. A Cardiff and Edinburgh political and public world in which everyone who matters knows everybody else has become ever more introspective, with the result that conciliation among the parties is quite as strong as it is in Westminster. Cosily, members of the Cardiff Assembly refer to each other by their first names in formal debate – a practice which seeks to further the appearance of democratic engagement but in fact contributes to the sense of an enclosed world – while the cost of building the new Edinburgh Parliament building confirms the suspicion that officialdom uses the public purse to aggrandize itself. Government money is also there, of course, in endless programmes of regeneration and reclamation, in industrial estates small and large, while agencies advise and claim job creation. But this is a decadent set-up. The newly regenerated Welsh and Scottish political elites sit on top of a wholesale collapse of industrial working-class culture. Within narrow corridors of prosperity, the money of the agencies tempts some businesses in, only to find that many take the money and leave within a few years. The elites certainly do well out of the deals offered them in both pre- and post-devolutionary worlds, and there have been some spectacular successes. The career of John Morris,[131] a Cardiganshire barrister who represented the steel constituency of Aberavon for forty-two years, culminated in his elevation as a Knight of the Garter, in which arcane Arthurian circle he may mingle happily with Scandinavian kings. But the careers of such members of the elite, and their endless capacity for self-gratification, should be measured not by their own ascent but against the background of a wasteland which is recorded accurately in the figures for long-term unemployment and for the various benefits which constitute the danegeld paid by the modern state to keep the people quiet.

## Immigration and Assimilation

Around the construction of so many politically elite careers, united in their methodologies of gaining and of exercising power, there hovers a major paradox which goes to the heart of what we mean by both England and Britain. There is a long history of speculation about what the national identity actually consists of. The arrival of a twentieth century which first of all got rid of empire and then forced Britain to deal with the consequences of immigration has been especially productive of such speculation. Confronted with the end of homogeneity, members of the elite have identified and acclaimed the diversity which supplies England with its roots. What was England and Britain, so goes the line, but a creation of invaders and immigrants, of Brythonic Celts followed by Picts and Angles, Saxons and Jutes, who were then followed by Normans, Huguenots and Jews? There have been opportunities for ethnic self-congratulation about toleration and diversity, but these have been essentially elite views designed for elite consumption because what was always acclaimed was the ability of these immigrants to assimilate and then rise. What is praised as exemplary is the fact that those who arrive are grateful and therefore do not question. Elite power therefore celebrates those new arrivals who concentrate on joining the national show so that they themselves may become successful operators and brokers of power. The reproach of some recent immigrants for failing to play that particular game has been sometimes implicit and sometimes explicit. Asian immigrants pass the test since so many are commerce-minded and the vast majority are unaffected by Islamic fundamentalism. They are therefore represented in both Houses of Parliament. But Britain has been unable to create a black elite and Afro-Caribbeans have proved stubbornly unassimilated to elite career expectations. These facts are testing ones for the political elite and its devotion to the facade of an accommodating, liberal openness. It is at this point of stubborn rejection that elite geniality tends to break down and the complaint starts to be heard that a welfare society requires a structure of common beliefs in order to justify the benefit cheques. But that refusal of some immigrants to assimilate and to play the power elite game is a reminder of a related, and older, truth about Britain and its exclusions. British political order, for all its supposed evolutionary capacity and its love of privacy and liberty, is based on the fact that the poor tend not to vote. Were they to vote, that whole political order would collapse, but the poor have been an absent voice in almost a century and a half of formal democratic enfranchisement. To that extent, the political elites have been successful in seeing off the biggest threat to their existence, the possibility of the politicized poor which is implicit in the very fact of a universal franchise and which has haunted both thoughtful and reactionary members of the elite. The absence of the poor from British politics allows the spread of consensual flatulence, and with it all the patronizing speculation about quiet, decent, non-extreme, property-loving, chronically garden-loving old England.

## The Death of the Region

But there is a further, and paradoxical, truth about the power elite in British politics. This is a highly integrated elite which has been extremely successful in setting out the terms of the national goals which need to be pursued and its own capacity to rule as a managerial class which 'delivers' that agenda. The apparently diffuse and extended nature of Britain's centres of social power has also been basic to that business. Britain is a highly centralized state when it comes to the implementation of power elite agendas, but it can also appear as a very ancient régime kind of society, one which seems no more than the sum total of many different societies. County society remains a fact of life, as the recent paper wars on fox-hunting and its abolition have demonstrated. The British army's regiments, though much diminished in number, are still organized around county loyalties and affiliations, although centralizing measures have been proposed. The ecclesiastical organization of England as a network of parishes weaves its way persistently throughout the English history of local government whose reorganizations now recur on a generational and cyclical basis as either efficiency or accountability alternately become the vogue of the moment. Public schools pride themselves on their autonomy and Oxford and Cambridge as universities are no more than an assemblage of individual colleges which claim their members' loyalties to a far greater extent than the idea of the central university does. And when the newer universities were established, many chose to imitate that collegiate model in order to show the legitimacy of their new authority. Political parties themselves pay tribute to this social charm of the locality with their regional offices and their professed preference for a local when it is time to select a candidate for a parliamentary seat.

Political mythology about the beauty of the 'organic community' builds on these social truths and has acquired both its conservative and its socialist versions in Britain.[132] But this is all pastiche stuff compared to the real business of who exercises power. The reality of small town and country town life in Britain is one of steep economic and social decline. Supermarket capitalism has been more effective at destroying the local corner shopocracy than any kind of socialism, as is illustrated by the rows of boarded-up shops in poor towns and rows of branded high street names in richer ones. Despite – or, perhaps, because of – these hard economic facts, Britain and its elites still love the appearance of antiquity and of gentility as a way of soothing the reality and accommodating us to the real facts about power. All those social and provincial settings are real enough as a stage on which the actors down from town can strut their parts and learn to produce those fakeries of tone, accent, clothes and manner which qualify them for elite roles. And the supposedly 'natural' hierarchies of many a Plumshire North is the natural aspiration of the early retired financier, the high-earning silk and the politician in search of a secure berth. The *Country Life* announcements of the engagements to be married of girls with pearls dutifully photographed in sub-Beaton poses are still a reliable indicator of social elite prestige, for the girls come from the grange and the manor, as well as from the vicarage and the rectory which are both now necessarily 'old' since they have been renovated to secular and expensive purpose. But it is the weekday addresses under the auspicious constellations of SW1 and SW3, of W8 and NW1, which are significant. Our elites turned metropolitan a very long time ago, despite what may be suggested by their patronage of the kilt, the Eisteddfod and the hunt, and they are not about to change now.

Britain's political elites do not on the whole lead fake-gentry, '*Country Life*' lives but they do inevitably lead urban–professional ones, and success means growing away from the region. It is the lives of their children which most often give the game away, those lives being determined by metropolitan accents, views and vowels. The elite which dispenses political power in Britain knows that it cannot afford to display metropolitan hedonism on the scale of the elites of fashion, sport and music, whose pockets are deeper and who can get away with a more evident, carefree, detachment from the lives of the masses. A formal obeisance both to the locality and to the people is still expected of our political elites, and that, like any facade of humility, is bound to be an uneasy and hypocritical affair. The third Marquess of Salisbury, modern Britain's least hypocritical Prime Minister as well as the one who was most sceptical about democracy, once described his horror of general elections with their 'days and weeks of screwed up smiles and laboured courtesy, the mock geniality, the hearty shake of the filthy hand, the chuckling reply that must be made to the coarse joke, the loathsome, choking compliment . . . the indispensable flattery . . . the wholesale deglutition of hypocritical pledges'.[133] The disillusioned view from Hatfield House at the turn of the twentieth century remains the view from Westminster at the beginning of the twenty-first. Elections tend to concentrate minds and sharpen prejudices, but the fear of the insurgent mass is a constant element in the thinking of the political elites. They therefore have a choice to make: they can either play along with what they take to be the 'democratic roughness' or they can conceal their aversion from it. In either event, there is a show which has to go on and the necessity of the local, the public and the democratic ritual accompanies and rivals the political elite's knowledge that it is party – a central mechanism – which has selected them and which now protects and sustains them in those various experiments in living that they call their careers.

*Chapter 3*

# The Professional Elites:
# A Collective Aberration?

## The Nature of Professional Power

The contrast between the elites of political life and those at work in the professions involves an important shift of scale. Elite activity in Westminster and Whitehall, together with its dedicated media, involves a small group of people united in a common function. Together they constitute a 'politics' which is only intermittently and faintly political. But the important business of who gets what is a much larger enterprise. Here we are in the realm of the lumpen-elites, the managerial–professional classes who have done well out of the Thatcherite settlement and its subsequent New Labour entrenchment. Considered collectively, this is numerically the largest elite group and, although concentrated in London, it is nonetheless a truly national elite. Its members secure decent salaries in the public and private sectors, and where possible they use specialist knowledge, or at least a convenient jargon, in order to keep them safe from the globalizing forces of competition that have casualized or removed entirely the work of the less fortunate and less nimble. This elite has grown out of the old professions, but it has mostly surrendered its autonomy in exchange for a privileged place in the corporate and public sectors.

The myth that Britain is a land of the inspired amateur dies very hard.[1] The 1980s vogue for the rugged virtues of entrepreneurial capitalism gave new currency to that individualizing ambition. The list of British worthies was brought up to date and now included figures such as Sir Alan Sugar and Sir Richard Branson, leaders whose Nelson touch was supposed to inspire a generation which was hacking its free market path through the jungle of opportunity. The echoing rhetoric has included a ready transference of the language of British military heroes to the world of civilian money-making. Popular and journalistic accounts of that world therefore describe captains of industry who survey the terrain and seize the moment before consolidating their gains in readiness for the next advance. The closer Britain comes to confrontation with genuine industrial and commercial competition from the Far East – and especially from China – the more vigorous becomes the language of buccaneering capitalism. In the 1980s that language was replete with formulaic praise of Victorian industrial might. Such pious blather has now yielded to uncertain millennial platitudes about 'technology', 'innovation' and 'creativity'.

This is especially true of political leaders who, for all their ready way with this kind of vocabulary, have little experience of such realities. There is a constant chasm between the embellishing effects of grand rhetoric and the disillusioned truth that industry in Britain has never been seen as a promising career.[2] This country's persistent bourgeois aspiration searches for something very different – namely the security, status and guaranteed pay which comes with being a 'professional'. Even the power structures of the business world pay respect to the honour and dignity of the professional class, for it is the company lawyer and the company accountant who tend to decide the policy and the direction of the firm. The interloping entrepreneur's insistent desire is to join those social and professional ranks as quickly as possible and then, if lucky, to find himself corralled among the honoured and the knighted.

These are old-established truths of English capitalism but they now exist in newly noxious forms since the nature of professional power and the forms assumed by its dominance have changed. 'Enterprise' is of course praised as the defining virtue of successful private businesses and it is a consensus wisdom that the same quality is exactly what the public sector needs as well. But in both these worlds the enterprising virtues are defined and applied in specialized and spurious ways. For those virtues have to be defined, measured and assessed by the new professional classes, whose tentacles of power have eagerly grasped the novel potency of management systems. It is these systems of bureaucratic power which have spawned the real growth areas in the British professions. They undermine the pragmatic ability of executive power to set its own goals on its own terms and their effect also undermines the freebooting energy of the entrepreneur. Inventing and making objects that people want to pay money for, discovering new markets that reveal new needs, devising services that fulfil a genuine purpose: these are all complicated, time-consuming and often expensive activities. It has been the peculiar genius of the new professionals to discover that there are surer ways to personal gain: looting corporate budgets and robbing the tax-payer.

There are social as well as cultural reasons which explain why English capitalism is so different from that of other countries.[3] There are few reflections here of the Italian tradition of family-based industrial enterprise or of the German fascination with creating shining objects of commodity desire fashioned out of metal and steel. The engineer in particular is a figure of fun – a designer of wobbly bridges who is easily absorbed within the quintessentially English tradition of Heath Robinson illustrations. In England, the inventor is a boffin, a weird and unworldly fool. When spectacular profits can be made out of industrial enterprise then the English are prepared, as they would see it, to get their hands dirty. But English capitalism, at this latest stage in its history, is averse to the long and slow grind of building up an industrial and manufacturing business within a world market. It likes nothing better than the cutting of corners and the quick return. The respect of both the talented and the lazy for the professional career means that English capitalism is a feebler beast than its American equivalent; with less mental energy to fuel it and less personal commitment behind it, its vulnerabilities are easily exposed. New Labour's early attempts to court companies such as Enron reveal the naïveté of the modernizers in the face of an American capitalism that is often dynamic but often unforgivingly rapacious.

The instinct which favours the professions, and which has guaranteed their growth and their status, has been around in English culture and thought for a very long time. The learned clerks who ran the households of mediaeval kings, and who wrote the histories of those institutions, were the leading professionals of their day.[4] Their heirs were the clergy and the bureaucrats who administered the Church and the state that emerged from the English Reformation,[5] while the history of Victorian England records the professional energy of a more secular elite which was making its careers in banking and science, the civil service, the armed services and the universities.[6] But it would be wrong to see the present professional scene and its growth as a mere accentuation of the long national trend. For what we now mean by a 'professional' changed quite markedly during the late twentieth century.[7] Once, the professional was a person who was defined by the possession of a kind of knowledge or by the performance of a particular skill – qualities which needed to be recognized by one's peers if one was to be regarded as a true professional. Personal accountability and professional self-regulation were meant to maintain standards and to ensure the competent performance of the task in hand. This kind of integrity was of course quite compatible with self-interested greed. But the professions did at least run their own show and they allowed the individual practitioner the freedom to set his own targets and to run his own career. However capriciously they might have been administered, the ethical standards which underpinned public confidence in those professions were applied by the professions themselves. But the growth of a 'knowledge' economy, of a service industry and of the management-driven state which is target-obsessed and consumer-focused has subverted these features of the old professional world and subjected it to management and manipulation by external forces.[8]

Enfeeblement of meaning and a diminished status have, however, proved to be perfectly compatible with expansion in numbers. A striking feature of professional elite activity in contemporary Britain is its newly energized role in the public sector. This is not merely a result of the great expansion in the health and education services since 1997 – although that has certainly created new career opportunities for the public sector elite. It is also a question of the rise of management theory, which is itself a by-product of the vogue for management consultancy.[9] Within this development, new tools have been used to exploit the persistent British respect for the professional and the desire to turn everything into a profession. But whether they find themselves in the public or in the private sector, the new professional elites are no longer experts within a body of knowledge but rather skilled workers in the service of either a corporation or of the state. The very word 'professional' has therefore lost its former clarity. All that remains of the old professional order is the security of its social status and the guarantee of its monthly salary.

'Professional', in this context, means respectability and safety. It guarantees insulation from all those adventitious features of commercial life which were supposed to give that existence its appealing and cutting-edge quality. 'Professional', in the jargon of evaluation and assessment which has itself become a mini-business in Britain, has become a synonym for reliability and honesty. The professional is meant to be endowed with esprit de corps qualities as well as being hardworking. A professional person, in this sense of the phrase, is simply a good human being. This invocation of 'professionalism' straddles the divide between public and private in Britain and makes the distinction between the two an increasingly irrelevant one within the general quagmire of an elite-run Britain. For a teacher, a doctor or a civil servant, an accountant or a lawyer, the prized and advertised quality is professionalism; the military proclaims the same virtue for its officers and its other ranks. But, when stripped of its former meaning in terms of knowledge and self-regulation, all that is left of this 'professional' world is a certain packaging. If a modern army has to be a professional one, then that means it must become more bureaucratic in its structures, adept at surviving the latest defence review and good at conducting press conferences,[10] while the 'professional police officer' is one who has withdrawn from the front line of policing and understood that an obsession with the latest software package is the best way of advancing a career. Clergy, too, had better be 'professional' if they are to survive the game of clerical snakes and ladders. Deans run their cathedrals as infotainment centres, promote concerts and aim to maximize visitor numbers, while a positive riot of bishops proliferates in a Church of England which has decided that the best way to deal with declining numbers is to create more and more bishops who have now become a tier of egregious middle management.

The new power elites in the professions have therefore risen at the expense of the old. In that process, the old idea of the profession as a morally elevated commitment to a skill has evaporated and left behind the mere shell of the professional idea – the notion that a profession is simply a well-paid and secure job. These new elites have proved malleable to the purposes of capital and of the state, both of which have subverted the independence of the professions and enjoyed great success in turning the members of professional organizations into employees. Power within the old professions has therefore shifted. The kind of self-confidence which used to typify the trained professional is now more likely to be found among head teachers who have re-branded themselves as chief executives or hospital managers playing with a PC, rather than among teachers struggling to hit the state-imposed targets or GPs working in their surgeries, while the legal profession sees an ongoing struggle between old patterns of independence and a new subservience to either state control or to financial power. Self-confidence does remain a psychological possibility for the professional classes, but only if they are prepared to lose their autonomy and become the manipulated objects of management power. Something very important has therefore slipped out of British life: the idea and the reality of a true public service elite – a cadre confident in its knowledge and imbued with a pragmatic understanding of what counts as the 'public good'. Whether in schools or hospitals, in government and administration either central or local, public sector 'reform' has invariably demoralized those once vital elites because it has shifted both initiative and status away from the practitioners and towards the measurement of delivery targets.

New forms of largely spurious professionalism can be found in various forms of management, among security 'specialists', IT functionaries and recruitment companies. These are joined by a myriad different forms of 'consultancy' – a word which trades off the original, authentic, use of the word to describe certain medical professionals. New professionalism's prestige requirements frequently demand just such a hijacking of established vocabulary in order to eviscerate it of meaning. Management consultancy, in particular, seems a prototype for all these new professional activities, since empty jargoneering and mendacity appear to be inseparable from their work. All these services are marketed to suit the demands of a new age, since they can be presented as 'entrepreneurial' endeavour. But this is entrepreneurial work of a rather specialized kind, based on the ability to extract large fees from a comparatively small number of decision-makers who allocate the budgets and make the decisions in both public and private institutions. This is, in the strictest sense of the word, a racket, since the fees which are handed over are really a form of 'protection' money. Those in charge of the cheque-signing may talk plausibly enough about the need to commission research into their company's potential for growth and diversification as well as into the possibility of cutting costs. But the really urgent need is to find as many forms of protection as possible against the threat of being sacked. The commissioning of the contractual agreement is designed to demonstrate one's executive probity and responsibility while not having to do anything very much oneself. These new services therefore provide a kind of protection service for the professionals who need to show their alertness to the available policy 'options'. They are also central to the development of those same individuals' careers: for the power to spend money, to commission and to act, in this instance, as the patrons of a mendacious cause, shows who really has the power within governments and large corporations.

For many charged with positions of responsibility in state and corporate institutions, a safe career is best built through spending money, not by making it: the pragmatic and sceptical English think that building a company is far less appealing than managing the orderly decline of an existing one. In this culture of faux-enterprise and faux-dynamism professionals who aren't really professionals collaborate in order to spend shareholders' and tax-payers' money. The process pauses only briefly while the players swap places.

'Professionalism' therefore is Britain's very own bourgeois version of the trade union and has invariably been a way of blinding the public, if not with science then at least with the self-confidence which comes with the ability to negotiate an apparently successful way around a field of knowledge. That process starts with the necessary command of certain key terms and phrases which provide the lexicon of power. Very soon thereafter, the professional elites of a modern and industrial society are able to organize themselves with a degree of hierarchy and secrecy which makes them the heirs to the earlier aristocratic elites. By such means, they can attempt the concealment of waste and stupidity, of ignorance and venality.

## The Knowledge Economy: An Informational Wasteland

It is in this area of manipulated knowledge that the rise of IT has led to an important access of power for the professional elites, for it has meant an extension of power, an enchancement of profits as well as some dramatic and expensive forms of incompetence which, however, can always somehow be explained away through the soothing cadences of a techno-power which is ever-ready with a plausible excuse. IT companies are the beneficiaries of an in-built obsolescence, with the speed of technical advance pushing up the profits as last year's software package becomes redundant. In the professional elite world this kind of information has become less of a tool and more of a subject. Far from being seen as what it is – the latest way of organizing knowledge and easing communication – IT has itself become a form of knowledge, a discipline which, once mastered, can then be used to encourage the superstition which is at the service of an unquestioned power running concerns both private and public.

This has been particularly obvious in government programmes dedicated, so ironically, to the 'knowledge economy' of an 'age of information' which knows less and less. Capita – that self-described 'leading provider of integrated professional support service solutions'[11] has been greatly favoured by government contracts, despite its previous problems. Naturally enough, the education business has been a prime target for forays undertaken by IT firms hungry for the government contract. 'Individual-learning accounts' was a characteristic government confection in its combination of market force with educational need set deep within that purchaser–provider hell which has now overtaken the British public services. The programme, run by Capita, collapsed owing £70 million over its allotted budget. That typical IT combination of speedy digits with absence of brain resulted in tens of thousands being paid out to those on courses such as 'crystal healing'. 'Contracting-out' has been a boon to private sector firms such as Capita, yet there is little real scrutiny, either of their methods or their invoices. The Criminal Records Bureau, run by the same company, ran £150 million over budget. Both government agencies and departments of state regularly stumble and fall within this wasteland and by the beginning of the twenty-first century Britain had witnessed a decade of other widespread government computer chaos. The Passport Agency's failure resulted in half a million unprocessed applications and some £12 million in compensation. The failure of the Child Support Agency's £456 million computer system resulted not only in error but also in human misery and injustice. Meanwhile, the Ministry of Defence's 'Trawlerman' system for dealing with classified documents has had to be abandoned after costing £41 million. In 2004 the government spent £20 billion on computer projects, a sum which is a testimony to the ability of IT companies to regroup and press on undaunted.[12]

Perhaps the education world's most startling example of IT wishful-thinking was the UK e-university. The product of a naive political imagination about life-long learning in the early 1990s. The e-university was paraded as the heir to over a century of noble aspiration and effective teaching through university extension and adult education. It would be the apotheosis of the Ruskin tradition of great minds elevating the condition of the workers. But in 2004 the e-university was wound up having spent £50 million of public money and attracting only some 900 students. Even in its first year the project attracted only a sixth of the numbers expected. Perhaps indeed the failure was, in the leaden words of the Parliamentary Select Committee on Education and Skills, the result of a failure 'to form effective partnerships with, or gain significant investment from, the private sector'.[13] But 'partnership' is one of those words used by the elite when aspiration must count for everything; it stands for lack of thought and, quite often, for questionable accounting methods as the private sector takes public money and is then relieved of all risk in its use. This is why the National Health Service University, another bold project, was going to be 'a partnership between the NHS, existing universities and the private sector'. According to the British government, this was going to be the biggest university in the world with more than a million students whose eyes would be glued to the screens in rigorous pursuit of their betterment. But here, too, 'partnership' has had its savage way and the NHS university ended in nullity.

## Old Mandarins, New Rules

This decadence cannot be attributed solely to IT superstition. It forms part of a wider and corrupting pattern of activity in which the governmental and public sector elites decide, quite consciously, on a policy of irresponsibility which is administered on the basis that an awful lot of the people can either be fooled or ignored for most of the time. The mental health charity Sane, for example, handles some 1,200 calls a week on its helpline and one-third of those come from those referred to the charity by the NHS. But in 2004–5 the Department of Health withdrew the £1 million grant it paid to Sane for the service while spending £6 billion on a national computer system which has been criticized by the National Audit Office.[14] In situations such as these the fast-talking computer salesman has, however unintentionally, become one of the major threats to the efficiency, the costs and the humanity of modern government. The noxious effects that may ensue through a failure to ensure that the public gets best value from such ventures are made more likely aided by the prodigality of government itself in its creation of ancilliary structures, such as the 102 Whitehall agencies which now have the power to inspect, assess and categorize hospitals. All those semi-governmental institutions bring with them their own forms of career opportunity and the main beneficiaries are those who run the agencies and the companies that deliver the contracted-out service. They include not just Capita, but also Jarvis, Atkins, EDS, KPMG, Arriva, Group4 and Carrillon. Companies such as these are the ones who really benefit from the modern state's activities and the ultimate accountability of those who run them is to the City of London. In education, the 200 new city academies, some already built but most yet to arrive, are the flagships of the government's plan to recreate grammar school values in a modern setting. But the cost of building them, at an average of £24 million, is double that of the cost of schools built by local authorities. The difference is spent on school administration which is now naturally provided by private management firms. In transport, a similar picture prevails of lazy and unregulated management systems taking the public sector for a ride. Rail subsidies have doubled in recent years but comparatively little of that money has gone into improving train services. The real beneficiaries have been the city consultancies awarded a £500 million cheque by the Treasury in order to help it privatize the tube; another £300 million has been spent on researching Crossrail, a network which remains a drawing-board speculation. Management consultants in 2004–5 earned a total of £1 billion in fees from the government, and to their numbers can be added the bankers and the engineers, the architects and the lawyers who all benefit from a regime of extravagant lushness, one whose confidence in its ability to bamboozle knows no bounds. The overwhelming effect of our third, technological, revolution, has been to line the pockets of those professional elites who, for an hourly computed fee, stand ever-ready to regulate, assess and measure the quality of the work done by those in the public sector who work for a fraction of their own salaries.

IT superstition, extension of government competence at the expense of government efficiency and the professional elites' capacity to negotiate and manipulate the public–private gap: all come together in the idea of identity cards. Intellect, the egregiously named trade body which represents the IT, telecoms and electronic business, is central to the debate and to the profits which will be made. It sponsors what it calls 'early dialogue between customer and suppliers'.[15] Since the customer here is the Home Office, companies such as EDS (which was responsible for the breakdown of the Inland Revenue's tax credit system) and Fujitsu have all rushed to be part of that promising dialogue in which companies, civil servants and politicians can get to know each other. Official estimates for the cost of the technology stand at £5.8 billion (or £93 per person). But the nature of the technology itself as it becomes more complex – and, therefore, more prone to failure and abuse – will both increase the costs and inflate the profits. Present governmental estimates exclude the administrative costs of handling the cases of those who refuse to comply. They are also based on the card having a ten-year lifespan. But it is hardly likely that all the relevant details of most people's lives will remain the same during so long a period. Rescanning in order to incorporate new information will be necessary at least every five years. Of course, such rescanning will require extra 'management'. An estimate of £14–£18 billion in costs (and up to, therefore, £300 per person) seems nearer the mark, given previous governmental form on programmes begun in ignorance, pursued in hope and ending in waste.

But the elite conspiracy in favour of ID cards is not simply a question of sanguine, or suspect, accounting measures undertaken on the public–private partnership primrose path that leads to the deception of the citizenry. It forms part and parcel of the wider professional elite onslaught on British freedoms, and in that onslaught almost any piece of specious reasoning will do. Once, it was the 'war on terror' which was the reason advanced for the introduction of the Identity Cards Bill. This rhetorical focus was then replaced by another – the assault on garbage. Rifling through the refuse, so the government has informed us without any supporting facts or statistics, is a cause of 'huge financial loss, distress and inconvenience'. It is supposed, in particular, to lead to identity theft with criminals abusing their knowledge of individuals' financial and personal circumstances. And so, by a convenient shift of key, the fight against organized crime has now replaced terror's threat as the justification. But the serious crimes of the white-collar class, which include money laundering and the frauds perpetrated on investments and pension funds, are corporate crimes, and as such they involve the manipulation of fake companies not of fake people. No ID card would therefore have an impact on that endemic feature of company, and criminal, life in Britain.

The ID card represents, and is meant to uphold, the professionalization of knowledge in modern Britain. Its true heart is the National Register, a vast central database which will store addresses, record criminal tendencies and business associates and also contain the biometrics – the facial scans as well as the fingerprints and possibly the iris patterns (both of which can now be forged) of 60 million people.[16] The state may have withdrawn from the planning of the economy and the micro-management of key industries, but the elite professionals, the class that once ran the nationalized industries, retain both the urge and the capacity to direct, invigilate and administer information about the self. A presumption, not always naïve but invariably stubborn, that the technology will mostly work is allied to the prejudice in favour of a central system of planned information which is meant to yield insights beyond the capacity of the local, the personal and the experienced. If the system fails sometimes, then that is a calculated price worth paying for the sake of a greater good. Lord Denning once stated that it was better that unfairly convicted Irish terrorists should be kept in jail rather than be released since that would lead to aspersions being cast on the objectivity of the law courts. On that sinister and utilitarian reasoning, the greater cause of a society's confidence in its institutions should take precedence over a particular and limited injustice. Behind the idea of an identity card there lies a similar readiness to gamble away an individual right – in this instance, the identity of the subject – in the name of a greater social purpose. In both cases there is a myth to be upheld, and the supposed nobility of that myth, along with the jobs created by it, means that the occasional act of injustice can be tolerated.

## Secrecy and Falling into Error

The gap created by hypocrisy – and the consequent public indifference and cynicism about motives – is not just a failure on the part of legal professionals. It also represents a failure of governments when it comes to the application of the law. Few pieces of legislation represented such high hopes as the Freedom of Information Act (2000), legislation which issued from the realization that the British state had become encrusted by secretive practices. The experience of two world wars did not just create an expanded intelligence service for the purposes of spying and more general information-gathering. It had also encouraged the assumption of governmental habits of secrecy which outlasted the particular war-time circumstances. The spying scandals associated with Philby, Burgess, Maclean and Blunt revealed a decadent intelligence elite which was as detached from British national interests as the City of London's financial elite.[17] Subsequently, the British government tried, and failed, to suppress the revelation of information about those scandals by taking action against the former spy Peter Wright for publishing his book *Spycatcher*.[18] As a result, government conspired with the intelligence services to appear both ruthless in intent and incompetent in practice. But the implementation of the new Act's more liberalizing intention has been accompanied by that frustration of intent which is the true genius of British government. All statute law has to deal with the subverting effects of another and less formal law – that of the unintended consequences which trip up virtuous aspiration. But the frustration of the Freedom of Information Act was an intended consequence since the government introduced legislation whose effects were vitiated by cautious prevarications and carefully crafted exemptions.

New legislation usually amends old legislation. But the drafters of the Act were consumed by anxiety about its effects and therefore created an exception so that in this case old laws had precedence over this new one and would have to be reviewed individually with a view to their possible amendment. In the interests of creating even further confusion, the Act was not even a self-contained piece of legislation which set out clearly all the circumstances in which information was to be kept secret. In the manner of dodgy practitioners throughout the ages government, with parliamentary consent, decided to use confusion as a weapon and so retained the mass of very specific exemptions contained in existing legislation. The Official Secrets Act itself was just the most famous of these exemptions but there remain over 400 laws containing some 500 prohibitions which are subject to review and the prospect of completing that process, having started in 2000, is now delayed indefinitely.[19] It has taken a government which is formally pledged to open democracy four years to amend just eight pieces of legislation. It is striking how many of these legal prohibitions relate to business interests so that it is illegal for a regulatory body, for example, to release the information it holds. The Medicines Act (1968) has now been amended so that there is no longer a ban on the release of any clinical trial information about drug safety. But the Fire Precautions Act (1971) still makes it a criminal offence to disclose to the public the result of safety reports about private properties and public buildings. Long before the 1987 King's Cross underground station fire a whole range of regulatory reports from the police and the fire brigade had reported on a possible fire trap within the building. But it took the deaths of thirty-one people and the subsequent official report to discover and disclose that fact.

The assumption, based on experience, that the state will be secretive forms an important part of the British population's cynical quietism about the power elites of the professional and administrative domain. It tolerates, on the basis of low expectations, not just the evasion of disclosure but also the most flagrant examples of error and stupidity. The establishment of the government Office for National Statistics (ONS) in 1997 replaced earlier and more ramshackle arrangements for the measurement and analysis of governmental activity. It was one of those regularly recurring moments in the history of British government when clarity and order are proclaimed as the order of the day – and, just as in those earlier moments, nemesis lay in wait to tease and subvert those optimistic intentions. In its short history, the ONS has produced flawed data on average earnings whose effect may well have been to cause the Bank of England to raise interest rates unnecessarily. It has also produced one of the major statistical errors in British economic history – a £100 billion discrepancy between two sets of figures on pension fund assets. Things were not much better when it came to running the national census, an exercise costing some £255 million and one which showed that the British population was a million less than expected. Pressed for an explanation, the ONS' Director advanced the idea that there were 'an unusually large number of young men in their twenties' sunning themselves in such places as Ibiza.[20] October 2004 produced a £43 billion error in the double counting of pension contributions, a fact which was then (according to the Commons Treasury Select Committee) 'covered up in the best spin-doctored fashion'. The idea of the institution's political neutrality was undermined when it ruled that the debt of Network Rail should not go on the government's books despite the fact of a £21 billion state guarantee to the company.

The points at which the merely ramshackle degenerates into the devious will vary according to the individual details of these and other examples of the culpably ignorant state. For Len Cook, the cheerful New Zealander who was Britain's National Statistician from 2000 to 2005, the mistake is simply the result of a lack of organizational 'resources'. 'In Britain,' he complains, 'you enjoy criticising everything that is professional.'[21] But that enjoyment is surely justified in a country where 'professional' has become just a synonym for the well-paid, secure and respectable job.

For the ONS the buck stops with the software, and the organiza-tion's official 'line to take' attributes its mistakes to the 'obsolete systems' at its disposal. That kind of confidence in its own authority despite all the facts of failure runs like a connecting thread through all the workings of British government. The moments of revealed in-competence can be embarrassing but a wider, political, dispensation will protect and keep the elite together. Which is, for example, why the ONS established its own Centre for the Measurement of Government Activity after the government was discomfited by official output figures which showed that state spending was being consumed by rising inefficiencies. It was a political response to a political problem, and a sign of the powerful convergence between the political and the administrative elites.

The convergence has turned the professional administrator into a *valet du pouvoir*, as can be seen in the valedictory remarks of Sir Andrew Turnbull[22] (subsequently Lord Turnbull) when retiring as Cabinet Secretary in 2005. From 1970 to 2005 Britain had, he said, seen a 'transformation for the better' and this was a result of 'a sustained exercise of political leadership over thirty years'.[23] In particular, the defeat of the miners' strike had 'established two principles which changed the course of history: that economic change could not be resisted and undemocratic trade unionism had no place in Britain'. The labelling of the civil servant as a bureaucrat was, he thought, a token of an insensitive failure to grasp the vitality of the official mind and its contribution to this transformative leadership. His own claim to a historical footnote was that he had helped to build 'out of the wreckage of the exchange rate mechanism, a macroeconomic system which is admired around the world'.

These unrealistic claims are examples of the self-confidence and the self-interest which come with high office. When viewed from this eminence, the past can be reduced to a series of edited highlights which then lead necessarily to the present. But the miners' strike came at the end of over thirty years of cumulative failure in the mining industry, and was the last whimper rather than the mighty roar that it suited both sides of the conflict to hear. The decision to wreck the coal industry has resulted in the damaging anomaly that Britain, alone among advanced economies, has no coal industry of its own. As for the other Turnbull claim, the ERM which ended in 'wreckage' was also a scheme faithfully administered by Treasury officials and it should really be seen as the final attempt by a British government at managing economic and fiscal policy. The 'macroeconomic system' which followed was really no more than a running up of the white flag by the state in order to advance one particular theory of markets and consumers. Since that process has coincided with Turnbull's career success he can therefore wallow in that elite explanatory glibness which comes with finding oneself at the top of the heap.

## Measuring by Numbers

'Turnbullism' is a form of intellectual arrogance which is quite as noxious in its effects as the more obvious and more exuberant forms of financial corruption which afflict the administrative classes of Mediterranean, US and Latin American societies. It results in that mutually back-scratching set of attitudes which helps to divide the spoils of power and of office. On the one hand, governmental elites have never been more addicted to pie-charts, bullet points, charts and graphs. 'Outcomes' are computed and 'inputs' are measured while numbers are generated to underpin argument. The McKinsey principle that if it can be measured then it can be managed has entered deep into elite patterns of thought. It seems therefore the most natural thing in the world that a McKinsey trainee, and an enthusiast for what she calls the 'knowledge industry' (Natalie Ceeney), should be appointed to run, inevitably as 'chief executive', the Public Record Office (duly renamed the National Archives).[24] It is surely part and parcel of the same industrialization of knowledge that the much-used archives which contain the celebrated census for 1901 should be run as part of a public finance initiative (PFI) deal, by the defence research company QinetiQ which, in turn, sold those archives to the commercial web site company Friends Reunited for £3.3 million in August 2005.

But the effect of all the measurement and all the calculation, all the renaming and the marketing, is merely to underpin not so much decisive argument as the banal whimper. That exemplar of elite thought, Lord Birt,[25] has attempted (in his capacity as the Prime Minister's strategy adviser) to produce a 'unit cost of crime'.[26] Crime has an obvious cash cost and the Birtian calculation adds a notional value in terms of trauma and distress. Taken together the two measurements generate the obvious conclusion that crimes of violence, which are few in number, are more important and more costly than other crimes. These trivial power formulations are the games that a power elite likes to play while justifying its existence to itself. The cult of management has replaced genuine policy and it finds more and more sophisticatedly numerate ways of stating the obvious. Our professional administrative elite, as Lord Turnbull's remarks show, engage in little independent-minded questioning of government. Mandarin mental self-confidence has diminished steadily and been replaced by chatter about 'line managers' charged with 'delivery of services'. Among those who offer the state some service, the neutral 'how' has replaced the enquiring 'why' because it is the safer option for the career builder – as well as a way of avoiding blame should things go wrong. The political elite therefore benefits from the existence of a pliant, administrative elite which is colourlessly neutral rather than independent-minded.[27] But the danegeld to be paid is the reinforcement of the administrative class as a group of tenaciously embedded officeholders. Governments will therefore talk of civil service cuts while presiding over a 'slippage' in their chosen 'targets'. Political and administrative elites lack the self-confidence required to advance the cause of a clever and forceful administrative class. But they also lack the will or the capacity to move to leaner government. Failing therefore to produce either form of administrative elite rule, Britain has the worst of all worlds – a rather stupid, and comparatively well-populated, administrative elite.

It is for these reasons that the Foreign and Commonwealth Office has a Human Resource Unit with 290 staff, five times the ratio for most world-class companies, while the Department of Transport likes to spend its money on jobs for consultants, with £10 million being spent (in 2004–5) on its contracts with IBM, Deloitte, KPMG and Halcrow.[28] The political elite feels obliged to bow to what it thinks is the popular, 'anti-bureaucrat', mentality while also knowing in its heart of hearts that this is one 'service delivery' about which it can afford to be relaxed. In 2004 the Chancellor announced, with all the predictable panache of the slasher, that 84,150 Whitehall jobs would go. One year later, the main result of that initiative was that 12,500 posts would be axed by the end of 2005 while, during the period 1997–2005, the total number of civil service staff had increased by 44,000 and the total number of public sector workers had increased by 650,000. 'Deployment' to the 'front-line' is the unhappy language, reminiscent of the trench warfare of 1914–18, used by all governments when they describe this change in elite function. If Whitehall is, eventually, somewhat diminished in numbers, nonetheless the staff are invariably redeployed in other areas of government, especially within the agencies. Governments therefore pretend to 'cut'. The attempt and the failure are both in their own different ways damaging because they promote the impression that governments are indifferent to the central administration of a modern democratic state. And that cynicism – along with the knowledge that the indices of performance are meaningless and the targets are a silly game – explains the indifference of the passive multitudes about a debate which, like so many English debates, is really a conversation between the different branches of a self-interested elite.

## Inequalities: Edbiz Elites

The superficial patter of claims to reform government, just like the awesome legal rhetoric about the fundamental rights of the free-born English, occur against a background of widening inequalities. Elite indifference to those disparities provides a further explanation for the popular indifference to both those claims and to that rhetoric. Acquiring the necessary patina of a professional existence has become progressively easier in Britain as long as you are born and bred out of that stock to begin with. Our professional elites are the beneficiaries of a state of affairs which guarantees them fairly minimal competition for desirable jobs since social mobility is now lower in Britain that it is in any other advanced country with the exception of the USA. In America it is race which explains that country's gross disparities, but in Britain it is the inequalities in education which lead to the children of the affluent benefiting quite disproportionately from the lottery of birth. In Britain 38 per cent of sons born in 1970 to the poorest quarter of families were themselves still stuck in the same bottom quarter of earners at the age of thirty, and a mere 11 per cent had made it to the richest quarter. But those who were born with a fair wind behind them stood a much better chance of retaining their advantages: 42 per cent of those born in the richest quarter of the population were still there at the age of thirty, while only 16 per cent had slipped into the bottom quarter.[29]

It is, largely, the function of Britain's public schools to insulate their pupils from the true competition which would come from the operation of a genuine and competitive market among the talented. Privilege, in this instance, arrives at the very start and skews both the market and its results. The public school educated boy may very well do worse than his state school contemporary once both have arrived at university. Armed with the same A level grades the public school-boy's chances of a good degree, either a first or upper-second, stand at 15 percentage points lower than those of his competitior.[30] Girls show no such disparity, and tend to carry on opening the books. That fact may also explain how the feminization of career opportunities has helped not just to reformulate but also to reinforce the power of the British elite. Socially alert feminism has concerned itself with the fact that most women who work do so in low-paid jobs, but the forms of career feminism which have been really influential within the British elite offer a grateful acquiescence in power rather than a critical dissent from it. Elite feminism has played the elite male role, and proved rather better at doing so than some dozy men.

Statistical demonstrations of comparative performances can be used to show why, and how, reverse discrimination is justified in order to create a genuinely open and clever elite among university students. But the benign effects of that discrimination are constrained by the fact that the class of degree is largely irrelevant when it comes to gaining elite power in Britain. That is not really the gradation that matters; the boy from a certain background can afford to slacken off because he knows that his elite prospects are not endangered. As Ben Fleming-Williams (Charterhouse) points out, now armed with a lower-second in combined arts from Durham: 'When you have spent most of your life being told that you are in the top 5% of the population, you are likely to think that you can relax at university.'[31] And a certain relaxed attitude among the elite is surely what is being commended, too, by Sir Howard Newby,[32] chief executive of the Higher Education Funding Council for England. If certain courses have to disappear in certain universities – if modern languages and science courses have to close – then that, he maintains, is no bad thing because it is merely a result of market wisdom discarding what is irrelevant and choosing what it needs. In particular, it would be wrong to succumb to 'moral panic' at the sight of the disappearance of separate scientific courses.[33] The division of subjects such as physics and chemistry is, in Newby's world, just a nineteenth-century invention, something which can be revised in the light of contemporary scientific discoveries that straddle the divide. But the ability to make the interdisciplinary connections presupposes the ability to know in the first place the differences between the subjects. The alternative is a multidisciplinary pap. Britain's 'knowledge economy', however, as run and understood by the administrative elite, is at ease with exactly that alternative. It happily criticizes a concern with 'standards' as elitist and talks of its desire to widen 'access' while at the same time guarding its own privileges as a power elite which is insulated behind a protective fortress of jargon. Elite power in Britain is nothing if not resourceful in its deployment of hypocrisy and all its lovingly deployed metaphors about the wide and the broad, the deep and the lean, are a cover for the maintenance of old hierarchy, which is why Britain now has an 18+ system of university education in much the same way that it used to have an 11+ system for secondary education. A small number of universities at the top cannot afford to expand while a vast number of others have become the new 'secondary-modern' sector.

Justified logic, rather than frightened elite establishment thinking, is what lies behind the public schools' desire to rebrand themselves as 'independent'. They do not stand for a genuine independence of the mind since practically all of them end up following the same curriculum as the state comprehensive. But the fact of their independence at an institutional level does separate them from genuine 'market forces' in order to achieve their true goal, the cosseting of some forms of low mental wattage among their customers. It is this institutional independence which is now aped by Britain's government in its attempt at creating an elite educational structure through the envisaged 200 city academies, which are effectively state-funded independent schools with private individual sponsors.[34] For £2 million such a sponsor gets the right to appoint governors and senior administrative staff and also the power to influence lessons within the national curriculum. This has been the British elite's most significant admission of failure in education and its consequent loss of nerve as it contracts out of its responsibilities in the provision of education – something which has been a core competence of government in all developed societies in modern times. The failure is one of the most derelict aspects of elite-run Britain, with only just over half of all children gaining those five pass GCSEs at A–C grade which themselves constitute a pretty modest goal. Almost a half of all boys and a third of all girls now emerge from their primary schools lacking the basic literacy which would fit them to cope with secondary education. But the academies already established, with their indifferent record of success, are largely a record of elite failure with one – the Unity City Academy in Middlesbrough – being officially failed by government inspectors.[35] They can offer their suitably high-sounding justification as institutions which can 'specialize' in certain areas. Islington's City Academy, for example, promises to specialize in 'global citizenship'. Their range of sponsors – city companies, Anglican and Catholic dioceses and a clutch of financiers including the founder of Saga holidays – are a representative selection of British elite significance, both old and new,[36] but this is a story of elite aspiration which struggles to justify itself even by its own chosen standards. A similar elitist impotence in the face of the facts is seen in the misapplication of market thought to already existing schools. 'Choice' is seen as the arm of the people's power and the ability to choose a school for a child is thought to raise standards by the inexorable logic of market magic. But there is no evidence that a successful school will necessarily want to expand and very many schools associate their success with the fact of their present size. Two-thirds of the best-performing comprehensive schools have said that they do not want to expand, and only one in six is prepared to consider it.

The distortions and the corruptions created by elite marketeering have also now entered deep into university life. Large areas of campus life are now dominated by the R & D needs of multinational companies – most markedly in the pharmaceutical, telecommunication and biotechnology industries. With that elite convergence between an academic and a business class there has arisen a new conflict – that between university teachers' paid duty to teach and the commitments of many to the consultancy or the spin-off company. But the conflicts engendered by elite greed go even deeper than those conflicting demands on time. A more rigorous application of the fair market – as opposed to the mere deployment of the manipulated version – would also ask what counts as a fair return for the public who can end up paying twice for the same research. They pay first through the taxes which pay for the university and then through the company profits based on the research costs which in turn are passed on to the buyer. These dangers have been most obvious in US universities where, for example, over 90 per cent of company-sponsored research into drugs' effectiveness gives those drugs the green light while only 60 per cent of non-sponsored research does so.[37] But British universities, too – with their new zeal to patent and license discoveries – are exposed to the same corruption.

## Legal Elites: An English View of Liberty

The legal systems of modern democratic societies, as run by the legal professionals, proclaim and defend a certain idea of equality. Those who appear before judge and jury, as plaintiff or defendant, are all 'equal in the sight of the law'. As a result, the citizens of a democracy and the subjects of a constitutional monarchy are not supposed to be able to pick and choose which laws they obey. The duke and the dustman are in this respect equal, and the blindness of justice is a chosen condition, a veil which is adopted so that she may not be swayed by the partiality which may arise from knowledge of social standing, the advantages of birth, or the endowments of beauty and intellect. Certain kinds of knowledge of some particular circumstances, of course, can and do affect the judgement delivered. Culpability may be diminished because of mental imbalance or distress; and guilt may be graver if advice has been ignored and the offender

111

can be proved to be particularly heedless of consequences. But to that fundamental idea of the equality enjoyed by the human personality's legal standing, and which governs how that person is treated procedurally, modern and democratically determined law pays an effusive regard. This is the legal basis of the means by which we are governed, and it is also the basis of the authority accorded to the elite of legal professionals who operate that system.

What has become a commonplace was once a revolution. The whole point of ancien régime Europe's society of orders was that different laws applied to different kinds of people.[38] In the most obvious case, the clergy of both the Catholic and (in England and its former empire) of the Anglican Churches were subject to canon law whose courts, trials and legal codes were separate from those of civil law.[39] European history is littered with disputes between Church and state as to where the boundaries should be fixed, where canon law's jurisdiction should end and the state's law take over. But even within the dominion of the state itself the aristocratic order for centuries was founded on a vigorously asserted inequality, otherwise described as a question of honour.[40] Nobility had certain legal rights that were not so much denied to non-nobles as deemed utterly irrelevant to them. The survival of an informal chivalric code allowed the practice of aristocratic duelling to continue well into the eighteenth century despite the formal interdiction of state law, while in Britain today substantial remains from that past are allowed to survive beneath the democratic facade. The opacity of land-ownership, for example, means that obscurity and ambiguity can conceal the fact of the old order's survival. If to measure a thing is to make it manageable, then the country's landed classes surely remain in a state of almost feral independence, while the notoriously complicated game laws of England and Wales, which govern the shooting seasons and protect the self-interest of men of landed property, are a tribute to the survival of Europe's last ancien régime state.[41]

The principles of the French Revolution[42] were the first decisive European step in the dismantling on a national scale of this idea of a society of orders, of different classes and occupations arranged in a hierarchical order with different kinds of laws in different areas applying to the various members of those orders. England's mid-seventeenth-century rebellion had witnessed an attempt to apply the democratic laws of the people objectively right across the social strata and so to strip both aristocratic and regal power of its mystique. But that experiment collapsed and was succeeded by a reactionary restoration of the old order. Calvin's Geneva and classical Athens had attempted a similar legal objectivity on the level of the city-state. Calvinism, however, had replaced an old version of aristocracy with a newly modelled theocracy: the laws might be applied objectively but they were administered by a hierarchy of elders who thought they were privileged by God.[43] The Athenian democratic record, though remarkable internally, is blemished by the imposition of regime change on conquered states who were then ruled as part of the Athenian empire by collaborationist local elites.[44]

Unlike Rome and Geneva on the one hand and the English rebellion on the other, the principles of 1789 applied at both the level of the nation-state and also proved to be long-lasting in their effects. In both civil and administrative law the legacy of the Code Napoléon with its rationalism and ideal of uniform efficiency has shaped the histories of those countries of continental Europe that were affected by French revolutionary principles. These modern states elevated the ideal of citizenship as part of the pilgrimage towards modernity. The legal equality of citizens was meant to cut across both the classes and the regions of particular countries. From now on, it was a sign of an antiquated and prejudiced social order when the legal bodies of particular areas produced laws that applied to their own regions but which might contradict the law that applied in other areas of the country. In developing this idea in so rationalist a way, the legislators of nineteenth-century Europe looked back as well as forward. For the traditions of Roman Law, marked by a similar kind of declaratory clarity and a deductive working out from first principles, had been a major influence on the evolution of European legal systems for centuries before 1789.[45] The same rationalism that had upheld the rights of princes was now used to enforce the authority of the modern state, its monopoly of force and its even-handed dominion over individual citizens.

Modern continental states therefore aspired to the condition of ancient Rome in denying the existence of legal obstacles to their dominion over individual citizens. They might allow the survival of social orders, just as Rome had done. The new aristocracy created by Napoleon and the recipients of the légion d'honneur were comparable to the Roman patriciate and its social prestige. But status, in both its modern and its ancient forms, was dependent on the support and the patronage of the centralized will, be it that of 'the people' or of Caesar.[46] This meant that these modern states diverged from the USA,

113

the other major political system to emerge from the political ferment of the late eighteenth century. The constitution of the newly combined American states retained important legal powers for the individual states within that federation, states which were run by local gentry elites. And in doing so the American constitution, though using the language of democracy, in fact gave new expression to many of the features of the old European and English aristocratic order, with different laws applying in different areas to different people. This explains the long toleration of slavery by some American states as well as the current regional variety of laws on questions such as gun control and the death sentence. The relationship between the federal institutions and the individual states was therefore diffuse and very different from the rational uniformity of the new European states with their subordination of the regions to the centre.

English legal thinking and legal systems stand at an oblique angle to these European developments, and that characteristic obliquity goes to the heart of the privilege and the power which are enjoyed and pursued in certain English ways. To a far greater degree than in continental Europe the whole question of law – how you learn it and apply it – is fundamental to this country's identity and its system of values.[47] The laws of mainland Europe were decisively affected by the political events of the great revolution, something which came from outside the debates of jurisprudence and then ended up changing not only those debates themselves but also how the courts decided on the rights and wrongs of individuals. The conclusions and rulings of our legal system permeate – as law should – every aspect of our lives. But what are also permeated are the procedural qualities of that legal system – the way law is communicated and taught, the means by which lawyers go about their business and express their views to each other, the whole texture and fabric of their existence as a life lived and a trade pursued. Until very recently, these qualities have shaped English politics and political thought rather than been affected by them. It has been a one-way traffic of influence, and this insularity has provided the ideal breeding ground for certain characteristically elite thinking and habits.

Instead of Roman Law, the English legal establishment glories in the common law of England. Legal history itself shows how the two traditions, far from being separate, actually coexisted and affected each other so that the one cannot be easily separated from the other.[48] But that fact of history is submerged beneath the weight of the rhetoric developed by legal elites, often assisted by axe-grinding political rhetoricians and misty-eyed historians, who maintain that common law is a stand-alone glory and a sacrosanct tradition which is therefore the most distinctive part of English law. It is a vast and rambling estate whose boundaries, quite gratifyingly, cannot be clearly delineated, and the lack of definitional clarity is what is meant to be attractive about it. The common law is an aspect of the mind of England for it offers and reflects a diffused and protean sense of the national self – unplanned, brilliantly improvisational, suspicious of theory, respectful of variety, adaptable and deep in its rich complexity.[49] As a result, when liberties are upheld and their denial condemned such acts are often described as assertions, or violations, of the common law. Those who ask for a definition of what 'common law' actually is betray, in the eyes of the legal guardians at any rate, their ignorance. That is an outsider's query. Part of the beauty of the common law – and also much of its propagandist usefulness – comes from the fact that there is no single code or principle which tells you what it is. It is defined instead by its methodology, a way of thinking which is highly congenial to the English legal mind because it concentrates on the object of special interest to that mind – individual cases and particular people rather than theory. If the common law can be understood only in terms of its methodology, then that is also a conveniently self-serving kind of elite understanding. The common law which is meant to be the cornerstone of liberty is in fact the possession of those who know their way around it. It is the property of the legal elite, a habit of mind and a style of life.

Common law no more exists in a single discoverable way than the British constitution is locatable in a particular document. Instead, rather like that constitution, it exists in a myriad different written forms and its judgements are the result of the comparison of different cases. Common law elevates a procedure into a principle, a way of looking at the world which rejects general theory as impractical and insensitive to individual circumstances. It is at the heart of the myth of England as a necessarily conservative place, a country whose laws and institutions embody that very specialized understanding of freedom which, through inspired insularity and the mystique of the nation, has been handed down and developed by successive generations, something felt along the bloodline and thought about with the heart. This is the view of England offered by T.S. Eliot and Henry James, two foreigners who brought with them a colonial mythology about the fondly imagined mother country when they started to burn their incense at an altar whose object of worship was an essentially country-house view of England. In determining the nature of legal power in England, the common law tradition has developed an elite power version of what these literary figures communicated in cultural terms. Instead of freedoms and rights, all those principles and declarations which issue from the arbitrary and capricious political will, it offers the supposed safety and provisionality of particular defined liberties.

So goes the view which presents itself as an unalterable fact. Great lawyers from Maitland in the nineteenth century down to Denning in the late twentieth century have enjoyed enormous success in persuading their countrymen that this view is simply commonsense.[50] It parades itself as a description of England rather than what it really is, a theory which has selected some helpful facts. This is, therefore, just the way we are and always will be – with English lawyers' arguments morphing into a Vera Lynn view of England. Any sense of the unusual nature of law in England is therefore lost. English law and lawyers may claim an exceptional version of national wisdom but, within the boundaries of the Dover Cliffs to the south and of Hadrian's Wall to the north the version is not considered at all unusual. Consequently, the observation from afar of European totalitarianism in the twentieth century, and its comparison with English benevolence or absence of malice, has resulted in some immensely self-satisfied notes of approval. Immune from revolutionary excess, England had the wisdom to preserve its ancestral constitutional understanding of liberty as set out in its laws. After all, didn't the new ferment of the democratic European societies of the nineteenth century also leave them vulnerable to the totalitarian grab for power in the twentieth century? Rousseau's will of the people all too easily warps into Hitler's will of the race and the mass emotion of the mob which can be all democratically virtuous at one moment can turn into mass intolerance the next. How much wiser, therefore, to leave those guardians of the constitution, the lawyers, in place along with all the other traditional features of old England in her winding sheet. Thus goes the theory which presses a native English benevolence into the career service of an English legal elite.

The cast of mind of contemporary English lawyers, their way of going about their business in the world whose difficulties and sadnesses, conflicts and tragedies, provides them with a livelihood, are substantially the same as those of their mediaeval predecessors.

Continuity with the past, or rather one version of that past, is the condition of their existence. Precedent is not only the substance of English common law as a subject, it also governs the more general procedure of English lawyers as a profession. It is all rather as if English politics had not had its Reform Acts and the English Church had not had a Reformation. Of course, there have been legal innovations that have changed the running of the legal business – such as the introduction of legal aid, together with the establishment of the CPS and of a Lord Chancellor's Department as the administrative arm of English legal bureaucracy. There have even been measures granting solicitors the right of advocacy in court, something which has gone against the grain of the deep institutional division between solicitors and barristers within the English legal profession. But lawyers, in ways both good and bad, have stood at more than an arm's length away from those new trends in British professional life which have emphasized 'transparency', measurement of 'outcomes' and 'market choice'. The mental habits of every other professional class – be they teachers, soldiers, the police, university lecturers, doctors, clergy or civil servants – have changed as a result of such managerial pressures. What has emerged is a new bureaucratic tone and a new bureaucratic elite which, having absorbed the clichés of management textbooks, uses that jargon to insulate itself even further from accountability and communication. In attempting to separate the legal profession from these developments, it is the barristers who lead the way and set the tone for the defence.

## The Bar: Elite Power by Social Negotiation

The Bar of England and Wales takes its elite status very seriously. Self-regulation for the profession and self-employment for its individual members have a more than totemic status. This is a professional elite which regulates its entry numbers tightly[51] and has an esprit de corps which has become rare among the other British professions which have been largely overwhelmed by the flight of talent and ambition to the City of London. That solidarity and that sense of belonging marks every aspect of life at the Bar. These professionals may be technically self-employed and treated as such for taxation purposes, but their individual status is expressed through, and affected by, a corporate structure which governs their lives and shapes their thinking in a communal direction. Government audits have more savage ways of reminding barristers of their dependent status. In 2005, the government cut the fees for representing defendants by between 1 per cent and 46 per cent after the discovery that officials had exceeded the £2 billion legal aid budget by £130 million.[52] The result – a withdrawal of labour by some members of the Criminal Bar – was in effect a strike against the employing state. But the incident also revealed the incompetence of that same state. It is the criminal legal aid stakes – as opposed to the civil legal aid ones – which have provided the richest pickings, with the top ten barristers working for the criminal defence service being paid more than £600,000 by that service in 2004–5.[53] James Sturman, QC earned £1,180,000 from this form of state pay during that year, most of which came from a two-year international software piracy case which, in his own view, should never have been prosecuted. Faced with criticism, Mr Sturman had his own defence ready: it was the reading of the papers that did it. Since the defence in this case had to read 2.9 million pages of prosecution documents this was, hour by computed hour, profitable business. Instead of taking the case to the civil courts and getting an injunction with a power of arrest 'the hi-tech crime unit brought the prosecution and once they served the papers we had to read them.'[54] In a characteristic touch of that elite power which knows how to protect itself by a touch of the demotic, Sturman reveals that he would have liked to have been a bass player in the Ramones band had he not become quite so high-earning a barrister.

As with the political elites, but perhaps even more so, the Bar is also a metropolitan grouping inducted into its ways of being, of communication and of self-recognition by membership of the four Inns of Court – the Middle and the Inner Temple, Gray's Inn and Lincoln's Inn. As a form of legal education the Inns are unique and there are no European equivalents. In their collegiate structure and style, along with the whole paraphernalia of chapels, dining halls with high tables and chambers which may be residential as well as a place of work, they hark back to their late-mediaeval origins. Right up until the nineteenth century the Inns were a kind of post-Oxbridge university at a time when the admission age for students at Oxford and Cambridge was lower than it is now.[55] After the mid-adolescence years spent at university came the really serious form of adult education, and the progress to the Inns by the banks of the Thames was a continuation of the same kind of collegiate existence that had started by the banks of the Cam and the Isis.

This sociality is not just an incidental aspect of legal education in England and Wales (Scotland has a less exclusive tradition). Nor is it some kind of anachronistic shell, something to delight the eye on National Trust and English Heritage terms, while the real work goes on underneath. It really goes to the heart of that education itself because, rather as in public school education, what is communicated by intuition is a certain code of conduct for those who are socially congenial as well as being mentally adept at the task in hand. That intimacy extends to the relationship between the barrister and the client as well as to those that exist between barristers themselves and between the barrister and the judge. As one eminent QC puts it this 'ability to condition ideas' is at the heart of what he does.[56] It is important for him to be able to influence his clients and if he can't carry them with him then 'the relationship does not continue'. 'The taxi-rank idea of engaging a barrister may still be the theory but in practice there are always ways of avoiding the client you don't want, don't trust, or don't like.' Elites at the bar – as in other areas of life – are useful, he says, because they offer 'a freedom of manoeuvre'. The freedom from constraint, which comes from earning enough money, gives him the freedom to use his judgement, to exercise responsibility and to display the awareness of privilege's responsibilities in ways congenial to him. All of this is a classic formulation of the barrister as a successful and independent practitioner within the elite. 'The beauty of the bar is risk.' But even this QC, a believer in elites and in the fact that there is 'an upper-middle-class basis to liberty', doesn't believe that the Bar has discovered 'the best way to identify its own elite'. 'We need a more elegant filtering.' All he can say with confidence is that 'if you really want to be a barrister then you do get there'. The statistics may be intimidating, with hundreds applying each year for just one or two pupillages at his chambers, but the ones who are ready to persist will attain their goal and 'everyone does get sorted out'. This apparent informality of approach has been typical of the recruitment proce- dures of the old English elite in general when it set about the business of selecting, really quite purposefully despite the superficially casual manner, those who were going to maintain the tradition. Its survival at the Bar shows how some lawyers remain at their post as embattled remnants of the ancient régime.

But in that process of 'sorting out' it is quite clear that the way in which the pupil-barrister displays knowledge of the law is quite as important as the content of such knowledge. The requirement to have eaten a certain number of dinners in the hall of the relevant Inn before being called to the Bar may be only a formality but it is also emblematic of a profession whose members need to be at ease with themselves and with their colleagues if they are to survive and prosper. This is not a profession for the angular, the difficult or the self-critical. The Bar is indeed more of a family thing than many suspect, with son – and now sometimes daughter – following parent into the same Inn. Indeed, the practice of senior benchers in the Inn awarding scholarships to help with students' fees sees many a friend of that parent helping out, and so keeping the whole business within the wider professional family.

The Bar is a sociable institution which cultivates a certain actorish self-regard. It appreciates that polished command of an audience and that easy way with a jury which also shows that the counsel is on top of the case. In the English manner, it rewards cleverness while rather looking down on intellectuality. England has only produced one major figure in the history of jurisprudence, the study of the philosophical basis of law. John Austin (1790–1859)[57] was an unsuccessful barrister with a temperament which made him a very odd man out at the Bar. His contemporary Crabb Robinson described him as being, variously, 'disputatious', 'offensive' and a 'loud talker', and those were judgements shared by most of Austin's legal colleagues.[58]

But it was Austin's views about law which explain both the originality of his genius and his own social and professional loneliness. Austin exploded the romantic–conservative idea that law is something discovered, a miracle which has been made by nobody in particular, has existed from eternity and is just lying around waiting to be declared by the legal initiates. Having studied Roman Law as well as German jurisprudence, he rejected the cosily consensual mythologies about English law and showed that law was not discovered but made, it was the result of acts of the human will and therefore reflected the truths of power and command. Every independent political society had a sovereign – which could be either a person or a set of persons – and law was the 'general command' of that sovereign. This inconveniently brutal insistence on the facts of power as the force which explains law accounts for Austin's early political radicalism as an utilitarian reformer. It also explains the hostility towards him of the legal professionals of his own, and subsequent times, those whose business was served by the concealment of these power truths and who preferred to cover the law with a comforting moral cloak. Professionally speaking, that cloak encouraged the idea that lawyers were a disinterested profession patiently at work discovering an objective legal morality. But if law is seen as the reflection of power then both the practitioners of law as well as its makers are placed on a less elevated level. They are no longer professionals with an expertise in the disclosure of how things ought to be (a subject which is the legitimate business of equity). Instead, they simply demonstrate how things necessarily are, given the fact of who has the power to act and who then does what to whom.

Jurisprudence remains an important component in the intellectual and professional formation of the higher branches of the legal profession on the European mainland. But the example of Austin's professional isolation shows how in England jurisprudence is strictly for the remoter branches of academic enquiry. That gap between the practising lawyer and the legal academic has grown progressively deeper in recent years. Although it was once common for the academic lawyer to be also a practising barrister that is now a rare combination and the rarity is a sign of the decline in the theoretical understanding of rights and freedoms in English law. That aversion to general theory has of course always characterized English lawyers. But the difference now is that the suspicion of abstraction is grounded on real ignorance where once it was grounded on intimate knowledge.

But this division between the academic theorist and the practical lawyer is only one element in a wider picture. The historic English constitution, with its thickets of prerogatives and peculiarities, of rights and obligations, required a certain kind of lawyer to interpret it. Classically, that lawyer was someone who had turned to law after an earlier, humanist education had given him the historical and philosophical background which then enabled him to understand the context of English law. These men were hardly philosopher-kings, but they had read their Plato, and though their study of English history was in some ways partial it was enough to provide the material for a reasoned, public defence of liberty. But the modern lawyer is by and large someone who started to study law as a first degree at the age of eighteen and who ever since has been immersed in the details of case law. It is perfectly possible, given the collapse of English secondary education, for extremely clever law students to be adept in the interpretation of law while knowing next to nothing of English and European history (apart from that ubiquitous subject of study, Nazi Germany), of literature and philosophy – that broader context which still supplies the background to the studies of their European contemporaries. The practical consequence of this is a 'hollowing out' of the common law tradition. The law faculties of continental European universities, at Padua and Bologna, Heidelberg and Tübingen, Montpellier and Salamanca, are teeming with students because such universities are less selective than British ones when it comes to the initial registration of students. And the dropout rate subsequent to registration is consequently higher than in British universities. But if their student base is wider, so is their conception of what counts as a legal education. It is now more possible than at any time in the past to do extremely well professionally as a lawyer in England as a result of having been educated and trained to think in an extremely narrow and mentally impoverished way. An in-built philistinism now operates as a new bias in English legal education. This supplements that hard-edged professional cynicism about human nature, as well as the inveterate determination to extract a fee from misfortune or criminality, which has earned the lawyer such an unhappy reputation in the history of English literature and of English public opinion. But the emerging legal 'professional' forms part of a cadre which is not only thoroughly isolated from the contemporary world but is also ignorant about the past which has formed the present. This is a new, and narrow, form of 'professionalism' whose pragmatism and briskness poses new dangers to freedom. A government which is indifferent to freedom has there-fore been able to benefit from an amoral professionalism.

This is a situation entirely different from the history of past legal elites, however unappealing some of the traits of character of those elites may have been. Oxford or Cambridge graduates with a good degree in law who join either a city firm of lawyers or a set of chambers as a trainee barrister have become instant members of an elite. But whether they decide to focus on civil or criminal, admin-istrative or employment law, they can experience success without having any depth of knowledge about the context and history of English law. Many commentators have remarked on the very narrow range of knowledge, the comparative ignorance about the past, revealed by Tony Blair in his judgements, speeches and statements, and have supposed this to be part of the make-up of a modern politician. Up until 1998, for example, he did not know what the Act of Accession was and its provisions, which include the prohibition on Roman Catholics marrying the heir to the throne, had to be explained to him.[59] But the real reason lies in his education and training as a lawyer who studied law – and nothing else – at university. His subsequent practice as an employment lawyer at the Bar also meant that he was absorbed in a particularly narrow specialism. This is a different matter from the question of not having any 'hinterland' – that background of intellectual interests which Denis Healey was so proud of and whose absence he lamented in modern professional politics. Given the particular nature of English law, its successful interpretation has always required practitioners who are versed in its contextual development. But the dominant tone of the new legal elite is that of a clever philistinism, which is not that different from the dominant tone of British broadcasting.

Alongside the new narrowness there runs a more ancient superstition. The law codes of early societies barely distinguish between human law and divine law. In both ancient Mesopotamia[60] and in early Rome, the priests were also the makers and the codifiers of law. The service of both the gods and of a society's collective solidarity marched hand in hand. All law in such societies was sacred law, the product of the divine will which was interpreted by the priests as a caste apart. And so to break those laws was to offend not just the social will but also the divine intention. Progress has involved distinguishing and separating human from divine law, but around the legal practitioners, and especially at the Bar, traces of the old sacral superstition remains. The English judges who parade in procession to Parliament after their service in Westminster Abbey at the start of the legal year exude an authority which is as much sacral as it is secular. On such occasions, heaven itself seems to have dropped down its blessings from above on the judiciary. Divine intent, it seems, has conspired to confirm worldly success as well as rectitude of judgement. The division of the legal year itself, with its terms that run from Michaelmas through Hilary and towards Trinity, follows an ancient liturgical pattern. But how did these British Solomons get to be there in the first place?

The method of selecting judges follows a procedure first systematized during the mid-Victorian era and from then until now it has repeatedly elevated much the same kind of people. Near the apex of the judicial elite stand the High Court judges, out of which group there emerges at a later career stage the Court of Appeal judges who in turn produce, at the very summit of the legal elite, those judges who sit in the House of Lords (the 'Law Lords'). Interest in this latter group concentrates on the twelve Lords of Appeal in Ordinary who sit, full-time, as the Appellate Committee of the Lords.[61] Past appointments were made on the basis of the Lord Chancellor's private consultations among other judges and criticism of this entrenched system of patronage and power has been a recurring, if largely impotent, feature of

British commentary on these matters. The judicial appointments system has followed less a pattern of self-regulation than one of admiring self-approval since the regime in place has indulged the career hopes of the white, heterosexual, male educated at public school and then at either Oxford or Cambridge, which is why the government elected in 1997 flirted with the idea of an independent commission to recruit and train judges. But the judicial regime has formidable powers of self-protection. Faced with implacable opposition from the judges the government initially abandoned the main thrust of its reforms. From 1998 onwards vacancies for the High Court appointments were advertised and candidates were interviewed by a panel of three: a lay person, a civil servant from the Lord Chancellor's Department and a judge of the High Court. But that was the sole example of a formal process of application operating for jobs within the higher judiciary, and even in this instance it was the Lord Chancellor who had the final say. He continued to make his own soundings and could consider those who had not made a formal application. In the case of the Appeal judges and the Law Lords there could be no question of anything so vulgar as advertising the vacancies that arose among their number: these judges were still appointed by the Prime Minister on the Lord Chancellor's recommendation. The new independent Judicial Appointments Commission promises to blow away some of these cobwebs but the appearance of reform is invariably a poor guide to the persistent realities of elite power.

The old regime therefore has remained substantially in place with all its whispers and gossip about the character and temperament of the various judicial wannabees. In no other country in the world are judicial appointments quite so much at the mercy of subjective views about whose face fits where. Sometimes malice plays its part as well. John Parris was a successful 1950s barrister who discovered only in the 1980s that his promotion to the High Court had been repeatedly blocked by a judge who told the Lord Chancellor (untruthfully) that Parris slept with some of his clients.[62] Candidates for judicial appointments are now told of any allegations of particular misconduct against them, but more general assessments of character are not disclosed, and this leaves plenty of room for prejudice and rumour, for arched eyebrows and sceptical intakes of breath to play their part in the undermining of a career.

It is harder than ever now to persuade high-earning silks to become judges, a job marked by peculiarity and solitariness of existence. The grander the judge the more hermit-like his existence within a well-appointed cell. Some members of this elite can undoubtedly turn a shade peculiar as a result. Lord Lloyd,[63] recently retired as a Law Lord, says that he has not washed his hair in years; rather than soap and water he has preferred to rely on the natural oils secreted by his judicial follicles![64] The lack of contact with the outside world can result in graver oddities. Lord Irvine's expensive 1997 redecoration of the Lord Chancellor's apartments in the House of Lords became notorious because the cost was borne by the public purse. Since his wife was involved, and she was a graduate of the Courtauld Institute, he claimed that no one could fault the taste on display. But it was the cloth ear for public opinion which condemned him. Judges can therefore earn headlines in the way that QCs do not, which is another reason for staying off the bench. The disparity in income is a further discouragement, with the earning capacity of the most successful QCs soaring above the level of judges' salaries. But for those with a taste for dressing up,[65] life among the senior judiciary undoubtedly has its compensations, quite apart from the knighthood which goes almost automatically with the job. The new High Court judge will be kitted out with black, red and purple robes which come with accessories fashioned out of ermine, fur and silk. Which accessory goes with which robe depends on the time of year the court is sitting and what kind of case is being heard. Day-to-day wigs are short with curly tops but special occasions dictate the wearing of a shoulder-length bell-bottomed number. If promoted to the Court of Appeal the lucky judge can then drape himself in truly sumptuous ceremonial garb: a gown of black silk decorated in gold lace is worn over a morning suit while a pair of knee breeches may, according to individual preference, be tucked into either a pair of white socks or into tights. And if the sight can appear outlandish that sumptuary excess is nonetheless a symbolic tribute to power.

The influence of the Court of Appeal still spreads across the world since its judgements, just like those of the Law Lords, affect not only the UK but also those former British colonies which still follow the English legal system and which therefore take note of the senior judiciary's judgements. The careers of some serving Law Lords illustrate what was once such a strong theme in English law: its imperial dimension and associations. Lord Steyn was a Senior Counsel of the South African Supreme Court (the equivalent to being a QC) before he moved to England, while Lords Hoffmann[66] and Scott,[67] like Lord Steyn,[68] were educated at South African universities. The old imperial aura also hovers around the court known as the Judicial Committee of the Privy

Council.[69] The survival of that council for almost a thousand years, along with the now empty honour of its membership, shows how British elite life excels at preserving the forms of honour even while its substance is disappearing. The shell which is allowed to continue then encases a hollowed out institutional existence. But the preservation of formal honour is an important power elite statement because of the soothing sounds which come from the shell. Novel and awkward facts about where power really lies can therefore be negotiated and new power be made to appear less dominating. The fiction of an evolutionary progress is particularly useful in this regard, since it helps to smooth away the rougher edges of a brutal truth. In the case of the Privy Council, power's objective facts show that Parliament has supplanted both the monarch and the council which once advised the monarch. But the swearing in of new Privy Councillors by the Queen can still be a symbolic moment for many members of Britain's power elite, a moment of formal arrival and an opportunity to declare, on their knees, a personal fealty to the sovereign.

The Judicial Committee of the Privy Council was established in the 1830s and as the final, imperial, court of appeal it reviewed every decision in every foreign territory over which the crown came to exercise its authority. By the end of the nineteenth century this was one of the great courts of the world, affecting as it did – because of the expansion of empire – the lives of some 400 million people who were subjects of the crown. During the mid-twentieth century several of the smaller jurisdictions among the newly independent colonies chose to establish a right of appeal to the Judicial Committee, but New Zealand is now the only major jurisdiction which clings to that remnant of the past. And while Commonwealth judges once served on the Judicial Committee on a regular basis they are now only occasionally invited to decide appeals.

The court and offices of the Judicial Committee are housed in No. 1 Downing Street. It is here that appeals are brought from tiny territories and statelets such as Antigua and Belize, Dominica and the Falkland Islands, Kiribati, South Georgia and Tuvalu. Further up and on the same side of the street government ministers come and go out of No. 10 as they scurry about the business of dividing up the spoils of elite power in post-imperial Britain. Within less than 100 yards comparative greatness vies, therefore, with comparative obscurity. But the measurement of these two buildings' significance, and of the institutions that they house, really is a comparative matter since there is a common theme which affects all who work within them: the narrowing of expectation, and the diminishing of greatness, in modern-day Britain. It is appropriate therefore that No. 1 Downing Street should also be witness to the tattered residues of the old, self-regulating, professional elite. For the Judicial Committee of the Privy Council also decides appeals by doctors, dentists and opticians who have been struck off by their professional bodies. And, as a tribute to that departing irrelevance which, although forgotten, is not yet completely gone, the committee also has the final say in disputes which have arisen within the Church of England. This is the only British court (apart from the Appellate Committee of the House of Lords) where judges do not physically look down on the counsel appearing before them since just one long dining table separates the two parties. This comparative intimacy also means that those judges who have had to retire from other courts because of their increasing deafness can always find work in this Whitehall backwater. A court which once held sway over one-fifth of the world's land surface has become a home for judges who would otherwise have to retire early. By such meagre means the institutional shadows of past greatness are allowed to survive among the decaying elite life-forms while the sun of true elite power spreads its rays elsewhere.

An aura of the predetermined surrounds the chronological details of the judicial career progress. Successful silks who become High Court judges are usually about fifty and those of their number who are promoted to the Appeal Court are generally in their late fifties. Having arrived, these judges learn to accept the constraints of their new existence, and public dissidence among their number is correspondingly rare. It was therefore something of a shock to the system when Sir Henry Fisher decided to resign after just two years (1968–70) as a High Court judge in order to become a director of the merchant bank J. Henry Schroder Wagg & Co. Ltd. As the son of a former Archbishop of Canterbury and then as a Fellow of All Souls College, Oxford, he had gone on to fulfil the career requirements of a legal and a judicial luminary. He was forty-two when he became a QC and was then appointed to the judiciary at the age of fifty. At which point something obviously snapped in the mind of a clever man, and he decided to leave for the City. It was something of a prophetic career move since so much of British elite life from the 1970s onwards would fall increasingly under the sway of the financial and business elites. Fisher obviously understood the power shifts of his time, although his decision to switch careers was much criticized and indeed considered to be an incomprehensible betrayal by his legal colleagues. No senior judge since then has followed Fisher's example, and that is hardly surprising. British banking's veneration for the traditional elites, and its consequent readiness to reward members of those elites with jobs, has been in constant decline ever since the socio-economic traumas of the 1970s.[70]

Law Lords are usually in their early sixties at the time of their appointment and, once appointed, they tend to stay in their eminent place. Lord Devlin became a Law Lord when he was only fifty-six and then suddenly retired only three years later probably because of his dislike of the famously reactionary Lord Dilhorne who served as Lord Chancellor (1962–4) during Devlin's time in office.[71] Government committees occupied Devlin's long retirement but hardly stretched his mind and that example of an underemployed eminence has kept most senior judges on the straight if narrow path of preferment. Having been a Law Lord, after all, what else can one do? Lord Slynn[72] is unique among present and recent Law Lords in having deviated from the conventional path to legal greatness. After five years as a High Court judge, he became first the British Advocate-General at the European Court of Justice in Luxembourg and then a judge of that court. In those roles he helped to frame the development of European law and to adjudicate its effectiveness right across most of the continent. But the call of the old legal establishment, despite the poorer pay and ramshackle administrative facilities, was too strong to resist and so he returned to Britain to join the Law Lords. That same predictability supplies the connecting thread in the modern history of the Law Lords as an institution. That history starts with the Appellate Jurisdiction Act of 1876 and only four of the 103 Law Lords appointed since then have ever studied outside the UK, while six of those who served since 1945 have been themselves the sons of peers. Their careers also demonstrate the traditional, although now fading, influence of university life and academic values on English judges. Many of the current Law Lords chose university teaching as a way of supplementing their meagre early earnings at the bar, and in some cases they went on to develop important academic careers, as Lords Goff,[73] Hoffmann, Lloyd, Mackay[74] and Slynn have all done.[75]

At an earlier stage in their careers all members of the senior judiciary will have passed through that elite rite of passage which allows some barristers to become Queen's Counsel (QC), and so to charge enormously higher fees. This method of selection in all its arcane obfuscation has been a paradigm of elite power in Britain – whether the power in question is that of the old-established professionals or of those newly arrived heirs who have supplanted them. The reforms currently introduced are intended to promote greater openness but have to contend against a history of august seclusion. In the past, applications to 'take silk' were made to the Lord Chancellor and unsuccessful candidates could try again. One particularly persistent barrister applied twenty-five times to become a QC.[76] Initial failure, however, could count against the aspiring silk when reapplying at a later stage. The timing of a successful application therefore required finesse and good judgement – or, perhaps, just being lucky on the day. Senior judges and some QCs looked at the applications, and their views were passed on to the Lord Chancellor's officials. Despite all the value supposedly placed on intellectual quality and ability, as an advocate the true measurement of worth has been a good deal cruder than either of these indices. It is a barrister's annual earnings which really show how good he is and which therefore determine whether he can become a QC.

The greed and cynicism[77] of lawyers mean that they can bond easily with the criminal classes, and the insights that they thus gain into the criminal mind is to their professional advantage as both prosecutors and defenders. However, once eyes have been averted from some of the more sordid and self-serving aspects of individual lawyers, law in general possesses an undeniable mystique in England. And if barristers and the judiciary are not exactly priests they are nonetheless draped and bewigged, set apart in a self-consciousness which declares that they are not as other professional men and women are. In the case of the judges this sense of mystery can seem positively numinous. Obliged, when travelling as circuit judges, to live in official residences, secluded from those who might meet them socially and so influence their views, judges lead a life which is as excluded from the world as that of any monk or nun in an enclosed order. The exclusiveness and remoteness of the old legal elites was partly due to the professional necessity which enforced the judges' separation from the world in the name of legal objectivity, and it was also the result of a social caste's desire to separate itself. Meritocratic ascent has changed and widened the composition of that legal and social caste, but exclusiveness is a persistent fact since, as is invariably the case with meritocracy, the difficulty is that of promoting it for more than one generation. Those who have risen tend to draw up the ladder after them once they've ascended and to identify too closely and uncritically with their new and chosen world. Indeed, a meritocratic elite, simply because it thinks it has got there as a result of its own merits and labours, may be more difficult to jolt out of its sense of superiority and acquired privilege than the more obvious elite of inherited privilege that it has replaced. This is why meritocracy hardens very easily into oligarchy. A visit to any favourite legal drinking den, El Vino's, say, in Blackfriars, Daly's Wine Bar on the Strand, or Ye Olde Cheshire Cheese beside Gough Square, confirms immediately the peculiar Harry Potterish sociality of the Bar – its abiding clubbishness which confirms belonging while also asserting exclusion. The indulgence of a laboured joke heard within an oak-panelled seclusion is part of that arcane self-referentiality which comes with self-reverence.

Cicero established these qualities as the in-house style of the lawyer, with his oratorical polish in the service of the *mos maiorum* – the customs and the laws that had made Rome great: a natural piety and sense of hierarchical stability, a stoic public-spiritedness and the graft of hard work. England's misty-eyed idealization of the lawyer's craft, and of the society into which he fits, makes our legal elites into continuers of a very conservative tradition. Cicero's lawyerly inability to recognize that brute force underwrites the social order made the Roman republican order more, not less, susceptible to overthrow because of the inflexibility he promoted. But in the English legal system it is the nature of reform itself, driven as it is by consumerist and bureaucratic demands, which has removed the system even further from democratic reality. Important moments still recur – and in 2001–6 they arrived thick and fast – when law can proclaim its opposition to executive and administrative arrogance, along with its rejection of the legal despotism which threatens individual freedoms. These are legal notes that have been heard before when political power has been thought to assume dangerous forms. Lord Hailsham raised the threat of a power, elected democratically but governing despotically, in his book *Elective Dictatorship* (1976). But that book was published in between his two periods in office as Lord Chancellor (1970–4, 1979–87) and for all the exalted language it amounted to little more than the grouse of a Conservative Party politician unhappy at being in opposition.[78] Once returned to office, Hailsham's constitutional fears were easily allayed and, as with so many members of the legal elite, his arguments for liberty merged imperceptibly with a defence of the Bar's most fustian practices and pretensions. His defence of the appointment of his successor Lord Havers,[79] who served as Lord Chancellor for just four months, was typically direct: 'I'm glad Michael got it because it means he'll get the pension.'[80]

Political power in Britain as a whole has certainly become more administratively centralized in recent years, more concentrated on the personal position of the Prime Minister and less subject to constitutional safeguards. When the law has, therefore, stood up to an overmighty executive it has fulfilled some of the previous functions of Parliament, as in the case of the rejection of the powers sought by the government in order to deal with terrorist suspects. Such episodes have been redolent of the ancient constitution at work, with its informal checks and balances. But it was the Law Lords, the product of an educational system equipped to interpret and defend that constitution, who led the charge. The emergent legal elites below them have become more narrowly educated and less sophisticated in their understanding, more exclusive once they have arrived, and less capable of self-criticism.

## New Legal Elites: Markets and Cartels

The cant of 'choice' is often invoked by the professional elites as they try to justify their powers. The reality is that of a cartel which seeks and finds mutual support through the arrangements and agreements arrived at among its component members. But that truth is overlaid by the manipulation of a neo-democratic fiction in which 'packages' of services and 'financial instruments' are made available, are sold and then bought by the alert customers who wander from stall to stall in this virtual reality market place.[81] Nonetheless, the attempt to present legal services in this light has run into difficulties and encountered hostility from some of the legal elite. The current proposal that outside investors might own law firms and that such firms could be partnerships between solicitors and accountants or other professionals has met with outright opposition from the Bar Council. The divide between solicitors and barristers remains a deep one, with the former pointing out, rather gleefully, the very high level of dissatisfaction recorded by the clients of high street solicitors.[82] Almost a quarter of such clients think that their solicitor did not listen to their opinion, a third feel that they are getting a poor service and almost a third did not consider themselves well informed about how much they would be charged for legal work. At the time of writing (November 2005), the Law Society (representing the 100,000 solicitors of England and Wales) is locked in dispute with the Legal Services Ombudsman over the targets imposed upon them for the processing of complaints, while the Bar's complaints system has scored an 87 per cent consumer satisfaction rate, a statistic which has been an excuse for trebles all round at El Vino's. But the self-regulation beloved of the Bar is on the way out, with the proposal to create a single office for Legal Complaints which will handle all complaints against lawyers. What will emerge will be yet another version of the regulatory body which, as in the case of Ofcom for broadcasting, will generate its own bureaucratic structures, a plethora of targets and further occupational career opportunities for a professional bureaucratic elite. It is the aim of the present Director of Public Prosecutions that the CPS should become 'a sort of public prosecution authority – in charge of criminal cases from beginning to end'.[83] The CPS has now taken over from the police the task of charging suspects and the effect of that change has been to reduce the number of cases which have had to be halted because of weak evidence. The authority of what is now best seen as the State Prosecutor's Office has therefore extended the authority and competence of the state. And, as in other areas of state authority, there is a consumerist justification at work: 'We have a major role in upholding the needs of victims and witnesses – it's clear they are not adequately catered for.' But the great beneficiary of this reform so far has been the status of the CPS itself, the largest law firm in the country with nearly 3,000 lawyers, while the biggest losers have been defence barristers, who see much of their work disappearing.

The new consumerism is also to be seen at work in the development of legal mediation or Alternative Dispute Resolution (ADR), which aims at a resolution of disputes before they come to court.[84] Business disillusion with the costs and complexity of the courts system drives the desire to avoid litigation. This is a form of legal business which has become especially important at an international level when the parties to the dispute are subject to different legal jurisdictions. The solutions provided by lawyer mediators need to negotiate their way around those differing legal systems, along with their associated differing cultural traditions. Following a now common pattern of influence, it was American business and consumer need which initially pioneered what is now also becoming a British business. And it is the large firms of solicitors which benefit from the consequences as cases are kept out of the gladiatorial arena of the courts. Those firms now train large numbers of mediators and identify with the corporate client's desire to cut costs at the expense of the barristers' silver-tongued, but expensive, advocacy.

The proposal to introduce 'victims' advocates' in homicide cases is another example of the new legal consumerism. As outlined in a government consultation paper the advocate, who might be a lawyer, a police officer or the representative of a body such as Victim Support, would read out a statement by the family of the victim after conviction but before sentencing. The intention is to give the victims a voice in court, but the effect would be to raise the expectation that such advocacy ought to affect the severity of the sentencing. This is the elevation of sentiment and of family feelings which, being feelings, will vary; some may be so overwhelmed as to be unwilling to share their grief. Others may feel particularly bitter on the day and repent of that bitterness later. In yet other cases there may be no surviving relatives, but the value of the life lost should not be diminished by that fact. The proposal shows how – as in so many other areas of elite-run British life – it is the quality of the collective which is being attacked. Some wrongs are so grave that they need be punished by the law which is the voice of society as a whole. Murder affects not just the victim's family, it is also an attack on a common humanity.[85] And the punishment of that crime has therefore to express the communal outrage which is felt at such a violation, rather than being merely the reflection of a vigilante sense of justice.

As in so many other areas of elite professional activity, there is an immense pressure on firms of legal practitioners to build up the working capital which arrives with the flow of outside investment. This was the rationale behind the building societies' move into buying up estate agencies in the 1980s, a development which led to partners making a financial killing before the almost immediate subsequent collapse of the businesses' value. Averting their gaze from such past disasters the legal reformers forecast a technology-driven future of 'wrap-around' legal services and call-centre operations where advice might be dispensed for a £50 fee over the phone. Companies may then be allowed to invest in or buy a share in a law firm, or even own a law firm themselves. High street retailers such as supermarkets will be able to set up their own law firms and offer legal services. Legal elites, some willingly and some resentfully, are having to respond to that fetishistic consumerism which by the early twenty-first century has transformed capitalism, deepened its inroads into the textures of everyday life, expanded credit supplies and deepened consumer debt while increasing profits. The elites at the Bar are putting up a fight against these excesses of management culture but solicitors are far more vulnerable to the spurious glamour of the corporate model.

There is an initial and beguiling simplicity to the idea of a consumer-led legal revolution. An ever-more sophisticated range of desires directed towards increasingly varied products and services is after all the force and the idea which transformed the western economies from the eighteenth century onwards. From that time onwards commodity diversity accompanied steadily increasing standards of living. Living longer and healthier lives has seemed the consequence of having more choice. But the desire to extend the consumerist idea to legal services – just like the idea of labelling and selling some financial services as 'products' – is the result of a problem which lies deep within the idea of consumerism itself. Beyond a certain level of craving, for food, drink and shelter, for warmth and mobility, we reach satiety. But that is a condition which consumerist capitalism finds impossible to accept since a market-driven existence depends on exponential growth.

'Market' reforms in legal services illustrate this same hegemonic impulse at work. They promote monopolies and thrive best in those circumstances when key individuals know each other and can fix a service or a contract to their own advantage, as has been alleged, for example, in the case of the Union of Democratic Mineworkers (UDM) and the Doncaster-based firm of solicitors, Beresfords.[86] The UDM has been given the legal right to handle compensation claims directly both on behalf of miners who have fallen ill as a result of their work and also on behalf of their surviving family members. This is profitable work, with the union charging a fee of around £350 for the handling of each claim and that fee then being subtracted from the compensation awarded to the claimant and processed by the union. In order to further this work the union set up Vendside, a claims-handling company which is wholly owned by the UDM. A further union-related company, Indiclaim, has received payments from firms of solicitors who have themselves earned millions of pounds by settling claims handed to them by the UDM. Both companies are the subject of extensive investigation. Beresfords, the chief beneficiary among these firms of solicitors, has in the space of just a few years transformed itself from a small local practice into a significant national legal firm operating from a £4.8 million headquarters. The firm's senior partner owns a seven-seater Super Kingair turbo-prop plane which is used for business purposes and the business has been paid almost £30 million for settling the compensation claims. It now stands to receive some £100 million more from public funds. The fruits of success included a profit of £1.4 million for the senior partner in 2003 and a country house bought in the same year by another partner for £840,000.

Gentrification of status is, after all, a persistent theme among successful English professional elites, who have regularly turned their cash into acres. With the present government expecting to pay out a total of £7.5 billion in compensation from the coal health scheme, the alleged reality in Doncaster appears to have been that of a hard-nosed legal professionalism which makes money from death and past suffering. Legal rapaciousness of this kind has of course always been around, but the emergence of local cartels illustrate a possible future: capital will seize the profession, encourage the dominance of monopolies and cartels and thereby replace partnerships with corporations.

The more arcane Gilbert and Sullivanish practices of the Bar and the very small minority of barristers earning £1 million a year attract their obvious critics. And for a very long time, up until the present challenges from all sides, the Bar illustrated that trend in English institutional life which accommodated itself superficially to new realities in order to preserve the substance of power. Edmund Burke,[87] the most misty-eyed of all the mythologizers of England, observed quite correctly that this capacity lies at the heart of English institutional survival, although what he noted as an intuitive and glorious wisdom was often really mere pragmatism laced with a squinty-eyed cynicism. But it is in the City that the true power of the legal professionals is to be seen. And here, as in other areas of elite life, it is the money trail which leads to power.

## The Solicitor on the Money Trail

If friends and relations, along with sociable ways, can ease the way to the top in the Bar, the solicitors who work in large firms, within the City and for important financial institutions show a more direct, less complicated version of elite formation. Unlike the Bar, pay is competitive in this area of the law right from the start and the companies hunt for the clever and the hungry. Connection can help in finding a job but only if there is cleverness there to begin with. But although this is a fairly meritocratic milieu it arrives with its own typical form of elite corruption. If these legal professionals are well paid then that is regarded as an automatic sign that they are worthy people. But their primary purpose is to serve the interests of the rich and the super-rich in the hope that they, too, may join those ranks. As one city lawyer puts it: 'I don't really think that my colleagues are professional people any longer. They have become businessmen.'[88]

An increasing number of the top corporate lawyers now earn more than a £1 million a year. Most are employed by the top four firms of Clifford Chance, Freshfields, Linklaters and Slaughter and May, the partnerships which, while lacking the civilizing patina of Bar life, have a greater and more practical involvement in the decisions that affect the way people live in Britain today.[89] Those decisions are made by a new legal class which has benefited from the new internationalization of business and legal life. The late 1990s and early 2000s saw a real 'bubble' of mergers and acquisitions as traditional law firms went on a shopping spree. Most famous of all these expeditions was Clifford Chance's takeover of the New York law firm of Rogers and Wells in 2000, which made it into the largest law firm in the world. Legal expansion into European and Asian markets has also been significant but has not been matched by any equivalent moves in the other direction. Gide Loyrette Nouel, which specializes in capital markets and structured finance, is one of the very few European legal firms to set up a London office and so to challenge the international Anglo-American supremacy. The 'bubble' may not have burst yet but the largely static, and in some cases shrinking, revenues of the firms shows that a period of stagnant turnover and heavy overheads has succeeded the earlier optimism of this particular English form of legal capitalism. Clifford Chance has had to close both its US west coast and its Berlin office, as well as losing a number of partners in New York. Its turnover has now fallen from £936 million in 2004 to £915 million in 2005, and in the space of just a year the firm's partners dropped from 635 to 580.

Adapting to these more awkward market conditions has meant pushing up the firms' profitability by cutting costs and stripping out the deadwood. Linklaters, for example, has been able to go against the almost universal trend and driven its turnover up by 12 per cent, up from £720 million in 2004 to £805 million in 2005. Its top-earning partners who were on £864,000 in 2003–4 now earn £1.065 million each; even junior equity partners in the firm earn £425,000. Slaughter and May, the only really major solicitors' firm not to pursue aggressive international expansion, has reaped the reward for being more insular. Here it is a small number of instructions, but ones with huge financial rewards, which have made the difference, with the result that the top partners at the firm earned £1.17 million in 2003–4. Slaughter and May were instructed in the case of Marks and Spencer's resistance to Philip Green's attempted takeover and also in the case of Santander Central Hispano's takeover of Abbey National. Such mergers and acquisitions are now the very lifeblood of the really powerful forms of legal elite power. Legal–commercial activity of that kind does not result in the creation of really productive jobs, goods or services. This is an elite activity in the very narrowest interpretation of the phrase, since it results from the ambitions entertained and the defensive postures adopted by a very small group of the super-rich who need to instruct. The decisions made on which law firm gets the instruction similarly depends on a fundamentally social network. Each of the proudly self-assertive major law firms contain partners who are capable of doing the necessary work; but which firm gets the work depends on who has met whom, along with where and when they met and talked, which is why corporate entertainment has now become such big business.

There are further parasites who prey on forms of legal business which are themselves fairly parasitic. Firms of headhunters, or 'executive search consultants', have been one of the great growth industries of the past twenty years. With fees paid by the City, by business and by the professions, headhunters trawl their way through comparatively shallow ponds in order to advise on the next appointment which, very often, turns out to be the one which would have been made anyway. Although an excuse for the kind of long and liquid lunch which has fallen out of favour elsewhere, the real reason for the headhunting executive's existence is the lack of confidence among those who are meant to exercise judgement and make the appointment but end up contracting-out. 'Executive search' exists because it benefits from the herdlike need to take refuge in those risk-averse forms of collective security which involve the avoidance of responsibility. Firms of head-hunters who deal specifically in legal appointments have been a particularly rapid growth and not all of their senior staff need to be lawyers. Mark Field, MP for the Cities of London and Westminster, attributes his success as a former legal headhunter to the fact that he was one of the few of his colleagues who had qualified as a lawyer. Just as with 'management' consultants, the expertise of executive search lies with the process rather than with real content. Which is why, when it comes to jobs in business and finance as well as in legal areas, there is no real need to have any particular knowledge about any of those worlds in order to advise confidently, if ignorantly, about who should get what. A connection with the political world, at a suitably maintained discreet distance, is a useful career tool for such hunters of heads. The careers of Mrs William Hague, Mrs Michael Portillo and Mrs Peter Hain all illustrate this pattern of elite convergence at work.

UK legal firms remain less profitable than their US counterparts, who have the typically lean American business model. The failure really to break into the much-admired, at least by the City legal elites, American legal market is really the result of an inability to match the salaries on offer from the American legal firms. But the surviving partners employed by the firms who took the risk and expanded but then had to cut costs can still feel pleased with their world. Although Freshfields' turnover dipped from £785 million to £780 million from 2004 to 2005, its average profits per partner were still up by 3.7 per cent to £700,000 and Clifford Chance's average partner profits of £644,000 represents a 15 per cent increase on 2004's £562,000. The high salaries also, of course, boost morale and are used to lure big-billing partners into the firm. These legal plutocracies, like the headhunters at work, represent the conglomeration of the elites. Their great riches are often the result of a decision made by many firms to pursue what Linklaters calls a 'broader and deeper' relationship with its clients. In effect, this means trying to persuade clients in one area of the firm's activities to engage the firm in its other areas as well. As English law, commerce and business come to exercise their dominance across more and more foreign jurisdictions, that means more work to be obtained by the law firm which can capture and keep its clients across a very broad front. As elsewhere in areas of elite business activity, there is an insistently monopolistic thrust behind both the business of mergers and acquisitions and also behind the expansions of legal firms themselves.

## The Threatened Elite

The high-finance world of the City's law firms is many worlds removed from that of the Criminal Bar and of legal aid. There are, admittedly, a very small number of practitioners at the Commercial Bar who can earn £1 million a year. In a few long and complicated cases there are examples of barristers earning a gross fee of up to £500,000 and in a very few up to that magic £1 million mark as a result of legal aid. But the earnings of a criminal barrister after qualifying average just £15,000 a year with those specializing in rape and child abuse cases managing to pick up some £35,000 a year. Day fees show how the lower and junior end of the Criminal Bar has been marginalized by the more powerful legal elites at the Commercial Bar and in the City. A bail application or other pre-trial hearing will pay £46.50, a sentencing hearing involving one day plus preparation yields just £60 in fees while a case management hearing involving substantial preparation will pay £100. Criminal barristers at the top of their profession can still earn an average of £200,000 a year on legal aid. One effect of these early years of low earnings has been to drive barristers to the richer pastures of the Commercial Bar, but it has also had the perverse effect of accentuating some of the Bar's own elite status, since those with some family money behind them are better placed to survive the comparative privations of the Criminal Bar.

Just 1 per cent of cases swallow up 50 per cent of the total budget for the Crown Court, and these high-cost trials tend to be fraud cases. The Jubilee Line fraud trial which collapsed with a total legal cost bill of £60 million included a legal aid bill of £14 million and the prosecution by the Inland Revenue of five individuals which collapsed in June 2005 involved total costs of £65 million and a legal aid bill of £6 million. Such cases represent a significant failure in the judgements made by the CPS in preparing and allowing such cases to go ahead. And, since the CPS is a government organization, the skewing of such legal aid costs is an important example of that persistent theme in modern Britain, the clumsiness of its officialdom. Recent decisions by the same legal bureaucracy, for example, have allowed the prosecution to present both hearsay evidence and evidence of previous convictions but this also amounts to extra, yet unpaid, work for the barrister.[90]

Criminal barristers have really nowhere else to go to in order to improve their lot. But the commercial practitioner can, and the reasons adduced by Murray Rosen, QC for leaving his chambers at 11 Stone Buildings, by any standard a leading commercial set at Lincoln's Inn, and for joining the City firm of Herbert Smith, bear some examination. Progressive law firms, Rosen says, look outwards towards the world and shame the introspection of the Bar: 'Faced with some really fundamental challenges, the people who could change the management of the Bar don't want to change. And if you can't look outside your own institution – if it's so cosy and such an extremely glamorous and comfortable ivory tower that you can't look out and see what's happening in order to prepare yourself for change – then you're probably doomed.'[91] Even the markedly aggressive and hungry Commercial Bar, with its steady stream of talented and specialist advocates, cannot really luxuriate in its own superiority.

The legislative changes passed by the High Court of Parliament, a body largely composed of non-lawyers, can and do change the legal business. The Construction Bar has lost much of its work because of procedural changes in the way disputes are now decided. After many years of good trading, libel lawyers have had to revise their earlier confidence about a rosy future since so many libel cases are now settled before coming to court. The kind of barrister independence which goes with self-employment is now increasingly at the mercy of the new kind of professionalism which is the basis of a really effective solicitors' firm. Extensive secretarial and research services, teams of lawyers who will work together to secure an urgent deal, and 'rain-makers' who will seek out new clients and new areas of work: these are the prerogative of large solicitors' firms who can absorb the overheads. In the case of an advocate working within a solicitors' firm the result can mean better preparation for a particular case as a result of having been involved in its preparation right from the beginning. For many barristers, the fine and careless actorly flourish is the necessary result of the inspiration which arrives with a last-minute preparation. It is part of that drama and improvisational genius which is built into the barrister's life. But it is that same individualistic ethos which may, ultimately, be its undoing. The barrister is a professional who is concentrated on his own self-interest, on the next case, on professional reputation and on keeping as much of the fee as possible. But in the City firm the link between the individual self-interest and that of the business collectivity is basic to the whole enterprise. And, as the highly successful Mr Rosen points out, the totemic allure of that £1 million barrister's fee for a case is really a kind of negative recognition: 'you end up with a certain amount of derision and jealousy when some enormous brief fee is announced and you are in the top twenty hit-list of fat-cat lawyers.' Such derision is not confined to the outside world. Like any profession, the real jealousy comes from the inside. The sanctioned greed of the City legal partner attracts hardly any of the same kind of scrutiny.

The capacity of judges to make law, along with the quality of their judgements, shows the continuing power of the English Bar and judiciary at both an intellectual and a practical level. And as the state has become more centralized, the readiness of some judges to exercise that capacity has become more marked. The circumstances of the times in which a Prime Minister thinks that legally speaking 'the rules of the game are changing' have placed them in a more exposed – and somewhat more sinister – position than ever before. Some judges have found this to be a frighteningly public experience and shied away from its dangers, while the more self-confident ones have been prepared to remonstrate. This has been most obvious in the case of the wave of legislation unleashed by the government's response to terrorism. But there are also other reasons why some judges are preparing for contentious times ahead. The Human Rights Act (1998), which has incorporated the European Convention on Human Rights (ECHR) into English law, has been one additional spur to judicial activity. And the UK's new arrangements for devolved government in Scotland and Wales will also in time throw up opportunities for politically charged judgements. The possibility of crisis in this area has been ignored during a period when the same political party has enjoyed dominance in all three countries. But in the event of a future dispute between the Westminster Parliament and the representative bodies in Cardiff and Edinburgh, it will be the Law Lords who will have to adjudicate between conflicting claims within the same kingdom.

These novel, current and possible forms of legal elite self-assertion, however, are rivalled, and in many ways undermined, by the harder-edged commercial and financial power of the City lawyers. The commercial and Americanizing pressures to which Britain has been subjected because of the transformation of its finance and business sector, has made the Bar in particular look quaint and sometimes silly, despite all the important issues of legal principle which are bound up in the history of this English institution. Meanwhile it is the management-driven state which dictates the pace of change for the judges. Under the Constitutional Reform Act (2005) the Lord Chief Justice takes over the Lord Chancellor's duties as head of the judiciary and, in the words of the Act, he will be responsible for 'representing the views of the judiciary of England and Wales to the Lord Chancellor and to Parliament'. For the first time in English history this legislation also enshrines the idea of 'the rule of law' in an Act of Parliament. The Lord Chancellor will now have to swear an oath to 'respect' that rule. Both he and the other ministers who have responsibility for the justice system will have to 'uphold the continued independence of the judiciary'.

On the face of it, these are profound changes which involve an access of power for the judicial elites. But what the Act calls 'the existing constitutional principle of the rule of law' is not so much a principle as an undefined aspiration clouded in uncertainty and therefore open to interpretation. In the absence of definition no member of the political or of the legal elite knows what that principle really means, or what its consequences might entail. There was a quality of pathos in the sight of Lord Woolf,[92] in one of his last

141

speeches before retiring as Lord Chief Justice, attempting such a definition. The eleventh hour of so distinguished a career was a strange time in which to have to confront the presumed basis of that career. Lord Woolf told the Commonwealth Law Conference in September 2005 that the 'rule of law' should include an unbiased judge, access to a court, a reasoned judgement within a reasonable time and a system of law that was 'reasonably certain, readily ascertainable, proportionate and fair'.[93] Nearly 800 years after Magna Carta the search has therefore begun for the definition of those qualities which were once assumed to be the bedrock of English justice and the Lord Chancellor, since he is a government minister and presumably therefore something of a suspect character, has to give an explicit undertaking to respect the rule of law. In the absence of definition, questions of interpretation will now occupy the legal, political and administrative elite as they attempt to protect their own position. The Lord Chancellor may not be challenged by a defined notion of the rule of law, but at least he knows that the Act's dreary verbiage requires him to 'ensure the provision of resources for the . . . support of the courts'. If, therefore, freedom is on the slide he can still plead in his defence that a contracted-out cleaning firm has been employed to keep the courts free of dust.

The new arrangements also include a little Whitehall ministry for the judges in preparation for the time when they take over the responsibility for their own budgets, complaints, discipline and welfare. There will be, rather inevitably, a media office as well as sixty civil servants to help them in their new managerial duties. But, by one of the instructive ironies of British institutional and governmental life, this devolution of power comes with a cost. Elite power in Britain now has to be exercised through a veil of management, and it is therefore the most natural thing in the world that top judges, including the Lord Chief Justice, should go on a course that includes psychometric testing, media training and instruction on 'performance indicators'.[94] The successful judge, from now on, is to be a management-driven judge, a fact which inevitably threatens judicial independence and authority.

In the past there was no need to exert an explicit political pressure on the judges, either in questions relating to their appointment or when it came to the daily exercise of their duties. This was partly because English judges, unlike American ones, have not been expected to interpret a constitutional document with all those embarrassingly explicit late-eighteenth-century clauses which require constant updating. Moreover, there has been until very recently precious little divergence of interest in modern English history between the legal elites and the political ones. As a result, judicial pronouncements on contentious political issues have not characterized English history in the way that they have punctuated American history. It was a convenient assumption for both the lawyers and the politicians that liberty would flourish within the capacious silences of English law, a system which offered no definition of freedom and which was persistently averse to explicit statements of principle. But it is the international dimension which has changed this cosy consensus.

In two separate hearings, in November 1998 and then in March 1999, the Law Lords decided that General Pinochet, the former President of Chile, could be extradited to Spain in order to face charges of torture committed during his term in office. These charges related to those Spanish citizens who were the victims of his regime and two international arrest warrants, issued by a Spanish magistrate when the General was in London, were then enforced by two English arrest warrants. The Law Lords were deciding on a specific point of English law which grants a head of state immunity from civil or criminal liability for offences committed during his time in office. But the final judgement against Pinochet leant heavily on the fact that Britain, like Chile, is a signatory to the Torture Convention (1984), which allows any signatory country to prosecute within its own boundaries an individual who is accused of torture within the territory of another country whose government has signed the Convention. Where English law has in the past been quiet about freedom it has now been allowed – or required – to become noisy, and it is the impact of law with an international dimension which has forced that development. Asserting liberty as a result of a negotiation among the forests of particular rights, prerogatives and peculiarities, balancing one form of freedom against another, rejoicing in the complexity of layers of precedents provided by the historic English constitution: these strategies no longer have the singular authority they once enjoyed in English law. The English legal elite which wishes to cling to these ploys as the basis of its career opportunities confronts an attack from two directions. First, there is the new legal philistinism which is averse to historic rights and wants to push ahead with both administrative despotism and legal consumerism. Secondly, the equally powerful world of international treaties, conventions of human rights and supranational sovereignty also subverts that traditional and informal

English legal understanding of what freedom means. Among barristers, it is the second challenge which stands by far the best chance of being incorporated within the potential of their own career opportunities (as the expansion of chambers dealing with human rights cases demonstrates), while among the elite of the city solicitors there is little contest between the two options: it's number one every time.

Both the judicial bench and the bar have been poor at defending themselves except in terms which suggest their own self-interest.[95] In this respect they recall the British trade union movement in the 1970s and 1980s. As a result, they are faced with the same loss of authority and influence through market ideology sustained by state power. The Bar, in particular, has become a soft a target for criticism because of some of its more self-destructively conspicuous elitist tendencies. Public schools continue to educate three out of four judges in the High Court and above. They also educate more than two-thirds of barristers at eight of the leading commercial chambers.[96] This is a picture which has barely changed over the past generation during a time when the consequences of trends elsewhere should at least have started to be visible as a result of the expansion of university education. Indeed, this narrowness may actually be intensifying, with an increasing number of younger barristers coming from the more obviously privileged backgrounds. But with the collective power of the Bar in such decline the truth of the matter is that we are witnessing a division of influence within the legal power elites themselves. The more important statistic is that half the partners at the big City firms are public school educated. The Rugby or Repton educated judge shares much the same background as the Marlborough or Malvern educated City solicitor and, within that shared milieu, it is the City solicitor who is more connected to the commercial and financial power which runs Britain today.

## Terrorism and Freedom: An Elite Debate

What counts as freedom and true security has become an issue which is debated within the elite itself. On the one hand, the Home Secretary Charles Clarke – the son of a senior civil servant and educated at that nursery of progressivism, King's College, Cambridge – tells us that he has 'spent decades of my life being patronized by lawyers, and I do not appreciate it'.[97] On the other hand, there stands an establishment of Law Lords who are ready to brandish the Magna Carta against an overmighty executive and in particular against that brand of security populism which has always been a powerful tendency in British governments, whether of the left or of the right, especially since the Second World War. That had been the first war which could be used as a propaganda in favour of 'Britishness', and the desire to pontificate, à la Orwell, about the values of an endangered Britishness which is quiet, hobby-loving, reserved and chronically fair-minded, continues to be a national sport among the literary and neo-literary elite who are paid to speculate and write about their compatriots. The judgement on what the war was for – the freedom to be independently British on the island state or the extension of collectivism – can go either way according to individual taste and experience. Much the same is true of the legal debate on security measures, and for similar reasons. For both are debates conducted within the elite itself.

In its relation to political power the law has become not only more openly critical than in the past, but also more obviously divided from it in career terms. The phenomenon of the successful QC who is also an MP is now effectively finished and the past convention of a barrister automatically qualifying to take silk if elected an MP has now been abandoned. David Mellor,[98] 'an undistinguished barrister' in the words of one QC,[99] was among the last MPs to be allowed to use this accelerated promotional ladder, and the fact of his mediocrity meant that the ladder disappeared soon after his elevation. It is now difficult to find MPs with the relevant legal experience to serve as the government's law officers, which is why Harriet Harman had to be pressed into service as Solicitor-General. The same vacuum also explains why Lord Goldsmith[100] now finds himself sitting in the House of Lords as Attorney-General. The debate over whether he was or was not leant upon by the government in order to revise his original judgement on the legality of the war against Iraq indicates the seriousness of the new divisions of view between the legal and the political elite.[101] The Prime Minister's own struggles – first attempting a solution in international law before then yielding to American might – show the division within his own mind.

In Britain therefore, at the beginning of the twenty-first century, the government can propose control orders against anyone it considers to be 'a threat' along with other powers of tagging and indefinite restriction, including the possibility of house arrest. The orders can regulate where people live and work and those with whom they are allowed to associate. These new scale of powers are subject to a judicial review but only by duly state-approved and vetted lawyers who will meet in camera and who do not have the right to see or to cross-examine evidence. Political power has also sought the right, when preparing a case against terrorist suspects, to present evidence extracted under torture in foreign jurisdictions. Such evidence could come from Syria, Egypt, Iraq or other states with a record of human rights abuses. The Court of Appeal conceded the government's case in a judgement which was then overruled by the Law Lords.

The state power which is at the disposal of the political and administrative elite therefore stands in an increasingly fraught relationship to the varying judgements of the legal elite. Sometimes that power may benefit from those judgements. But when it does not get its way then the machinery of government is invariably prepared to attempt further subversion of the legal elite's views and judicial conclusions. The government's measures are a response to the Law Lords' decision (16 December 2004) that Part 4 of the Anti-Terrorism Act (2001) authorizing the detention of suspected foreign terrorists breaches the ECHR. That measure was judged to be both discriminatory, since it does not apply to British nationals, and also lacking in proportionality. And that in turn was the resolution of an argument which centred on the detention without trial of terrorist suspects in Belmarsh prison. But the striking fact about the government's response is that it has also been an implicit admission that none of these men need to be imprisoned or even subjected to house arrest since they can all now be adequately dealt with by the control orders that restrict their liberty. The House of Lords' judgement was therefore correct, but it can still be ignored. Both house arrests and detention orders may now be imposed by the Home Secretary simply on the basis of 'reasonable grounds for suspecting' that a person is a terrorist. English law knows no such low standard of proof. In respect of control orders (though not so in the case of house arrest) there is no right of appeal from the government's decision to a judge. Following the bombing of the London underground (7 July 2005) the government has also proposed a revival of the offence of treason, a provision which until then had been left in a dusty abeyance on the statute book.

Considered together, these are powerful, and symbolic, measures – an assertion by the elite of state professionals that they are both privy to intelligence which must not be disclosed and that they must have the capacity to act in defence of the people as a result of this private knowledge. The alternative step would be to seek derogation from the ECHR which a signatory state has a legal right to do in the event of a 'public emergency threatening the life of the nation' (Article 15). But such a derogation would not have the attraction of demonstrating that busy governmental activism which has now overwhelmed the British response to terror. In a world in which the cliché of globalization affects all activity, from trade through to charity, the response to a 'global' terrorist threat has to be equally global in its sweep. Reliance on the current provisions of the criminal law is scorned for a very good, if reprehensible, reason. Those provisions, properly enforced, would deal with the threat as a criminal disorder and, after due process, would result in convictions on the same scale and of the same kind as the new provisions. In their effects and consequences of loss of life, criminal injury and damage to property, Britain's terrorist outrages are no different from any other kind of criminal act and they fall well within the scope of the criminal laws already on the statute book. More effective street policing from a less management-obsessed police force would lead to better detection in the planning of such crimes. But what the British governmental elite craves is the drama and the glory of a display of symbolic power, something which shows who's in charge now.

Measures proposed for the deportation of suspects to countries which, such as Egypt, Algeria, Morocco and Tunisia, have a record of human rights abuses, raise the possibility of torture, and that in itself ensures the prospect of years of court battles. This, therefore, is not the proposal of a short sharp shock, and is not really designed for an immediate response to a terrifying danger. It is rather the use of such a danger in order to consolidate state authority by the most effective immediate means available to it – the spreading of fear, the appearance of majesty and the upholding of dignity. And it is here that the revival of treason is particularly significant. The ministers of the current British government are, after all, the highly successful representatives of a right-wing, 'market-facing' ideology pursued by Trotskyite means. A vanguard of true believers have infiltrated a movement, the British Labour Party, and changed it from within. In the process these partisans changed the meaning of the word 'treason' so that what was once a betrayal of that party's principles should henceforth be regarded as loyalism. Having used that movement in order to advance their own careers and to seize the central machinery of government, they continue to use the same vocabulary of treason, betrayal and loyalism but do so now in a specifically legal sense. Their own self-interest is no longer merely equivalent to that of their party, it is also the cause of the state itself. This is an event, and a claim, which is unique in British history. At least the varieties of aristocratic cabals that used to rule Britain, like their immediate democratic successors, had to subscribe to the idea that the government was conducted in the name of the crown.

But this has also been an event and a claim which has caused comparatively little outrage. The democratic elites that one would expect to be offended, including the professional legal guardians of the constitutional liberties, duly express their horror. Left-leaning civil rights groups raise the banner of fundamental human rights, lawyers object to the dismantling of due process and the commentating classes opine in newspaper pieces. This, it might seem initially, is one of those causes which has the power to unite in a potent resistant force those who are otherwise politically and socially divided. But the popular response is one of shoulder-shrugging passivity. Britons show a marked willingness to give up their civil liberties when told that such a sacrifice will lead to greater effectiveness in state anti-terrorist security. It is the oldest mistake in constitutional law to think that the eradication of particular human beings' wickedness requires the reduction of liberty enjoyed by human beings in general. Totalitarian societies may make that claim and boast of the disproportionately violent forms of state punishment which have abolished thieving. But democracies are supposed to place themselves beyond and above that moral ambit. Yet the public mind has shown itself ready to travel to that terrain. An ICM poll[102] conducted on 12–14 August 2005 showed that 73 per cent of those questioned backed the plausibility of a trade-off between abandoned liberty and increased safety, with only 17 per cent rejecting it. And, like those elites who have shown a unity in their opposition to the use of law to restrict liberty, the popular will is also a cross-party agreement, with 79 per cent of Tories, 72 per cent of Labour supporters and 70 per cent of Liberal Democrats approving the measures. The idea, implied in the question posed, that there can be a strict balance between freedom and security, is an example of that artificial questioning which vitiates most polling. But the consensus is nonetheless overwhelming. There is some residual respect for judicial power, with 40 per cent thinking that judges are the guardians of civil liberty and that they should continue to overturn anti-terrorist measures if they think it right to do so. But 52 per cent thought that they should not be so cheeky since, specifically, government measures had been passed by Parliament acting in the people's name. The prospect of torture held little terror for the 62 per cent of respondents who favoured the deportation of radical Islamists to countries with a penchant for that practice.

Even after allowing for crass questioning, such polling helps to dismantle the myth of a freedom-loving Britain which defines itself in terms of individual freedom. But the explanation for this state of affairs does not lie within a psychological soft spot and a tenderness towards authoritarianism. The reach of a regulatory state which measures, calculates, prescribes and proscribes not just in economic and financial affairs but also in questions of behaviour and conduct has certainly changed the mind of Britain over the past century. As a result, the largely conservative idea that the function of law is to reflect, rather than to mould, society has taken a huge knock. Within the space of a mere generation legislation on race relations has objectively, and for the better, changed the content of what can be said about, and the kind of behaviour that can be tolerated towards, those of different racial and ethnic groups. But the notion that religious groups also have a right not to be offended by what is said by others about their beliefs is also now beginning to hover on the legal horizon in Britain. The Incitement to Religious Hatred Bill currently under consideration is in effect an extension to other religions of the current, but unenforced, historic laws relating to blasphemy against Christian beliefs. This represents a populist and appeasing response by a political and governmental elite to the rise of fundamentalism, a development which has disfigured not only Islam but also Christianity in the late twentieth century. The law of the land in this instance would be used in order to protect not just the individual freedoms but also the sensibilities of a minority whose views are, at best, opaque to the majority.

In these circumstances it is unsurprising that Britons have become progressively indifferent to the elite proclamation of fundamental legal rights and liberties. The genially anarchic strain which impels them to leave work early in order to heckle a cabinet minister remains in place. But these enjoyments are seen as the occasional expression of temperament rather than the assertions of indivisible rights. The advocates and practitioners of the historic British constitution have no hold over the imagination, the loyalties and the self-interest of their countrymen. Napoleon's 'nation of shopkeepers' is still attached to the idea that their economic freedom to trade and shop, to choose and consume as they wish, is fundamental to their identity, although that freedom is in fact tightly hedged in by the monopolistic constraints of monolithic capitalism. But when it comes to political and constitutional freedoms they see no connection between their daily lives and those historic arrangements which, accordingly, can be abandoned as a fustian irrelevance. Between the high rhetoric of the legal elite about 'freedom of the subject' and the day-to-day reality of British life there is a deep chasm which is the result of a lack of shared experience and a common context. As a result, the legal rhetoric sounds like the ingenious verbal exercises of those who are protecting their own professional careers rather than as the wise words of prophets inspired by that disinterested care for the protection and advancement of individual liberty which would mark them out as the successors of Pym and Hampden, of Wilkes and Cobden.

In early twenty-first-century England, preposterously, the best arguments for legal freedom and some of the values of the eighteenth-century Enlightenment come from the Law Lords, a group of elderly men occasionally draped in ermine and operating as the judicial committee of an unelected upper chamber. This has been taken to be a sign of the peculiar excellence of the English tradition and its deep-rooted institutional strengths. But the reality is a more precarious one since the prospects for the survival of that kind of legal elite is uncertain along with its long-term capacity to defend liberty as both a lived reality and in a way which makes sense to the nation. When accused of 'aggressive judicial activism' by one member of the political elite, Michael Howard[103] (himself once a member of the legal elite as a QC), the elite defence is cogent enough. Lord Bingham, the senior Law Lord, points out that the idea that 'the judges in some way seek to impede or frustrate the conduct of government' is 'a complete misunderstanding'.[104] Judges overturn government decisions not because they disapprove of the decision but because it is contrary to law. And on the particular issue of the deportation of terrorist suspects they are legally bound to consider the likelihood of such suspects facing torture or inhuman treatment if they are returned to certain countries. If, says another Law Lord, judges 'are prevented from mediating between the individual and the state and from ensuring that ministers act within the law, then both democracy and the rule of law will suffer'. But what is revealing about these remarks is the very elite-based pessimistic view that democratic, mass, opinion will invariably condone a feral injustice. For Lord Bingham, it is unsurprising that human rights laws protecting vulnerable, and sometimes despised, minorities: 'should provoke howls of criticism by politicians and the mass media – they generally reflect majority opinion'. But if that is so it is an indictment of the condition of English liberty and a dangerously isolating view of how the legal elites see themselves – a minority manning the barricades.

English liberty, when it existed, came from a deep critical under-standing of English history, an understanding which is now on the way out among the legal elites and is certainly absent among the wider public. Publishers and television stations feed that public on a diet of island-story glory from Nelson to Churchill, martial and vigorous but defensive in its relation to the wider world and apolitical when it comes to individual freedom. It was not newly minted documents but shared memory among the educated minority, along with a certain quality of mindfulness and alertness to individual cases, which used to sustain the case for English liberty. That kind of liberty was a quiet presence and a tacit force which was allowed to exist rather than a challenging itch to say truth to power. For much of English history, liberty depended for its continued existence on its being something that most people knew very little about. And, therefore, when the social pressure to sustain it is no longer around that liberty has always been vulnerable to the possibility of being undermined by mere neglect. The real threat therefore has been not so much that freedom might be trampled on but that it can be put to one side and forgotten. This precariousness of English freedom is hardly surprising since the vast majority of the population have no formal education in law. Not only have they never been informed where constitutional liberty and personal freedom might be located, they have also been told that, given the peculiarity of our historic arrangements, the document which might specify that liberty does not, should not and never will, exist. The legal elites – at both the exalted level of the judicial theorists who see freedom as the possession and preoccupation of an elite and also at the more mundane level of the rich servants of corporate power – share a responsibility for the sudden prominence of the threat to freedom. The one group thinks that the people do not care about liberty while failing to see that it is their own class- and group-based notion of freedom which is responsible for the popular indifference. The other, overwhelmed by the cash nexus, shares that same indifference. English liberty is no longer a shared purpose. Is it, therefore, any surprise that the two persistent vices which typify our two types of legal professionals should therefore be thrown into sharp relief: vainglory on the one hand and venality on the other?

## Elites and Crime

Legal elites exist because of crime, disorder and criminality. And the maintenance of their power depends on the deployment of a certain kind of language and rhetoric about social threats.[105] Whether in the case of the inner-city riots of the 1980s, the Tudor fear of the unruly apprentice, the Victorians' concern about hooligans and street gangs – or, most recently, in the case of the government campaigns for 'respect' and against 'hooded' youths, the language of English public debate and opinion has shown both fear of disorder and a perverse fascination with its manifestation. Governmental definitions of Britishness and of Englishness themselves have a long history of legitimized violence against the outsider. Jolly Jack Tar and John Bull emerged because the new eighteenth-century British state wanted to define itself as a true fighter against continental Catholicism. These were iconic emblems of brute force who were to be opposed to a foreign world which was, paradoxically, both effeminate and threatening. Luxuriousness and profligacy would sap the newly invented antique British virtues that animated the national and isolated interest. Ideas of manly virtue acquired a widespread political currency far beyond the military–political–Protestant classes. Elite views of the necessarily thuggish nature of the population became part of the defence of England, just as in the case of the rude and valiant soldiery whose corpses littered the fields of Waterloo. The people might therefore be brutes, but at least they were brutes in the service of England and therefore performed a service for the elites who ran the place. Even the artistic avant-garde at the beginning of the twentieth century saw itself as contributing to a revitalization of imperial and British values through its emphasis on the hard and the clear, the vigorous and the unsentimental.[106] Wyndham Lewis and other English precursors to continental fascism represented just the latest chapter in what has been a continuously authoritarian national style.

Contemporary English film and television has been ready to sentimentalize, sensationalize and glamorize the violence of crime, and it has had many precedents to build on both within and beyond the country's shores. Film noir from California to Paris has given the tough its sheen of allure, and in literature the crime novels of John Buchan, Geoffrey Household and Ian Fleming are just the most famous examples of an English fascination with brutal violence which gains respectability by expressing itself in the language of martial vigour and manliness. The novels of P.D. James and of Agatha Christie portray crime against a background of bourgeois–professional propriety on the one hand and of a fantasy, squirearchical England, on the other. The true denouement in both these authors' works is the delicious security of that social order which is reasserted when the criminal is detected. But the marketed Britishness of the 1990s produced something novel – a wave of pathological treatments of working-class criminals by largely privileged film directors whose origins were far removed from those they sought to portray – and sometimes to elevate – but most often ended up demeaning. *Lock Stock and Two Smoking Barrels* (1998) directed by Guy Ritchie, the son of one of Britain's first advertising moguls, was the most famous of such films and the release of Nick Love's *The Business* (2005) showed the continuing fascination with geezer gangsters. That classist manipulation within the cinema is supplemented by a steady stream of television dramas from *The Bill* to *Silent Witness*. These developments in film also occurred at a time of new emphasis on lads and laddishness as part of Cool Britannia's vigorously Union Jackish reinvention along with stereotypes of national masculinity. Criminality in film added an extra sheen of the sick-chic. As represented on the screen, the south London gangland of the 1950s and 1960s mingled the classes to nasty effect and communicated fantasies about hard men whose thuggery was expressed in operatically flowery language. These were spectacles for the observer who could experience a frisson of revulsion before retreating to class security.[107] And a public school Prime Minister who could affect estuarized English at the drop of a vowel at one moment, before then preaching on the need for renewed respect for social order, showed the calculating reality behind this confusion. Status, after all, comes from the demonstration of an ability to imitate the demeaned without suffering degradation oneself, which is why the mockery of the working classes through the parody and imitation of their voices and their accents by middle-class actors is such an insistent feature of English entertainment and comedy.

The same impulse to dominate is evident in the power elites, who enjoy the frisson engendered by their contact with a touch of the rough but also know that their authority is defined by the distance between the classes. The Tory peer Lord Boothby[108] hanging out with the Krays and the Labour MP Tom Driberg[109] fellating working-class men both illustrated that queasy truth in the 1950s. It has always been the job of professional elite authority to enforce that distance, but in contemporary Britain this has become an ever-more attractive option. This, after all, is now a country which has been ruled for over a quarter of a century by governments which think that they can do nothing to 'buck' the markets. Compared to any of their twentieth-century predecessors there is therefore much less for them to do. But they still need to convince the electorate that they are worth paying for – that there is a method and a purpose to their professional existence. They are therefore reduced to frantic displacement activity centred around 'anti-social behaviour' which is really a code for punishing the poor and stupid through the self-important proclamation of edicts and the imposition of legal orders.

## Locking Them Up: The Prisoners of the Elites

The methods used to enforce both discipline and distance behind prison walls involves complacency and cruelty – complacency about the consequences of imprisonment and a cruelly class-based understanding of what makes a criminal. Here again it is television, an industry which reflects the attitudes of an entertainment elite, which holds a mirror to the reality of dominant attitudes. Few comedy series have been as popular as *Porridge* – but what made for the laughter was that acute British sense of hierarchy which allows itself to be superficially softened round the edges in order to reinforce the acceptance of its power. Cons and prison officers are presented in entertainment, as they often are in reality, as members of the same working class who are therefore able to collude with each other. All the teasing and all the slang, the invigilation and the lack of privacy, the dress code and the silent, sly subversions which are found on either side of the cell door in prison are replicated in other hierarchies of British power. The professional elites that run the prison service, just like the ones that run public schools and regiments, political parties and business corporations (including football teams), see that the best way to preserve authority is by building up the communal team spirit. But in prison that spirit means the toleration of decadence and the inculcation of despair. The authority of prison officers is based on their toleration of drug-taking, bullying and minor criminality, which is why the condition of the prisoner in elite-run Britain has slipped into the squalor of the pre-Victorian houses of correction. Britain contains a persistent group of 155,000 people (150,000 men and 5,000 women) whose recurrent patterns of behaviour make them responsible for practically all the most serious crimes and a half of all crimes committed in Britain today.[110] And in all the statistical litanies of penology perhaps the most melancholy is the fact that 50 per cent of the victims of crime are also offenders. The kingdom of crime, therefore, is a true 'community' formed by shared experience.

It took an unusual Home Secretary, Douglas Hurd, to point out that prison was 'an expensive way of making bad people worse'. As British elites have consolidated their own form of class power over the past generation so at the same time the statistics for offending, for imprisonment and – crucially – for reoffending have soared. For every five prisoners who are now released from prison three are reconvicted and back in prison within two years, while among younger prisoners in the eighteen–twenty-five age group four out of every five of those released go on to reoffend and are jailed within the same two-year period. The authority which condemns and sentences is but another aspect of the same authority which tolerates prisoners' illiteracy and drug-taking. As many as a third of all Britain's prisoners cannot read or write at all which condemns them to that life in penury and vagrancy on the outside which is but the preliminary to the existence back inside. A further third have literacy abilities which are below the level of an eleven-year-old child, a standard which is barely adequate even for that lowest rung of employment which is represented by the packer of supermarket shelves.

British elites did not acquire power by being stupid – and it would be foolish to think that our elites actively desire the creation of a vast cohort of prisoners poised to reoffend. Attacks on property, rather than on persons, constitute by far the great majority of offences committed, and since property in its various forms supplies our elite with some of its greatest ambitions it is hardly likely to wish that property endangered. But self-interest can itself fall a victim to perverse consequences when it is short-sighted. The toleration of the causes of criminality, along with the cynicism it displays about reform, is just such a perversity. The big Victorian debate about criminality and prison reform relied on a certain idea of the nation as a genuine and moral project. Morality in this respect, far from being hypocritical, led to self-reproach because it was somehow shaming to the national sense of self-worth that crime should be committed and that offenders excluded from the moral nation should exist in squalor. But the men and women who run our elite structures have largely lost any sense of Britain as a national project and are largely disengaged from it. It is that absence of common purpose which lies behind the toleration of criminal Britain, and also the occasional delicious sense of a vicarious glee which the elites allow themselves on an entertainment basis when they envisage the criminal at work.

Prison officers are therefore the custodians of a contracted-out morality which, like all such contractual arrangements, is averse to responsibility and shuns consequences. As a result the modern prison measures itself by those targets and benchmarks whose hollow sounds mock the modern British state's effectiveness. Modern 'professional-ism' excels both at producing targets and at engineering that ticking of the boxes which means that a target can be scored while its real intent is ignored. In much the same way that proudly professional teachers promise themselves that a certain capacity of a particular pupil has been defined and tested so the equally highly professional prison officers will delude themselves that they have presided over those four hours a day of 'purposeful activity' which are promised to each prisoner, but very little of which is either meaningful or particularly active. Only 10 per cent of prisoners are ever placed in prison workshops, factories or in jobs which might equip them with a trade, while the rest are doped out of their minds most of the time. Serious drug use in prison (according to an estimate by the House of Commons Home Affairs Committee) now affects some 80 per cent of prisoners. This may have started with a recognition that a druggy prisoner is likely also to be a pretty passive one, and that, lacking in energy, he will therefore be easier to control. But what started as a weary cynicism and a method of group control has galloped into a continuous crisis of authority.

## Policing the Elite Society

The idea of an elite officer-class charged with law enforcement, although often attempted, has never really taken off in the police force which has remained wedded to a trade union idea of solidarity. The police hierarchy is based on a shared level of experience and of training which creates an unusually communal esprit de corps. As the force has become an increasingly graduate profession so those original features have also become more evident. This professional grouping exists as something of a fortress and its hierarchies are notorious for their unwillingness to attribute blame and place responsibility on individual colleagues when things go wrong.

In becoming more professional, therefore, the police have become more of a self-interested elite.[111] There are at the moment forty-three independent forces in England and Wales, many of which share their boundaries with city and county governments. Just as in the case of local government officers and executives, those police forces of

England and Wales are subjected to repeated bouts of restructuring and administrative change.[112] Sometimes these reviews stress the degree of local accountability and create comparatively smaller units. Then, by a kind of predetermined antithesis, later reviews end up recommending larger units in the name of efficiency costs and economies of scale. This constitutes the cyclical tedium of what passes for British reform. Greater effectiveness in the fight against terror is the specious plea used to justify that cycle's current enthusiasm – the merging of smaller forces to form larger units. But the passing of the years will see the fashion change, as it has done in the past. In that process, new units are fabricated while others wither. Thames Valley or West Mercia suddenly appear, or – in the case of other confections such as Avon or Humberside – disappear. Nobody of course has ever declared an identity as a West Mercian since the eighth century, and the valley of the Thames as a focus of meaning exists only for house agents and owners of boat moorings. But perhaps the weirdness of the invented identities is the true point of the exercise, for it underlines the remoteness of power structures from the lives of those who are meant to exercise democratic control. Meanwhile the same people doing largely similar jobs remain in place – in much the same way that inter-war French governments would fall every few months to be replaced by new governments that might differ in form but would still see the same ministers in power. Change of office, title and function should after all ideally accompany continuity of personnel in a true elite society; and in policing issues that continuity may be one way of ensuring the job security of those who hold the thin blue line. Perhaps a less secure state of mind would have sharpened the reactions of the Thames Valley policemen who were sent round to the house of Mrs Vicky Horgan in Highmoor Cross in 2005 when both she and her sister were being threatened by the estranged Mr Horgan.[113] Despite being equipped with helicopters and full body armour they moved too slowly and failed to intervene in time to prevent the women being killed. It was the same force which, in spring 2005, unveiled a system of awarding points to its officers for making arrests.[114] A seemingly whimsical system decides that detaining a shoplifter is worth two points and that an endorsable motoring offence is worth five but that getting hold of a rapist should be something of a career red-letter-day since that achievement scores ten points. But English whimsy is never entirely unselfconscious. As in other areas of modern management the performance criteria that measure and enumerate also reflect and categorize current 'best practice'. They thereby uphold the decisions of the elite career structures from within rather than challenging them from outside.

Thames Valley was therefore an appropriate enough management training ground for Sir Ian Blair,[115] the current Commissioner of Police of the Metropolis. His time there (1994–7) as Assistant Chief Constable was the preliminary to his rise to high office and he is a figure who encapsulates the hesitancies and the dilemmas, both self-chosen and self-serving, of the professional elite. A mid-1970s Oxford graduate in English Language and Literature had many options open, but the smarter establishment type with a sheen of liberal culture knew just what to do – join an institution with residual authority and public status but a declining reputation. The really clever ones would be avoiding such an organization, but the fact that only the comparatively thick were joining up was also a great opportunity since the only comparatively clever would therefore also be the ones in line for the baubles. This is what led Sir Ian's Oxford contemporary Tony Blair to politics and the Labour Party, and it is also what led the new Commissioner to his choice of career with the police force.

Blairist policing is the mirror image of Blairite politics, since in both cases regular television appearances are required, along with an evasiveness about truth. Sir Ian had to hesitate before eventually admitting that his officers had no justifiable grounds for thinking that the Brazilian electrician Jean Charles de Menezes whom they killed at Stockwell underground station in July 2005 might have been a terrorist: 'It was a mistake not to have corrected the misinformation. I wish we had done that earlier.'[116] Slipping into that collusive comfort of the first person pronoun has become a technique of elite power when finding itself on the ropes. The proud banner of diversity and reform in public services flutters above both Blair careers as a justification for ambition, and when considered solely as a career-building move the sloganizing is undoubtedly capable of working its murky magic. When Britain's professional elite turn to the public sector for its jobs, it likes to boast of bearing the cares on its shoulders while also baring the scars on its back. It is the echoing sound of a liberal conscience which stands so self-admiringly on the bridge when all save its own vainglorious self has fled the scene. This elite also needs to measure and define itself by its calculating distance from the structure it wants to reform and change. That is why an excruciating jargon of delivery is used in order to support and explain its defensive tone. For Sir Ian, policing is now in a debate about 'How it delivers its service. Is it customer shaped?'[117] But the idea that people choose a policing 'service' in the way they choose a brand on the shelf is a preposterous one. The victims of crime are not market-led customers picking their way between different forces' statistical performances before finally alighting on the one that just hits the spot and suits them best.

The distance between the enlightened leader and the purblind forces at his command is what gains the headlines for the liberal professional elite member on the make, but when things go wrong evasive measures and special pleading are required to salvage that professional career. The elite professional in charge of an inadequate institution can always find excuses within that very inadequacy for is he not engaged in what Sir Ian himself calls a 'culture war'? In his case the daily drama is that of one brave commissioner who has to define himself against 31,000 officers. When three white officers of the Met were disciplined over allegedly racist remarks they sued the Met itself, and were awarded a total of £90,000. That was a setback to the Blair campaign in favour of a police force which would be as intolerant of racism as it would be effective in its criminal detection. But the same arts that elevated the career professional must also be used to defend him in a sticky patch. Which is why Blair then ordered that 100 staff at all levels of the Met should be phoned to discover whether they believed the charge, reported in the *Daily Mail*, that he had manipulated the case against the officers in order to prove the depth of his own anti-racist attitudes. He was, Sir Ian said, 'aware of what an enormously powerful newspaper the *Daily Mail* is'. Those who have risen by the manipulation of opinion tend to know that they can also be destroyed by that same force.

But if the Metropolitan Police find it difficult to communicate with some aspects of a modern capital they can also find themselves in situations where they can't even communicate with each other. 'Connect', inevitably a PFI communications project, is being built by the City Link consortium for a hefty £1.2 billion spread over a very generous twenty years, and aims to establish a new radio system ('Airwave') for the tube. But the scheme is not only running predictably late it is also incompatible with the police's own radio system (MetRadio), with the result that any policeman operating underground is out of contact with colleagues above ground.[118] The perversity of contracting-out arrangements, compounded by PFI shadiness, ends in a public service which is not only neutered but also, in this instance, mute.

## Conclusion: The Hollow Crown

Popular and electoral awareness of the reality of the elite professionals' power, their easy ability to dominate argument by jargon,
evasion and enclosed systems of thought, explains the lack of a
genuine rejection in Britain of the European Union's supposed 'elites'.
Traditional 'Euro-scepticism' has now become as much an established
feature of the political landscape as the dividing lines between public
spending and private enterprise, between tax and spend, or between
direct and indirect taxation. For over a generation now an enormous
amount of emotional and political capital has been invested in the idea
of a virtuous British polity which is being attacked and subverted by
unelected Brussels elites. But a response of genuine and popular
outrage, something which would correspond to the gravity of the
supposed anti-democratic violation inflicted on Britain, remains a
minority affair. Euro-scepticism contrasts Euro-elitism with the genuine, albeit threatened, realities of a British democracy in which elites
are held accountable. But the truth of the matter is that there is a broad
continuum between the EU elites and the British ones. Both thrive by
the same means and the wasteful, duplicitous effects of their work on
our daily lives are fundamentally similar. Which is why noisy Euro-
scepticism's impact is undermined by Brito-scepticism's quiet but
stubborn witness. The only real difference between the two sets of
elite professionals running these related shows is that the native British
ones are more numerous, more deeply entrenched in national structures and less immediately visible as an object of attack than their
Brussels equivalents. They are more cunning and therefore more
powerful.

We have become so used to our professional elites that we acquiesce
in their local and national monopolies of power rather than initially
displaying, as we should, offence and then resorting to scepticism
when confronted by the evidence of their dereliction of duty in the
matter of running Britain. Around their existence there hovers the
mystique of 'professionalism', a form of knowledge and a set of
practices which have always been used to proclaim their separation
from the rest of the population. But the distinctive knowledge of the
old professional elites has been largely taken over and suborned by the
spurious practices of the new professional elites. The result is a hollow
crown: the appeal of the professionals in Britain now is simply that of
a dignified existence and one which is immune to genuinely forceful

criticism. And it is therefore unsurprising that so many want to get in on the act and to benefit from the credulity with which the professionals are treated.

Some professional elites do still require the mastery of a complex body of knowledge. Most scientific and medical professionals, along with the legal professionals, are of this kind and those elites need to demonstrate that kind of mastery before they can start organizing their career structures. University teachers and scholar–professionals in the humanities also try, with variable success rates, to imitate this notion of an objective corpus of truths which can then be pressed into service as the basis of their career-authority. But the administrative elites which affect our lives do not come close to commanding any such body of knowledge. They simply work their way around forms of information – some held secretly and others which are more widely available – but in all cases comprehensible to a numerate and literate person.

But whether their power comes from this kind of generalist information or from the possession of more specialist and technical knowledge, the capacity to get on and build a career is becoming much the same right across the professions. Success requires malleability to the demands of the new professionalism which has been taken over by capital markets and by the state. It is these two forces which are the new regulators of professional conduct and professional thinking. Beyond a certain point, any original questioning of the hierarchical structures that they enforce is self-destructive to a career.

The conformity of the new professionalism means that once you're inside the professional group – and as long as you play the game which balances the need for deference with the opportunity for self-assertion – it's very difficult to get expelled from it. That fact owes less to the probity and high-mindedness of professional groups in managing entry procedures than it does to their manipulation of the established prejudice which runs in their favour and which maintains that we need them more than they need us. Britain's professional elites are powerful as well as being often incompetent and venal. But they can afford the incompetence and be indifferent to the venality because of the mystique which surrounds them and indulges them. Evidence of their failure recurs to an increasing degree in everyday British administration because of the concentration of power at the top in British institutional life. As our professional elites become more influential and their ambitions more and more dizzying so their power bases become more concentrated and intense. Holding such undue concentration of powers in their hands it is not surprising that they – and those they govern – have to pay the price in human error.

The professional elites, however, can invariably walk away from their mistakes – or, at the very least, explain them away – because they are the beneficiaries of that irrationality and that conformism which parades itself as a collective wisdom based on practice and experience. Although they have accommodated themselves to the new market conditions and state demands, our professional elites can still justify themselves in terms of an old cultural model. Their authority is supposed to have arisen organically by trial and error from the rich soil of old England, to be the fruit of experience and its various modes rather than the consequence of anything so vulgar as a grab for power and elite control. This collective wisdom presents knowledge as a self-justifying process rather than a specific outcome. It is meant to be an experimental dialogue in which the idle and apathetic play as important a role as the informed and engaged. This is a true enough description of stock markets with their two kinds of traders: those who place their bets because of sentiment and superstition as well as those who gamble on the basis of knowledge and experience. That mixture is the reason why stock markets create their own speculative frenzies. But, when applied to the ideas that sustain power, the picture is a false analogy because it can justify mental obscurity. What was witch-burning in the seventeenth century – that social consensus of the age – but a form of collective wisdom?[119] It resulted from a convergence of opinion between those who claimed special authority on the subject and others who relied on hearsay, sentiment and gut-instinct to support their views. The stubborn belief in the power and the necessity of professional groupings, both old and new, is no different from that earlier belief in the existence of witches and the consequent desire to exterminate them. Professional elites, just like the witch-hunters and the witch-burners, exist only because of the lazy acceptance of the fictions and lies promulgated by a spurious and self-interested authority. But although the product of a collective aberration and the beneficiaries of prejudice, they and their bogus authority are, happily, vulnerable to the solvent of enquiry.

# Chapter 4

# The Financial and Business Elites: Dividing the Spoils

## The Control of Capital

Every year, at the spring equinox, an ancient fertility ritual is celebrated within the boundaries of the City of London. City workers, businessmen and a few local residents who belong to the Ancient Druid Order, a pagan group based in the City, don their white robes and hoods to perform a ceremony which has been staged in London since 1717. Prayers for peace and prosperity compete with the roar of city traffic while the Goddess of Spring, a figure dressed in a long yellow robe, presents seeds and flowers to the Chief Druid. For just a few hours this part of London reverts to its pre-English past and memories are revived of the Celtic tribes who used the services of the druids as judges and doctors, mystics and scholars. The eyes of curious commodity brokers and traders in derivatives may spare the antiquarian scene a few moments of their time before returning to the more insistent forms of power displayed on their computer screens.[1]

The mingling of the pagan prayer with the grey flannel suit is not as surprising as might at first appear. The City of London is, with Wall Street and Tokyo, one of the world's three leading financial centres. The City, in combination with New York, now controls 90 per cent of the world's wholesale financial activity.[2] At the end of 2003, 311,000 were employed here, 145,000 of whom worked in financial services. The UK's financial services trade surplus of $25.3 billion in 2003 was more than double that of any other country.[3] The upward thrust of the steel and plate-glass buildings symbolizes the central preoccupation of Britain's business and financial elites: the control of capital and the expansion of markets. All the other forms of power pursued by Britain's elites now have to accommodate themselves to the greater

163

power purposes of the financial institutions run by this particular elite. Sometimes the accommodation has ended in the straightforward subordination of a master–slave relationship. In other instances there has been a subtle slide through appeasement into an acquiescent recognition of the facts of power. And, occasionally, there have been tussles and resistance along the way when dissidents have attempted their forays. But this is the power track which all the elites now have to respect if they wish to maintain their own kind of eminence, since at no previous time in British history have the financial and business elites been as dominant as they are today.[4]

The City exemplifies the shock and the awe of resurgence and novelty but its roots as an institution – along with the fetishistic veneration for what it represents – lie deep in English life and attitudes. The spurious playfulness of post-modern architecture within the Square Mile promotes the occasional illusion of openness with its exposure of pipes, ventilation shafts and lifts. But the majestic shadows and cavernous interiors of the Bank of England offer a visual illustration of those truths whose roots lie deep in the City's past and which yet persist despite the raucous sounds of the new hegemony: discretion is expected from those who have been initiated into the mysteries of capital, and sometimes an advertised secretiveness is a more effective statement of power than any explicit pomp. Sir John Soane therefore designed a fortress–temple to house the Bank and the Masonic symbolism of its architectural features shows the ancient power of City connection, the appeal of secrecy and the bonds of ritual despite all the hard-edged modernity of the surrounding buildings.[5] The building both dominates its environment and keeps the outside world at bay, which is why even the massive form of James Stirling's avant-garde building, Number 1, Poultry, has to pay tribute to its neighbour by imitating the orders of that implacable classical facade.

The druids stage their ceremony within the City because their lore maintains that one day this Square Mile will revert to its natural, ancient, state. The metropolis which has grown around the banks, the finance houses and the exchanges, with all their gleaming towers and august facades, will then crumble away at the unimaginable touch of time. But the sacred quality of this plot of earth will, they think, survive. Celtic prophecy may be just fantasy and City prosperity certainly has little to do with prayerful efficacy. But the druidic ceremony is something more than just a demonstration of that weirdness which, like the river Fleet, runs below these concreted-over surfaces.[6] City continuity and City magic are part of the energy concentrated within this space. The rest of London – indeed the rest of Britain – could disappear tomorrow and the City would carry on functioning quite happily. For this is its own place governed by its own Corporation of the City of London and by its own power rules about what counts as success and failure. The City may lie geographically within the British capital, but its attitudes are resolutely offshore even when its assets are not. The ripples and waves of its economic effects determine the whole nature of the British economy as well as shaping the country's politics and moulding its social attitudes. But the loyalties of the elite who work here are not particular to Britain. A largely benign tax regime and system of financial regulation makes this the best place in the world for these workers to find themselves at this moment in history. At the end of the working day the bankers and traders, the accountants and lawyers, along with those agents who are ancilliary to their purposes – the PR people, the consultants and the advertising executives – travel by tube, train and car to their homes in the rest of London, its suburbs and surrounding 'home' counties.[7] But the location of those homes is really a foreign country so far as City attitudes are concerned and the City toiler, whether a grandee or a corporate minion, is a bearer of colonial attitudes when he travels outside the imperial centre which is his place of work. He has, after all, been told repeatedly by everyone who matters in Britain that the City is one of the glories of Britain and the source of its prosperity, so that the rest of the country now depends for its very existence on what the City does and thinks. And it is doubtless true that the decision whether Britain for example should, or should not, opt for closer European integration has been a debate largely governed by what suits the City and its needs as a centre for foreign exchange dealing. It is unsurprising therefore that a certain pro consular self-importance should creep into the City worker's voice and affect his bearing when he moves about the rest of London and of Britain.

Other organizations have seen and heard that importance and therefore moved to the east hoping perhaps that some of the sheen of that power will rub off on them. There was once a cosy contiguity to the geography of power in Britain. The half-hour walk from Westminster in the west to St Paul's in the east took the observer through all the relevant centres of power – from the political life and the administrative life of Whitehall, past the Royal Courts of Justice in the Strand, along the newspaper offices of Fleet Street and then up

Ludgate Hill and so into the heart of the City. But the move of newspaper offices from Fleet Street to the City's new dockland developments was more than just a geographical shift. It showed how journalism had become a facet of corporate life and was closer than before to the power of capital whose masters and servants worked in tower blocks very similar to the ones in which newspapers now found themselves. Similar conditions of labour started to breed, unsurprisingly, some unanimities of view as two sets of drones both stared at screens while stuck in work stations spread across open-plan offices. The Fleet Street dispersal broke the old geographical link and showed a new truth: the residue of political activity at Westminster now seemed not only distant but also irrelevant because so much power was being absorbed into the very belly of capital itself. There were other changes, too, at work because the latter-day Dick Whittingtons who came to work in the City were no longer exclusively British provincials. London by stages from the mid-1980s became an international metropolis. What attracted the foreign nationals to this new Babylon, with all the lushness of its night clubs, bars and restaurants, was not cultural freedom or political liberty but the lure of money. Britain's London-centric financial elites have therefore grown in numbers and they have also been supplemented by the workers of the other European economies as well as by their Asian and North American counterparts. Their service needs have attracted in turn other, humbler, immigrants who, along with many native-born Britons, clean and decorate the houses of this elite, look after their children as nannies, train and buff up their bodies as personal trainers, advise them on their appearance as groomers, cater to their whims as therapists, drive them in taxis and cars, serve them food and drinks at restaurants, bars and clubs as well as catering to their commodity tastes and choices in Bond Street and Oxford Street, Harrods, Selfridges and all the other centres of gratified desire where the tills may sing as the credit card slips are collected.[8]

No other capital city or country conspires to make quite such an awestruck fuss of its financial centre, endowing it with a collective authority beyond the understanding of mere mortals and a mystique which enforces worship. Germany does not become starry-eyed about Frankfurt and the Paris Bourse is not an alternative focus of loyalty within the French Republic. Wall Street comes closest to the City in terms of the attitudes it engenders, but even there the culture of money has to exist within a wider cultural dynamic which has been created by political radicalism and a cosmopolitanism with deep central European roots. But the business of London is business and what matters in the life of the capital is capital. Entertainment and diversion, culture both high and popular, are London industries which are driven by mass-opinion because that is what mass-market capital requires. London is admittedly the world's musical centre since the diversity of its orchestral repertoire and the vitality of its popular music scene have no rivals. But precious little intellectual life is allowed to affect the capital's purpose and direction. London's universities are a sideshow locked away inside their own enclaves: they offer no comparison with the way in which Berlin's university has affected its environs since the nineteenth century and with how Paris has been shaped by a university culture since the twelfth century. The difference is partly a result of the modest size of European capitals compared to London's scattered population of 7 million who struggle to travel across a capital which is the equivalent of several small towns and cities. As a result the voices of chattering dissent and organized opposition have no natural, geographical focus compared to the cafes, bars and meeting places which have been the setting for continental European debate and have helped dissent to acquire a critical mass. Capital in London, however, has shown that it is a jealous neighbour: it brooks no rival and its insistent accent rises above the noise of any competing clamour. The supremacy of finance and business over any other form of elite power is proclaimed at the Lord Mayor's banquet, that annual rite of central, symbolic, importance when the Chancellor of the Exchequer is expected to travel to Guildhall so that he can explain to the City his actions over the past financial year before going on to offer reassurance about his future intentions.

At both ends of the scale of employment, from directors and partners at the top to traders on the floor, the City is a place which exults in its own form of cleverness. Essex barrow-boys may now have given place to wide-boys from all over the south-east of England and beyond. And 'boys done good' pop up all over the City – both of the cheerfully self-nominated variety and of the kind denominated as such, de haut en bas, by their imagined superiors. This is almost invariably a boys' place, which is why boastfulness about the size and success of one's latest financial conquests is so very evident. But even among those who do the name-calling and the categorizing there is an abiding egalitarianism at work – one which comes from the knowledge that money is the only reason why anybody should want to work here. A readiness to use mental power exclusively in the service of money markets – along with the frank acknowledgement of that abasement – is the one necessary qualification for City success. As a result there is no need here for any of the native British hypocrisy about virtue and the City has no room for the management techniques and the management theories which prop up elite life elsewhere in modern Britain. The contrast with the enfeebled professions could not be greater and for this much brutality in counter-point, perhaps, some thanks.

Joyti De-Laurey, a personal assistant at the investment bank Goldman Sachs, offended against this world in very many respects. She stole more than £4.5 million from three managing directors of the bank by forging cheques and was sent to prison for seven years in April 2004 on twenty counts of fraud. But De-Laurey's offences went beyond the technicalities of fraud. An outsider, a woman of Indian descent and one who worked in a relatively humble role, had shown how easy it was to steal money from people who were supposed to be money experts. Her activities had exposed a world in which it was customary for secretaries to forge their bosses' signatures when they were not around and bills needed to be paid. A bank trades on its reputation for trust and security and therefore as one former Goldman Sachs employee has said: 'It might have been better . . . if they had sacked her, recovered the money and kept quiet about how much she got away with.'[9] The case gave much innocent pleasure to observers and De-Laurey was clapped and cheered on the tube as she went to Southwark Crown Court for her trial. But internal considerations of prestige militated against those of PR which is why the case went ahead amid so much loss of face. The pride of City lions means that they regard PR executives as part of the chino and cafe latte brigade – unnecessary, not very clever and a mere tribute to the silly demands of an age whose newly spun conventions are best ignored.

There have been other periods of fiscal frenzy – in both the history of Britain and in that of other countries – when the money power of the financial elites have also dictated the terms and conditions of political power. The palaces of the capitalist barons on Long Island show the grandeur that was Vanderbilt and the greed that was Pierpont Morgan at the end of the nineteenth century – before anti-trust legislation affected some of the monopolist thrust of those corporate machines.[10] The colonial expeditions of that age, such as the building of the Panama Canal and the creation of Panama itself along with the activities in Cuba of Theodore Roosevelt's gang of land-speculating 'Rough

Riders', were the reflections in action of America's money markets and their capital demands. The Orleanist regime of King Louis Philippe of France rejoiced in that injunction to 'make yourself rich' which was also the motive behind the colonial regime's expansion after Algeria was annexed in 1830.[11] And it was the gold and silver of the New World, along with the expansion of credit opportunities, which helped the Spanish Hapsburgs to maintain their foreign policy adventures and to attempt a European dominance, until the long revolt of the Dutch made that ambition an impossible exercise in imperial overstretch.[12] The British money craze of the late twentieth and early twenty-first century has been exceptional because of the absence of any political or economic counter-weight within the country itself. At various stages in British history from the eighteenth to the early twentieth century the 'money power' of the City had to contend for predominance with both the manufacturing interest and with some forms of the landed interest. Subsequently, it was forced to struggle in order to retain its power against first radical and then Labour agitation. But at the beginning of the twenty-first century it stands on a lonely eminence as the global division of labour leaves Britain to pursue its comparative advantage in the two activities which form the core competence of the City of London: reckless gambling on the one hand and well-spoken, beautifully suited, sharp practice on the other.

Britain now enjoys an undoubted eminence as a service economy, and especially in its provision of all those City-based financial services. But the precariousness of that eminence means that it can be blown off course very easily. In August 2005 Britain's overall deficit on trade in goods and services plunged to a record £5.3 billion in the month, having stood at £3.9 billion in the preceding July.[13] This reflected the record importation of £2 billion worth of crude oil and also the decline in oil exports as a result of production problems experienced on the country's North Sea oil rigs. But the balance was also hard hit by the impact on British insurers of Hurricane Katrina in the south of the USA. Estimates from the ONS suggested that the catastrophe would cost Lloyd's insurance syndicates some £1.4 billion. As a result Britain's normally healthy surplus on foreign trade in services was cut to just £284 million. This was the worst trade balance on services since the deficit of £919 million incurred because of the insurance losses which followed the terrorist attacks on Washington, DC and New York City on 11 September 2001. The City's development over the past two decades has accompanied, and built on, the emergence of a British 'virtual' economy – one sustained by telecommunications and IT systems while trading in services which, though intangible, are measurable because they are bought and sold. But an economy built on a basis which can be so easily undermined by natural disasters and by politically inspired attacks is a precarious construct despite the smooth tones of those who defend it. And the impact of the deficits is measurable in the consequent reduction in the rate of growth for Britain's GDP.

## The Triumph of the City

The transfer of power to the financial and business elites has been an unusually smooth one, with London finance dictating the pace for the rest of the country during an exercise in financial dominance which started with the deregulation of the City institutions – the 'big bang' of 1986. That dominance has both accompanied and explained the increasing silence of politics during that period, and has ended in an epoch when the normal rules of party politics have been suspended. The only part of Britain where those rules have continued to operate during this time has been the province of Northern Ireland, a place which is an useful control experiment for those who have either forgotten what politics really is or have never seen it at work on the mainland. Issues of principle about identity, rights and freedoms continue to divide – and so to explain – party politics in the province. And because there has been no takeover here by extra-political forces the politicians remain in their natural state of being at each other's throats. The silence of English politics is now thought to be almost normal while Northern Ireland's vituperative condition is considered abnormal. But it is English politics which is exceptional while Northern Ireland is the forgotten norm. Not even the British government's best attempts at turning the province into a major centre for the military–informational complex have produced a peace dividend by concentrating minds on jobs rather than divisive politics. Raytheon, the third largest arms manufacturer in the world, is now based in Derry where it develops e-commerce software. John Huddleston Engineering, providers of missile and helicopter components, the happily named Spirent which produces software for the US airforce and Thales Air Defence, which makes missiles: all have become an important part of the Northern Irish economy and help sustain conflicts in other parts of the world while the graver local battle remains the one for local political power.

Meanwhile the politics of continental Europe, because far less exposed than Britain to the dominance of capital, is still comparatively vital in debate and confrontation. French socialists may be rudderless after the scandal-ridden Mitterrand[14] years but French politics still reflects sharp conflicts of interest between some free market globalists and those who adhere to the charms of France's social models. Germany – although a country with a strong tradition of consensual politics since 1945 – also has a distinguishable centre-left tradition which opposes an equally defined Christian Democratic one. The European country which comes close to Britain's state today is the Italy of Silvio Berlusconi[15] where, in classic fascist style, the interests of big corporations, businesses and financial institutions have merged with those of the central government itself. As a result of this takeover the voices of Italian parliamentary dissent are almost as silent and impotent as they are in Britain. The only difference is that Britain's Prime Minister – unlike Italy's – does not personally own the television stations, football clubs and advertising companies which are favoured by state power.

The extravagant triumph of the City is a recent development. It has assimilated all the other elites and it therefore feels that it can get away with an exuberant shamelessness. The gleeful noise contrasts with the reserve of the past, for Britain has had a long tradition of that quiet money which glided easily up and down the passages of power. Quiet money liked a quietly influential life and, historically speaking, it was in its interests to be on easy terms with the other elites. Its natural habitat was the boardroom of the merchant bank, and it needed to cultivate relationships with the other forms of power in order to achieve its ends. 'People can say what they like about Bob Maxwell,'[16] once mused Sir Michael Richardson,[17] an arch-survivor of that world of discreet money and a sleek director of Rothschild's, 'but the great thing about Bob was that he always knew how to look after his English bankers,'[18] which is why Sir Michael made his way to Jerusalem to attend Maxwell's funeral and carried on defending him even after the exposure of his abuse of the *Mirror* pension fund. Quiet money needed, in most circumstances, discretion and it liked that silkiness of tone which, in the case of once-British-owned institutions such as Lazard's, Barings and Cazenove, used to accompany the mid-morning tea served in bone china cups. The tone was often associated with a certain blueness in the bloodline while its outward and visible sign was the purring of the chauffeur-driven Jaguar. Such people were the backbone of the grander kind of gentlemen's clubs in St James' and, even today, some of the directors of these great institutions, themselves often the heirs of forebears who were also directors, can be found loitering in White's, Brooks' and Boodle's among the shades of their ancestors. Sometimes they had a racy edge to them for these men were after all gamblers by trade despite the patina of gentlemanly capitalism, which is why they could also be found in the Turf Club tucked away in Carlton House Terrace. A lot of them are still there, since racing – with its long history of corruption, fixed races and bent jockeys – is a game well suited to the manipulations of City financiers.[19] The sport is uniquely English in its combination of proletarian popularity with aristocratic enthusiasm and so the concern of the turf with the line of the bloodstock fits easily with some old-style City snobbery. Corporate exclusion, mostly with less ancestry to exult in, can also be witnessed in Mark's Club in Mayfair's Charles Street, where Mark Birley's deeply cushioned sofas allow the plumpest of business behinds to sink into pampered luxury. The City is busier now at lunchtime than in the past and dealers certainly are fixed to their screens monitoring the morning moves on Wall Street in the London early afternoon. But when their bosses opt for lunch it is usually best to return to those ancient habitats of St James' and Mayfair where the eyes of fellow lunchers on other tables may be less prying than would be the case at a City restaurant.

These providers of financial muscle have influenced British power ever since the country started on its journey towards a global presence. But those ancestral voices of money power often had to argue their corner and to confront forceful criticism on a scale which has now become quite unimaginable. The establishment of the Bank of England (1694) – and with it the provision of reliable credit supplies for government – lay behind the acquisition of Britain's first continental empire in the mid-eighteenth century.[20] French foreign policy had to rely instead on the shaky household finances of its kings in order to raise the money needed for wars, armies and navies. Britain's national bank eventually proved to be as powerful a weapon as any cannon or musket in the race for global supremacy because it could raise more cash than any French king burdened, as such monarchs tended to be, with a dodgy credit record. But the idea of establishing a national or public bank, as well as that of institutionalizing a national debt, was a controversial innovation in Britain. And the political–financial elites who argued for it could easily be presented as an alien, Europeanizing group who had seized power as a result of that aristocratic coup d'état of 1688–9 which had ejected the native Stuart dynasty and installed a Dutch prince, William III, on the throne of England.[21] The very idea of a public bank was copied from the Dutch who had, in turn, built on Italian experience. Europe's first real public bank was the Banco della Piazza di Rialto which, after its founding in 1587, reformed the Venetian currency and payments system. The Amsterdamse Wisselbank (1609) performed a similar public role in Amsterdam and it was followed by equivalent banks in Hamburg (1619), Delft (1621) and Rotterdam (1635).[22] Once England's own national version of these banks had become associated with military victories, territorial expansion and sound money it was, retrospectively, justified by events. But to begin with this was an authentically City game of chance, one which was initially designed to meet the costs of Britain's involvement in the War of the League of Augsburg (1688–97) against French continental dominance and also an experiment which required thereafter a stream of military victories in order to justify the gamble and redeem the loans. Over a century later, in the aftermath of the Napoleonic Wars, critical voices could still be heard. William Cobbett in the 1820s attacked the institution of the national debt because it had created a new class of unproductive plutocrats, idle rentiers, 'loan-jobbers', 'stock-jobbers' and bondholders who 'have had borrowed from them the money to uphold this monster of a system'.[23]

Since Britain's national bank was based on the need for good and successful wars it is unsurprising that the first empire of the British was always an explicitly financial and commercial affair. The territories that came under Britain's control after the Seven Years War (1756–63) in North America and India were used to make money. An imperial concern with spreading Christianity and abolishing superstition, with establishing rational improving government, better law, decent sanitation and communications: all of these would come only much later in the nineteenth century. Money showed then – as it has done ever since – that it can establish good terms with power as long as it gets its own way. Perhaps its ideal condition for coexistence was that rather Venetian oligarchic structure of eighteenth-century England. The directors of the East India Company ran the sub-continent as a business and governed it through their fellow oligarchs, the local native aristocracies. There was an easy congruity of interest as well between the old unreformed House of Commons and the men who ran the Company.[24] Britain's modern democratic experiments have posed their own particular challenges to the City. But finance has seen off in succession the threats to capital from the early Labour Party, from syndicalism and from the trade unions. It first of all learned to live with the nationalized industries and then took back power to itself through both the privatization of those same industries and then by the vast expansion in activity since the deregulation of financial services in the late 1980s. Finance has had, of course, its ups and downs during that time, since that is in the nature of markets. Perhaps no more irrational a system for distributing human goods and resources has ever been invented, for markets attract the ignorant and the venal, the nervous and the temperamental, as well as the cool and the informed.[25] Rumour and suspicion swirls around them quite as much as knowledge and expertise does, which is why frenzies and fears can suddenly seize the collective imagination of the buyers and the sellers. But in cases of reputation, as well as those of stocks, what goes down very often ends up going up.

The scandals of the past twenty years have given rise to new forms of regulation which have been imposed upon the City. Insider dealing was the worst of these scandals, but the process of reform was also a chance to reassert some forms of old power in the City of London, since those who were guilty could often be dismissed as spivs. The City's chief watchdog – the Financial Services Authority (FSA) established in 1997 – works smoothly enough within what is really a form of City self-regulation by any other name. But the FSA can also be easily frustrated on those occasions when City finance finds it an inconvenience. Under the regime in place since June 2005 the FSA stipulates that customers in the market for financial products must be given full information on the charging structures for those products and the maximum charge for each deal needs to be shown against an industry average. But the advisers who have to provide this information have pleaded, implausibly, that it has been difficult to enforce this rule. The FSA's web-based 'commission calculator' – which is meant to help them work out the charges in relation to the market average worked out by the calculator – is, the advisers complain, incompatible with many of their own computer systems.[26] By such obvious manipulations Britain's financial elites can keep the weary old regulator waiting in the ante-rooms to their power.

The FSA can claim its occasional necessary scalps, as in the case of Carl Rigby and Gareth Bailey, the former chief executive and chief financial officer of AIT, who in October 2005 were sent to prison for three-and-a-half years and two years, respectively.[27] In 2002 they had used false contracts in order to support their case that the company would meet forecasted profits. The impatience of shareholder power denied its profit expectations can be a nasty experience, forcing many a listed company director into evasions and half-truths. But the AIT case was an unusual one since the FSA almost invariably uses its civil enforcement system rather than the courts in order to punish cases of market abuse. The complexity and the length of fraud cases means that they are an expensive legal gamble. Juries, perplexed by the complexity, will often acquit despite the strength of the evidence in the eyes of the experts and the authorities. Fines and a City ban for a number of years, rather than prison, are therefore the real threat to the corrupt director and the City can be remarkably indulgent when it comes to readmitting a repentant fiscal sinner into its circle. However creative their ways with truth, therefore, very few company directors will ever find themselves in court. And they can take comfort in the sounds emanating from Downing Street. In a speech delivered on 26 May 2005 to the IPPR, the Prime Minister described the FSA as a body which was 'hugely inhibiting of efficient business'.[28] Mr Blair, having been nobbled by City interests unhappy with the costs of compliance, was once again performing his regular role as the mouthpiece of those interests and thereby distancing himself from his own government's official policy.

When, however, the regulatory regime in question reflects a true political and military power real teethmarks become visible on the corporate body. Companies that have US listings or legally binding alliances with US-listed companies are subject to the rules of the Washington-based Securities and Exchange Commission (SEC). Where US shareholder interests are concerned that SEC body now recognizes no geographical boundaries to its imperium.[29] Much of the SEC's new powers and concerns relate to the need to avoid a repetition of the Enron and Worldcom financial scandals and it is especially concerned with the detection of possible conflicts of interest when auditors conduct lucrative consulting work for companies whose accounts they also audit. New powers (Section 404 of the 2002 Sarbanes–Oxley Act) require companies to report on their internal controls and auditors need to pass judgements on the effectiveness of those controls. Faced with some British and European protests the SEC has given non-US companies just one more year before they, too, must fall in line with US companies. British capitalism's more relaxed attitudes means that it has avoided rigid standards and prescriptions about how a company runs itself. Concerns about costs of compliance vie with some bridling at being subjected to the draconian might of a foreign power but the SEC monitors access to the most liquid markets in the world and those who want access to those markets must pay in order to play that game. Since this is an instance of American influence on the world stage there are no signs of British governmental resentment at this kind of regulation's inhibiting of efficient business.

But when corrupt judgement affects the holy of holies itself there is an audible sound of heels being dug in and of lawyers drawing up bills for services offered in the protection of reputations. In 1975 the Bank of England, the institution with the deepest pockets available, decided to become the supervisor of the Bank of Credit and Commerce International (BCCI). When BCCI collapsed its creditors decided to sue the Bank and, after a case which lasted twelve years, they were unable to gain any acknowledgement of responsibility.[30] In this case the creditors had to prove actual malfeasance or dishonesty – something which a central bank could never admit to. Politicians can quite cheerfully survive allegations of dishonesty and thereby squander the credit of their own personalities, but a Bank – and especially the Bank of England – is something quite different: its opponents have to be refuted and its reputation has to be upheld, however great the legal costs. That is also the nature of the difference between power which is merely apparent and real power in modern Britain.

But perhaps the City's most precious victory has been an intellectual one: the almost uniform acceptance in Britain today that markets work and that competition is the basis of capitalism.[31] As a result the truth has been forgotten that a market is just an invented metaphor rather than a neutral description of what is supposed to happen 'naturally'. But even the original market place of the trader is a contrivance since all those stalls do not just arrive from nowhere and there are comparative advantages and disadvantages to their positioning. A market is always regulated, even when it pretends to be free: the only question is who does the fixing. Business and the City have been aided in this easy victory by the loyalty of commentators, for financial journalism is surely the least critical of any form of journalism. The City commentator feels unusually privileged to be in on the action as the confidant of merchant princes for he mostly shares their world view and any radical commentator on City ways risks being condemned to the sidelines. In a world where so much is based on rumour – where speculation, after all, is the substance of daily activity rather than being an occasional amusement – that isolation spells professional death. Meanwhile, think tanks such as the Institute for Economic Affairs have also played their loyal role, funded as they have been by those sympathetic to City and financial interests.[32] At the same time, a generation of innocents among conservative intellectuals have affirmed and rejoiced in the City view of life – with frequent, and frequently misunderstood, extrapolations from Adam Smith. All have failed to observe, or chosen not to see, how powerful is the thrust of monopoly in capital's command of the world, and how the urge to create larger and larger units is the true lifeblood of its existence and its motive for being.

But of all these forms of victory none surely was sweeter than the one that arrived with the election of the Labour government of 1997 – an administration which was pledged quite explicitly to reassure the City of London and which then went on to mollify it on a scale not even attempted by any recent Conservative government. At least some Tory governments contained experienced businessmen such as Peter Walker[33] who understood the power of capital, and who therefore also knew what capital could get up to unless it was controlled. But no recent Labour cabinet has contained a major businessman who might cast an equally sceptical eye on City and financial interests. Lord Haskins (of United Foods)[34] and Lord Simon (of BP)[35] were used for comparatively brief periods as junior ministers but the period in office of Geoffrey Robinson (a former chief executive of Jaguar) as Paymaster-General[36] may have discouraged further experiments of that kind. However, a government which is devoted to the betterment of millionaires has always kept Downing Street doors open to members of that fiscal tribe for social, political and business purposes. The experience of the two parties in government therefore offers an instructive contrast in terms of their approach to the financial elites. The Conservative governments of 1979–97 certainly gave the City what it wanted in terms of sound money, deregulation and reduced taxation rates. That dedication to City interests was rewarded by directorships in the privatized companies for retired Tory ministers.[37] But Tory survival instincts also dictated a degree of cynicism about capital, a cynicism which was based on insiders' knowledge. A City poacher turned Tory ministerial gamekeeper could blow the whistle on sharp business practices which had the potential to harm Conservative governments precisely because such governments were so vulnerable to the charge of a partiality for plutocrats. Tory cynicism in this respect contrasts with Labour naïveté. An ignorant and bedazzled veneration of the commercial interest means that New Labour has in some ways been a far more pliant 'party of business' than its Conservative predecessors.

## Britain's Two Nations

As Peter Hain once observed when discussing market capitalism: 'It was always a mistake for the Labour Party to end up on the wrong side of that argument.'[38] The fruits of that recognition have been many as well as being, for the consumers of those fleshy delights, particularly succulent, lush and decadent. The sheer ubiquity of money's new noisiness when it goes out to play today distinguishes it from the discretion of some past forms of English capitalism. In September 2005 a hedge fund manager decided to celebrate at the Aviva Bar in Kensington's Baglioni Hotel after he had been awarded a bonus of £3 million on the basis of just one deal. Having decided to share his good fortune with the rest of the bar's customers he ended up with a bill of £36,000 for the drinks consumed in one evening by his friends both old and new and, apparently unsated by this display of conspicuous, if self-serving, generosity, he tipped the waitress who served him £3,000.[39] If this particular tale seems exceptional it can be matched by the experience of many others who work in the Square Mile which once was square but has now turned perennially golden. Gluts of mergers and acquisitions mean that City dealers trading in complex financial instruments such as credit derivatives – ways of parcelling up and passing on financial risk – are now qualifying for bonuses of between £5 million and £10 million, far more than the average bonus of £1.6 million they earned in 2003–4.[40] That may be the end of one particular boom, with just £7 billion worth of contracts now outstanding, but who can doubt that these pashas of opulence will find other ways to make money quickly and spend it publicly?

In terms of salaries alone, the disparity between the successful elites and those who toil at the bottom, as well as with those who survive in the middle, is now so great as to justify the suspicion that Britain is – once again – two nations who know little of each other. A small and confident class enjoys expectations of life and samples pleasures which are at such odds with the experience of the rest of Britain that it would find it difficult to communicate with that other nation were it to encounter it in any serious way.[41] Mervyn Davies, for example, the chief executive of Standard Chartered Bank earns £2 million a year while Dame Marjorie Scardino, the chief executive of Pearson, is still earning £645,000 a year along with bonuses of £1 million despite the strategic misjudgements made during her time at the top. Public service feels obliged to keep up with these pay scales as well, which is why Mark Thompson, Director-General of the BBC, now earns £495,000. Stepping into the domain of the managers of the hedge funds requires a good head for heights when it comes to reading the salary slip. Stephen Butt, hedge fund manager at Silchester International Investors, earns a basic salary of £10.63 million and £5.1 million in dividends while Elena Ambrosiadou, hedge fund manager for IKOS UK, earns £15.9 million including dividends. At the same time the payroll manager at a City firm who processes some of these payments is lucky to get £40,000.

Such are the forces, and the differentials, which are matched elsewhere in 'enterprise' Britain since every form of employment is now driven by these business expectations and by the need to maintain the differentials even when the pressures and the risks vary hugely. A floor manager in a bookshop will not earn much more than £20,000 while the chief executive of the HMV group, Alan Giles, earns £976,000 plus bonuses. An experienced postman with the Royal Mail earns about £16,000 and an office manager with London Underground can earn £30,000 but the chief executive of Network Rail, John Armitt, earns £480,000 and the chief executive of P&O Nedlloyd, Philip Green, earns £550,000 with bonuses worth more than £1 million. Sport, too, itself now a major corporate activity, shows the divide at work, with Jose Mourinho, Chelsea's manager, earning £5.2 million and the average football referee earning about £50,000. The NHS, too, has its masters and its servants: the chief executive of Guy's and St Thomas, NHS trust, Jonathan Michael, earns £214,000 but an NHS switchboard operator is on £8.40 an hour and a hospital porter is worth about £10,000 a year. However hard the conditions may be for retailing in the high street and however tasteless the foods of Britain's supermarkets, the onward march of the high-earning corporate prince in this sector is unstoppable and the difference between his magnificence and those who toil to create his profits must also be rigorously maintained, which is why Sir Terry Leahy earns £2.9 million as chief executive of Tesco while a shelf-stacker for the same store working in London earns £6.89 an hour. The fitness and leisure trade thinks that it, too, must maintain the same hierarchies while it pursues its own capital goal of turning the body into a commodity which has been trained, buffed and expensively billed. The Body Shop has been expert at turning ethical pleasure about using natural products into healthy profit, and so its chief executive, Peter Saunders, earns £828,000 while a personal trainer at a rather grand gym will earn barely more than £20,000. These are the differentials that underpin our new age of deference.

The political and administrative government of London as a whole illustrates the same inflation of salaries and of fees since it reflects the expectations of the business and finance interests which are now thought basic to the capital's existence. In the space of three years (2002–5) the use of consultants employed by the Greater London Authority (GLA) grew five-fold and the cost of special contracts rose from £900,000 to £4.9 million.[42] City Hall may have its own economics unit employing sixteen staff but that has not stopped the Mayor from paying £225,000 a year for part-time advice provided by Volterra Consulting, the company of the GLA's consultant chief economist Bridget Rosewell. When the auditors Deloitte investigated the GLA's use of consultants and chose ten contracts at random they could find a paper trail for only seven of them. But with a dynamic city buzzing away on the doorstep and equally dynamic elite careers in sore and daily need of servicing, perhaps the practicalities of invoicing are disposable items. The bosses of Britain's remaining public services require and demand similar treatment. Adam Crozier[43] runs a massive business since the Royal Mail has an annual turnover of £9 billion and his pay package is presumably meant to reflect that fact. In 2005 he earned £704,000 in salary and bonuses and also received £1.845 million as part of a long-term incentive plan while four other Royal Mail executives were paid £1 million each. During Crozier's period at the top the Royal Mail's business improved, having been in a chaotic state before he took over; but he has, in a rather typical power elite way, been rewarded for being a successful manager rather than a genuine provider of a service. He runs a monopoly and his solution to the Royal Mail's problems was to cut the number of deliveries from two to one while increasing the cost of using that service. Even with the advantage of providing a service which does not have to deal with competition the Royal Mail could still only arrive at its £537 million operating profit as a result of indulging in some odd accounting decisions. That profit figure excludes a provision of £138 million to cover the contributions to the company's very sickly pension fund and the £218 million needed to cover bonus payments of £1,000 to each of its discontented staff.

Bonus payments can also compensate four directors of Network Rail to a total of almost £900,000 in 2005 while they come to terms with the fine of £3.5 million levied on the company by the courts in October 2005 because of its liability for the Hatfield rail crash which killed four people and injured 102 in October 2000.[44] Taking their bonuses into account the chief executive, John Armitt, will earn £755,000 in 2005 while his deputy, Iain Coucher, will get £433,000. One in six trains may still be running late but that did not stop the company's remuneration committee from ignoring the rail regulator. Failure to give enough notice of engineering works and a delay in issuing emergency timetables meant that millions could not buy discounted fares in advance. The company was therefore, as the disobliging regulator pointed out, 'seriously in breach' of its operating licence and any bonuses should take that fact into account. But what, after all, is a remuneration committee for if it cannot operate as the directors' friends? Meanwhile the big train operators continue to report big rises in rail profits.[45] In 2004–5 FirstGroup announced a 36 per cent rise in profits to £67.7 million and a 10 per cent rise in dividends. In the last quarter of 2004 only 68.9 per cent of the commuter services into Paddington run by the company were on time during the peak period – the worst record for any company in the south-east. On the TransPennine Express run by the same company in association with Keolis, only 68 per cent of trains ran on time during the same period. South Eastern Trains, a company which has been relatively successful since the state took over from the feeble Connex, is now going to be reprivatized so that it too can join the ranks of those rail companies run by bosses who, above all other considerations, derive comfort and joy from the timely arrival of the annual bonus.

However, the corporate plan to reward Lord Hollick[46] a bonus of £250,000 on his departure as chief executive of United Business Media ran into difficulties.[47] The Labour peer left in 2005 with a combined final-year salary and bonus of £1.44 million as well as a £14.5 million pension which will pay out £726,000 a year. But the bonus, weirdly, was justified by the remuneration committee on the basis of the need to secure an orderly transfer of power to Hollick's successor, at which point shareholders revolted with three-quarters of those meeting to discuss the proposal voting against it, and Hollick eventually complying with their wishes. It may seem odd that a departing boss should

181

need to be paid to stop him behaving badly when he leaves, but the corporate elite often works on the basis of assumptions and expectations which are utterly disconnected from those of daily reality.

The banking world which has been so swift to condemn European stagnation and lack of entrepreneurial ambition is in fact one of the chief causes of those ills. If nascent British and European technology companies have failed to develop a global presence in the manner of Microsoft the reasons lie in certain predetermined patterns of corporate elite behaviour in banking and finance.[48] Of course, the absence of a huge monolingual and homogeneous domestic market for goods is one inhibiting cause. But European and British companies who want to develop in an innovative and challenging way experience unusual difficulties from their own domestic banks when they approach them for money in order to raise seed capital – a difficulty which is not typical of the experience of their US counterparts. As a result European technology – which is quite as innovative as the American variety – repeatedly fails to break into the international market. Looking only at electronic technologies, the American success story is a dazzling one and includes not just Microsoft but also Intel, IBM, Applied Materials, Hewlett-Packard, Comcast, Oracle, Qualcomm and Texas Instruments, to list just the most famous. Europe, however, by comparison, can offer on that global scale only the examples of Britain's Vodafone, Germany's SAP which specializes in business software, Finland's Nokia and ST Microelectronics, the Franco-Italian semiconductor group. Marconi, Britain's last major producer of high-tech communication systems, failed in April 2005 to win the BT contract designed to help the telecoms firm build its new £10 billion data network.[49] The contract would have been worth £500–£700 million spread over three years and the failure throws into doubt its survival as an independent British company. The reason for the failure was Marconi's smallness as a company, its inability to pay for really significant R&D costs and also its inability to offer those economies of scale which lead to a competitive advantage.

In this respect the competitive individualism of American culture is an advantage since, in banking terms, it means a readiness to lend on the understanding that while failure is probable, success is also a possibility. But the introspective and self-serving world of corporate banking rewards the banker rather than the customer, the shareholder and the consumer of the financial product. In this kind of power elite existence the most successful kind of individualism is the one which goes along with the communal, the corporate and the collective mentality. The bankers' Christmas bonus is now a regular feature of corporate existence and the justification for it is quite as predictable as the fall of the autumn leaves which so often precedes it.[50] If a banker generates additional revenue for his bank then, somehow, the bonus is earned. But the bonuses are discretionary and come from a pool based on the bank's revenues unlike those commissions which may be earned by the employees of other kinds of businesses. Even those new and noxious forms of business power, the pharmaceutical companies, do not hand over a share of their sale profit to the scientist who has invented a new drug. The perverse, but almost universally accepted, practice within elite banking circles sanctifies the position of those who are in power while also protecting them from those market shocks that they are otherwise so eager to elevate as the justification for capitalism. The divide between the ownership and the control of a company is sharper in banking than it is in any other area of elite business life. And if the general truth is that shareholders – rather than employees – have the right to any residual part of a company's income, that idea is turned on its head in banking circles. Half of the revenues earned in banking end up stuck to the employees' sticky palms in good years and compensation remains high even when the trading profit declines.

## Demolition and Development

Salary inflation and bonuses have a measurable impact on what matters most in the British economy – house prices. The effect is felt first in central London where a clutch of good City bonuses can have a sudden artificial effect of boosting prices in certain areas, just as the absence of the bonus results in an equally artificial depression in prices. As a result of the inflated prices there has been a massive movement of the workforce out of London and into the south-east in recent years. British homes are now 70 per cent more expensive in relation to wages than they were in 2000 and the average house costs six times the average annual income over the UK as a whole and seven times as much in London and the south-east.[51] Some of the pressure on Britain's green belts is the result of the spread of the second home, but whereas it was once the affluent who left the city for suburban green pastures now it is the helotized workforce on low-to-middling incomes which seeks affordable places to live beyond London. Governments have therefore become the agents of building contractors who set about proposing and facilitating new plans for housing. On current plans almost 600,000 new houses will be built in the south-east during the next twenty years at a rate of almost 30,000 a year.[52] But the spread of an urban blight along with the problem of how to pay for the new infrastructure needs of this suddenly and vastly more populated area are really the consequence of a failure to develop London as an affordable place in which to live. As a result London's future is that of a city sharply divided between those who can afford to live in part of its historic centre and the rest who exist on the margins and beyond the boundaries. Britain's tax regime and inheritance laws will allow the large and steadily growing number of the children of the owner-occupiers to inherit properties and therefore to exist as, effectively, rentiers who will never be able to buy on the basis of their own incomes. Meanwhile, in the decaying industrial areas of the Midlands and the North government continues to be the property developers' companion rather than the servant of citizen needs. The decline in the quality of the professional abilities of those who work for local authorities means that it is now quite easy to find a surveyor who will declare that a house or a whole street may be 'unfit for human habitation'. What follows is a process of compulsory purchase and land clearance by the councils. The declaration that a process of 'development' is under way then accelerates the local process of decline, as it is designed to do, so that shops, schools and pubs close. The aim of demolition is to provide a builder and a private developer with what looks like an attractive sight for 'development opportunities'. But the demolished houses were often structurally perfectly sound Victorian and Edwardian houses which would have been worth half a million pounds had they been in Fulham. The very high costs of demolition are underwritten by a government subsidy when it would have been cheaper to restore and renew the housing stock.

The plans for 'regeneration' and 'Regional Economic Strategies' drawn up by the country's nine Regional Development Agencies with their combined £2 billion budget have been basic to this destruction and this hollowness. Big budgets mean big rhetoric. Who could disagree with the proclaimed goal of the South East England Development Agency that it should create a truly 'inspirational region', one in which all the workforce are, of course, 'skilled' and the 'rich cultural heritage' is protected. But, as usual with the provincial quango, what is striking about these Agencies is the closeness of their collusive

184

relationship with some favoured companies and the indifference of other businesses to their very existence: 30 per cent of those asked in a survey of IoD members had either never heard of their local Agency, or considered it irrelevant to their work.[53] But when it comes to the development plan, the land reclamation and the bulldozing of entire districts, these quangos are fundamental to the local power elite business of who gets the right contract and who benefits most from the available grant.

## Global Business Shifts

The government which serves the interests of capital is also much given to preaching about the dangers of global markets unless Britain in some unspecified way improves its productivity and generally pulls up its socks. In this general exercise designed for the chilling of spines it can rely on the assistance of bodies such as the CBI, whose Director-General Sir Digby Jones maintains that Britain has just five years of competitive edge left before the Chinese arrive at the gates.[54] The statistics are powerful weapons in the armoury of the British power elites who still think that the necessary sacrifices will be made not by them but by the millions who work as part of Britain's untrained and ill-educated workforce. China experienced a 9.5 per cent annual rate of growth in the past two decades and in the 1990s the number of state-controlled companies halved from 300,000 to 150,000.[55] The evidence of its initial penetration into western markets shows the scale of Chinese global ambition. Lenovo, the Chinese computer company, has now bought IBM's PC division for $1.75 billion. But Chinese technology, unlike that of the Japanese of the 1970s and 1980s, remains derivative rather than pioneering and the country's competitive advantage is overwhelmingly based on what the western business elite calls 'low production costs' – a euphemism for a low-paid and ill-educated workforce which is barely one generation away from peasant ignorance and poverty. The computer screen-maker BOE Technology made international business waves when it bought into Korea's Hynix Semiconductor company in 2003 since it seemed to presage a global dominance. But the end result was a mountain of debt for the company and a persistently poor rate of technological development.

The futuristic game of which economy will rise and which will fall has a statistical and an economic base. Speculation about the consumerist wave sweeping across India is based on the fact that Gandhian socialism is dead and that India is far more than those thousand villages defined by the ascetic as being the country's heart.[56] The average middle-class Indian family's disposable income grew by more than 20 per cent between 1999 and 2003, and a capitalist ingenuity in the face of market saturation is seen at work when Mauj Telecom and Rediff Mobile, hit by falling sales, introduced Hindu devotional options on mobile phones so that a sacred bell can be rung and an image garlanded at the press of a key. At the same time the fact that the average national income per head during that period rose from £238 to £292 also shows the persistently grinding nature of Indian poverty.

The wilder end of the speculation about the impact of these global shifts remains an abstract matter and, where the elites are concerned, the more abstract, speculative and imprecise the better in order to spread the fear and dismay which reinforce their authority. Self-reproach, it is not so subtly suggested, should be the sentiment of the poor, the unskilled and the low-waged at the sight of these economically burgeoning giants yearning to be free.[57] Had they applied themselves in time the marginal and the marginalized would have been better prepared for that hurricane from the Far East which, however, is now poised to destroy them. The sermons of the power elites are really therefore counselling a certain fatalism as the best available option to be adopted by those they rule. For these power brokers – the servants themselves of capital's haughty hegemony – equate success with virtue and regard failure as always culpable. That was a defining evangelical truth of early American capitalism summed up in Emerson's remark that: 'There is always a reason, in the man, for his good or bad fortune.'[58] As Britain's economy dances increasingly to the demanding rhythms and invocations of American capital's needs and ideas, it is unsurprising that the rhetoric which accompanies that dance should also sound increasingly similar. It was the unsustainable booms and busts of nineteenth-century capitalism with its regular series of crashes which first exposed the lie that failure is the result of improvidence. Thrifty depositors could end up as bankrupts in that giddy cycle. And the dream of total independence, which fuelled the myth of the virtuous entrepreneur, becomes just a silly lie when most workers have become wage earners dependent on their employers' success or failure. The New Deal programmes of F.D. Roosevelt followed on from the insight he announced at the beginning of his presidency in 1933 that: 'If I have read the temper of our people correctly, we now realize as we have never realized before our interdependence on one another.' But the rise of the American New Right in the 1980s has meant a return to the old fable which takes comfort in the fact that the poor are only there because of their moral fallibility and in the consequent conviction that the hierarchies reflect a just reward. Repackaged English Conservatism accepted – and dutifully reflected – those same insights during that same period. The greatest success enjoyed by the movement has not been within the domain of the political elites, for this form of conservatism has not needed to be in government in order to be in power. It has, rather, consolidated the power of capital markets and given new authority to those who run those markets.

In that process of confirming power it has been necessary for the business and financial elites to offer a parody of other countries and other economies, and there have been times when those who serve those elite interests have toppled over into self-serving geo-political fantasies about 'old Europe' and the 'end of Europe'. This is usually done with a good deal of shrill denunciations of the European elites while being blind to the fact that the USA – so admired by these same fantasists – is a business run by the narrowest of senatorial and gubernatorial elites. Luke Johnson,[59] the business mind behind the success of Pizza Express, therefore proclaims himself overwhelmed by the sight of labourers working seven days a week in Shanghai at a rate of less than $5 a day. Looking down at the scene from the seventy-fifth floor of a sky-scraper hotel he acclaims that 'miracle of modern China' which exposes 'Britain's serious vulnerability as a first-world economy' and the delusion of European welfare systems that 'undermine ambition and discourage effort'.[60] Speculation of this kind is sometimes rewarded with the adjective 'maverick', but it amounts to no more than a set of conventional views.

Gallons of crocodile tears are also available for public viewing when it comes to the imposition, for a limited period, of EU quotas on the importation of Chinese textiles and the effect of that measure on the country's textile workers.[61] But complete freedom to trade right across the board in every area of activity is as much of a chimera as the supposed opposite, a rigidly protectionist system. The equilibrium attained by the free flow of goods would become possible only if both buyers and sellers held equally perfect information. And since that is an impossible achievement all economies have at times resorted to some degree of protectionism in some sectors, as the USA has done with its steel industry. The parody of the modern European economy as an entity doomed to irreversible decline finds a few all-too-resistant facts staring it in the face. Germany has now overtaken the USA as the world's largest single exporter and it has been propelled to that position by the fact that new Asian and Eastern European economies are buying its hardware.[62] The country's trade surplus is greater than that of China, Japan and India combined and amounted to 16.8 billion euros in just one month (June 2005). There is little here to justify some Spenglerian gloom about the fall of the West. Germany's proportion of state spending as a proportion of GDP stands at 46 per cent, which places it right next to that supposed model of deregulated leanness, Britain, with its 45 per cent. It is a German company, Bertelsmann, the world's fourth biggest media group, which owns both Britain's Channel 5 and the publishers Random House. In the first half of 2005 its operating profit rose to 644 million euros, an 8.1 per cent increase.[63] German as a language of the boardroom has established its own, albeit uneasy, coexistence with Anglo-American, many of whose business terms it has incorporated into its own phraseology.

Cultural self-confidence dictates that French is still the language of the French boardroom despite the inroads of Franglais, and it is that self-esteem which explains the uneasy British relationship with France, that top-of-the-range model of state spenders where the public sector takes up 54 per cent of GDP and where 42 per cent of the country's young people say they want to join the civil service as opposed to just 14 per cent who like the idea of international business. Half-enviously and half-resentfully, Britain maintains a 'mésentente cordiale' with its nearest neighbour. France is the continental country most visited by Britons on holiday: 12 million go there every year and half a million own French second homes. Francophilia has a deep hold on the British imagination because cross-Channel differences evoke a lost British world. France is what Britain was before the present age of the dominant corporation enforced uniformity and diminished variety. Bakeries stay open because the price of a loaf of bread is fixed by law, controls restrict the growth of supermarkets that might destroy the shopping centres of towns and villages, the elected mayors of local communes determine local planning issues and make sure that small schools and post offices are kept open. Here the capitalist economy is at the service of the state which embodies most of the nation. The sole exception is the French capitalist class whose upper echelons are consumed by an envious astonishment when they look at their English counterparts. France is also the country with Europe's highest birth rate because the total economic package of the supportive state is a family-friendly one as opposed to the artificial and bureaucratically managed stimulants of Britain's tax regime of credits and allowances. With its heart and also with a good deal of its head much of contemporary Britain knows that the French condition is superior to its own domestic wasteland.

The fiscal and the business elites – together with the pens and voices that represent their interests – have therefore had to invest much time and energy in their discouraging, and counter-intuitive, portrayal of a decadent continental European tradition which wants to cling to a cherished consensus. It ascribes that perverse desire to the reaction against the class conflicts, the wars and implacable ideologies of the first half of the twentieth century. This is a curiously complacent and offshore view as well as being a lazily ideological theory whose main purpose is to prop up self-esteem. But there is nothing lazy about the interests which are the material substructure beneath the world view. When Werner Seifert, chief executive of the Deutsche Börse set out to acquire the London Stock Exchange he did so with confidence having gained the approval of his supervisory board. This was a bold adventure designed to turn the Frankfurt Börse into a major international trading exchange. But Seifert also needed the explicit approval of his shareholders and, since the dominant voices among those shareholders were US hedge funds and asset managers working in London, they voted against a measure which they thought would be bad value for their investment and also, perhaps, a European step too far.[64]

## In the Service of Corporate Power

The self-confidence which has always been required for successful membership of Britain's financial and business elites is now matched by self-satisfaction since so many want to join their numbers and participate in the glories of all that 'corporate governance'. The Darwinian competition of the market place has established the supremacy of just one way of running a business – the publicly owned company which is based on the strict separation of labour from capital. Ideas of employee share-ownership are easily dismissed as a romantic nineteenth-century myth of cooperative endeavour, even when the aim is to engage workers' sympathy for capitalism through their self-interest. The partners in John Lewis plc are a quixotic survival. The proposal of the Royal Mail's management to hand over half the business to the postal workers in a partial privatization package is just a ploy dictated by union hostility to full privatization. Elite arguments point out that if new employees are granted stock when they are hired then the established workers see the value of their own stock diluted, and if the new arrivals are not granted stock the result is a divisive one. But this presupposes that a company so governed is always going to be stagnant and therefore unable to offer that prospect for future progress in which employees can envisage the growth which will benefit them. The true, short-term, elite benefits of the alternative – and now dominant – form of doing business in Britain is that capital in bad times can always force labour to bear the burden with cuts in pay and pensions. That is the truth which also gives the lie to all the tedium of the management textbook truism about the workforce being a company's greatest asset. In this model of activity it is the function of the upper band of workers – the management team – to organize the lower band of workers inspirationally and then raise their self-esteem by promulgating the vision of a better corporate tomorrow. But labour – especially its lower ranks – is not that easily persuaded, since it knows that most of its work is dull, that management theory is bogus and that it will always be the first to go when the profits fall. That is why the disillusioned comedy of *The Office*, with its portrayal of boredom and futility, led to such a popular television success. It is also probably the reason why employees steal on the scale that they do from employers. In 2004 the retail industry alone, admittedly a vulnerable target in this respect, lost £11.5 billion because of thieving employees who may well justify their takings as an anticipated form of redundancy payment.[65]

Endowed with their entrenched advantages company boards can always attract those who may be useful to their purposes. Rupert Murdoch was able to rely on the friendship of the former President of China, Jiang Zemin, when News Corp's Star TV set up the joint venture Phoenix satellite TV and gave CCTV, the Chinese mainland's chief broadcaster, a stake.[66] Phoenix – with its indulgent reports on the official party leadership – pleased the Chinese establishment, and the occasion in 2003, when Mr Murdoch addressed the Central Party School which trains the future leading Chinese cadres, was surely a mighty moment of East–West elite fusion. But a greater power in this instance can also be a capricious one and the new President, Hu Jintao, has not been such a News Corp-friendly power broker, as a result of which Star TV's joint venture with Qinghai Satellite has been cancelled by the government. Happily, though, Rupert Murdoch and News Corp have found Britain's New Labour Party leadership to be a far more reliable business partner and has been granted the effective right of veto on any future British adoption of the euro. Irwin Stelzer, the chosen Murdoch intermediary in these and other matters, continues to liaise with both the Prime Minister and the Chancellor and has done so ever since the days when Labour was in opposition in the mid-1990s. Bored by his early retirement in Denver, Stelzer discovered his salvation in his neighbour Rupert Murdoch: 'Rupert asked me to travel the world kicking arse for him – and that's what I do!'[67] Stelzer delighted in the rapid ease with which he could travel on his trans-Atlantic missions in the days when Concorde still flew and would land him on the Heathrow tarmac where he would then be collected by the corporate car and motor along in anticipation of the permanent welcome inscribed on the No. 10 doormat for this august ambassador from a foreign power.

But elite business power connection depends mostly on less exalted minions. Former civil servants, unused to soaraway directorial salaries and bonuses, are happy to accept the tens of thousands which are offered them as non-executive directors. Lord Kerr,[68] therefore, former permanent secretary at the Foreign and Commonwealth Office, lends his dignity to the board of Shell and Lord Wilson,[69] a former head of the Home Civil Service, has been happy to join the board of BSkyB where he may provide some patina of respectability for Murdochian roughness of edge. Lord Burns,[70] a former permanent secretary at the Treasury, has been appointed deputy chairman of Marks and Spencer while also sitting on the board of Pearson and of British Land Company plc. His Treasury predecessor, Sir Peter Middleton,[71] is a former chairman of Barclays and is now chairman of Camelot. Lord Powell,[72] having been the Prime Minister's foreign affairs adviser during the Thatcher years, has become – inter numerous alia – a consultant for the arms manufacturer BAE Systems. He also achieves something of a hat-trick in uniting political, business and professional elite activity with his appointment as the present Prime Minister's special envoy to the Sultan of Brunei in which role, according to Downing Street, 'he discusses a wide range of bilateral issues and regional issues'.[73] Capital power finds it useful to have these dignified individuals safely tucked away on board. Few are there because of their contacts or their 'experience' since business advance makes past knowledge of people and events irrelevant on an almost daily basis. The mandarin experience in emollience may well be useful in some circumstances: Lord Burns' task, for example, will be to unite a boardroom divided over strategy as the company's market share falls. But these individuals' most relevant function is give a gloss and a sheen to the coat of a corporate power which can then go on to trade off the appearance of a borrowed majesty while it prises open new markets.

There are, however, a few spectacular cases of a fortuitous link between the policies advocated in a professional job and the subsequent business career. Dame Pauline Neville-Jones[74] was political director of the Foreign Office, 1994–6, and a prime influence on the British government's policy during the break-up of Yugoslavia and the war waged by Serbia against Bosnia. As the chief British representative at the Dayton peace talks she argued energetically for an end to sanctions against Serbia. Both she and her colleague Douglas Hurd, the Foreign Secretary at the time, treated the Serbian leader Slobodan Milosevic (in Francis Wheen's words) as: 'a moderate and necessary middleman, refusing to accept that he was in fact the genocidal thug who had instigated the violence'.[75] Even while she was at Dayton, however, Neville-Jones was already negotiating with NatWest Markets about the possibility of a private sector job. Hurd had become a deputy chairman of the bank shortly after resigning from the government in 1995 and Neville-Jones became managing director in July 1996. The two, liberated from officialdom's constraints, then travelled to Serbia in order to negotiate one of the consequences of the abolition of sanctions: 'At a "working breakfast" in Belgrade, Milosevic signed a lucrative deal whereby NatWest Markets would privatize Serbia's post and telephone system for a fee of about $10 million. For a further large fee, [NatWest markets] agreed to manage the Serbian national debt. Hurd and Neville-Jones claimed that this hideous partnership with the Butcher of Belgrade was "in the interests of the West" since it committed Milosevic to a process of "liberalization".' But the partial privatization of a 49 per cent stake in Telecom Serbia was simply a way of raising government cash in order to finance the next military offensive against Kosovo, which duly went ahead.

The former representatives of government can therefore influence – or exalt – the interests of a financial and business elite. But the traffic of influence can work the other way as well. The management consultants McKinsey have been pioneers along this particular dual carriageway.[76] Sir Michael Barber,[77] the former head of the Prime Minister's 'delivery unit' is now ensconced as an 'expert partner' in McKinsey's public sector practice. High statistics for still births in 'public sector reform' need not therefore discourage the administrative power elite which seeks to move into the business elite. Travelling in the other direction, David Bennett moved from McKinsey in 2004 to become head of the No. 10 policy directorate. It is a move for which he is appropriately prepared since he has already worked as a McKinsey consultant to the Department of Health's cumbersome IT project for the NHS. And if he steps into the neighbouring government department he can take comfort in the company of those officials who embody the extension of McKinsey patterns of thought by any other means that may come to hand. The Cabinet Office's chosen method for an anti-bureaucratic campaign has involved the creation of a Better Regulation Executive and a Better Regulation Commission which will, naturally enough, 'challenge the role played by the Better Regulation Task Force'. 'Misunderstandings' and publicly voiced accusations of conflicts of interest inevitably emerge when Whitehall hires private sector executives whose commercial ethos may conflict with established civil service rules. For example, Martin Banfield, an export promoter, was brought into the Department of Trade and Industry only to find himself at the centre of controversy over a payment by a Swiss bank of $200,000 (£115,000) after a machinery export deal had been arranged.[78] Such developments worry the secretive McKinsey organization, a group as mandarin in its occlusion as the senior civil service itself, which is why Lord Birt, an unpaid government adviser with a contract which ended in the autumn of 2005, has had to sever his links with the consultancy. But the official severance of that connection does not affect some salient facts. McKinsey has won £40 million worth of contracts from the Ministry of Defence alone since Lord Birt was appointed to the government service in 2001. It has also benefited greatly from Monitor, the regulator of the NHS foundation trusts, which spent £10 million on McKinsey consultative fees in its first fifteen months, more than half its £19.4 million budget.[79]

However, there are occasions when the civil servant need not wait until retirement before being pressed into the service of corporate power. When the government's Gambling Bill was published in October 2004 the public reaction was one of distaste at the prospect of the spread into Britain of a Las Vegas-type world of supersized casinos. But officials from the Department of Culture had been hard at work negotiating with the casino bosses and trying to prepare public opinion. Lord McIntosh,[80] the minister in charge of gambling, had visited casinos in France, South Africa, Atlantic City and Las Vegas itself in order to prepare his brief. Officials from his department had also visited Las Vegas (in October 2004) where they met executives from the main gambling companies: MGM Mirage, Caesar's Entertainment, Kerzner International, Las Vegas Sands, Harrah's Entertainment and Ameristar. Both officials and politicians had to deal, however, with the concerns of the British police about money laundering, and the fear that the proposed huge increase in the number and the size of British casinos would make it easier for criminals to clean their 'dirty' money. The proposed counter-measure was a new directive requiring that gamblers spending more than £700 should give proof of their identity – a measure which, in the view of the casino companies, would frustrate their aim of really large-scale growth. When, therefore, Richard Beston, an official at the Department of Culture, prepared a brief for Lord McIntosh in early 2004, in advance of the minister's meeting with Lord Nathan, MGM's European chief, he was dealing with a sensitive issue and one which had become a subject of negotiation with the Treasury. But the briefing was optimistic: 'We have asked the Treasury to consider revising the third money laundering draft directive to exempt casino members from showing ID on entry to [sic] when they enter the actual gaming floor . . . If these discussions fail I will consider with the industry how best to resolve this issue.'[81] Appeasing the men from Las Vegas had therefore become an important part of British government policy, but these useful vulgarians also needed advice on how to conduct themselves if they were going to get their way. The enthused remark by Terry Lanni, MGM's chairman, that the proposals had 'the potential to make the UK one of the most exciting gaming markets in the world' had been particularly unfortunate in this respect. As Beston pointed out to his minister in a document dated 9 October 2003, McIntosh should tell MGM 'not to talk up your ambitions for the UK's casino market. Gambling is still a sensitive subject in the UK . . .'

## Pharmaceutical Dependency

Pharmaceutical profits, however, are far from being the sensitive subjects that they should be in Britain. Old age is big business now in Britain, along with the drugs, pills and other medicines that prolong life for the elderly and also ease pain in the short term for large numbers of other people. Britain is now meant to have a drug problem among both its young and its not-so-young, whether the setting is Notting Hill or Nuneaton, Guildford or Glasgow. But the problem of the recreational drug bought on the street corner, whether it falls into category A or B, is rivalled by that pharmaceutical and drug fraudulence which runs right through both the NHS and private medicine, and which in the process sustains big business profits. This is in part a question of corrupting mental attitudes with both the GP and the patient establishing a collusive understanding that the easiest response to a problem is to prescribe a drug. But the patient's ailment may be more psychological or social rather than straightforwardly physical – and the easy scrawl on the doctor's pad which leaves the patient satisfied in the short term leads to long-term, compounded, problems. A political world which preaches so vigorously against the dangers of state dependency allows, nonetheless, a form of pharmaceutical dependency to spread its tentacles. And since the costs of that dependency are borne mostly by the NHS budget it is the state which meets the bill which maintains the pharmaceutical profit. As a result, prozac and valium have now supplemented the more conventional forms of state benefit. In no other instance is the abject condition of those manipulated by the power elites more obvious, whether those victims are to be found in old people's homes where dozens of expensive but unnecessary medicines surround the bedside, in sink estates where the popping of the pill in the morning helps the victim survive the day, or in the more affluent suburb where neurosis, guilt and fear are sustained by the pharmaceutical means that once promised to be a palliative. In 2003 doctors in England wrote some 19 million prescriptions for Seroxat, one of the anti-depressant drugs collectively termed SSRIs (selective serotonin reuptake inhibitors). Fears about the suicidal consequences of the SSRIs led the UK's Medicines and Healthcare Regulatory Authority to launch an eighteen-month inquiry as a result of which it concluded in December 2004 that the drugs were overprescribed but could still be safely used by adults. But evidence about the link between the taking of these drugs and attempted suicides continues to accumulate. A study in the journal *BMC Medicine* (August 2005) concluded that adults taking GlaxoSmithKline's top-selling drug Seroxat are more likely to attempt suicide. Because of this risk drug regulators in the US and Europe already advise against giving SSRIs such as Seroxat to those under eighteen. GSK claims the study is misleading 'because it focuses on incorrectly selected data'.[82]

But charges of a more directly legal nature are also now current in the world of the drugs' companies because of their collusive relationships with each other, with the doctors who have become their clients and with the NHS which is their biggest single customer. For careers and profits are at stake here, sustained in the first place by that power of connection which is the defining feature of elite-run Britain and then by the insistent monopolistic thrust of the corporate boardroom. Up to a dozen senior executives at six major British drug companies are currently under investigation concerning allegations relating to the operation of a cartel, which cost the NHS more than £100 million, in order to fix the prices of generic drugs and share the profits.[83] Penicillin-based antibiotics and the anticoagulant warfarin used in cases of heart disease and strokes are among the most-prescribed drugs within the NHS. They therefore represent a huge market opportunity, especially if the market can be controlled, and it is the sale of those drugs which is at the centre of the investigation into executives at Kent Pharmaceuticals, Norton Healthcare, the Goldshield Group, Generics UK, Ranbaxy Laboratories UK Unit and Regent-GM Laboratories Ltd. Generics UK and Ranbaxy have agreed to pay compensation of £12 million and £4.5 million, respectively, without admission of liability.

Pressure of costs as well as of supply and demand provide the pharmaceutical companies with their cartel opportunities. In Africa they can conspire to keep costs high because of the immense demand for drugs to treat the 26 million who are infected with the HIV virus across the continent. The situation in Britain is complicated by the fact that the market is dominated by the needs of just one large consumer, the NHS. It was that consumer's cost-cutting demand for cheaper drugs which led to an increasing number of doctors prescribing 'generic' drugs – ones which are no longer covered by the patent which applies for twenty years after the original invention and which enables a company to recoup its R&D costs. Once the twenty years are up other companies can start marketing their own versions of these drugs, and such 'generics' can cost between a half and a tenth of the drug in its patented form. Between 1989 and 2004 the percentage of generics prescribed as a percentage of the total number of written prescriptions shot up form 43 per cent to 79 per cent. The pharmaceuticals could therefore go for bulk sales as a way of keeping up their profits. But even more profits could be made if a restriction of supplies could somehow be applied. And if, as the prosecution case maintains, companies could pretend that their supply of particular drugs was dwindling then higher profits would kick in as pharmacists would no longer be obliged by the NHS to discover the cheapest available forms of those drugs.

## Too Much Choice

The demand for ever more refined, sophisticated and powerful drugs is meant to illustrate the power of the market demand which can force ever greater variety of provision and therefore produce the choice which drives up standards. But in the case of the pharmaceutical trade it is the companies which have often dictated what the market should pay. And in many cases the promotion of ever-greater refinements of existing goods has been the method used by elite financial and business power in order to try and expand a market which has become saturated, jaded and bored. Mobile phone companies, for example, have tried to recover their past rates of growth by promoting text and picture messaging. But the market in such cases may be genuinely inert, rather than eager for greater choices if suitably prodded. The choices offered can be peculiarly futile. Gillette's launch of its two-blade razor in 1971 came seventy years after King Gillette's invention of the original safety razor. The Mach 3 followed with its three blades in 1998, after which the market competitor Wilkinson Sword stepped in with the four-bladed Quattro in 2003. Gillette's predictable reaction was to launch the five-bladed Fusion model in 2005. And since it is so hard to trim facial hair accurately with so many blades the Fusion arrives supplied with a sixth, single, blade attached on the back of the razor for that purpose. Innovation at this level has degenerated into a lazy form of silliness.

Many of the problems of the western economies, from their work-force's obesity to the overcrowding of their roads, arise in fact from having too much choice rather than too little. And even the most innovative of companies can sometimes come up against the barrier of consumer commonsense. In these circumstances a market still has to respond somehow to the fact that it has reached the optimum size, for sheer inactivity is never an option for capital which must always be engaged in some activity or other. As a result the competing businesses will often turn upon each other with the energy of wild animals and seek each others' customers instead of looking for new customers in new directions.

Another response to the banalization which comes with largely satisfied consumer desire is to try and find new and luxurious ways of selling the same old product. The association between a particular brand and a celebrity endorser may not say anything very much about the product itself, but it does seek to establish the product as part of a newly discovered, emotional need and as an image of the desirable self. That kind of branding helps to keep the price up, which is a necessary goal since the celebrity package is a niche luxury good which is not intended for the mass-market. A frustrated market is one which is always trying to find new ways to break out of an enforced stability – and that impatient energy can get angry and even petulant if denied an outlet, which is why it imposes irrelevant forms of competition, as in the example of the consumerist marketing of legal services. A hegemonic system of financial system has already bent the self-interest of the professions to its will. Moreover, that same force has closed down thousands of local shops, built out-of-town supermarkets and thereby killed off active civic, urban and village life right across Britain. As a result areas which were once scenes of commercial activity either become dormitory suburbs (if the scenery is pretty) or, in the case of decayed industrial areas, they degenerate into the desolation of empty streets with boarded-up shops. Town centres in Britain acquire an eerie uniformity of appearance as the big chain stores move in, aided in most cases by local councils bent on re-development. Initial choice then collapses into homogeneity and, even in prosperous towns, the effect is economically destructive since the money spent in the stores ends up in corporate profit rather than circulating in the local economy

## The Methods of Corporate Power

The takeover and the merger which supply work at hundreds of pounds per hourly fee for the banker, the accountant and solicitor are the basis of British business and financial elite activity. Their consequence is often the loss of jobs in order to convince the City of the new company's profitability. Norwich Union is now called Aviva since pompous neo-Latinity is one of the methods used by corporate life when it tries to dignify itself in a rebranded existence. In March 2005 it took over RAC, the land car breakdown service which was bought by Lex in 1999 (before that company then re-christened itself RAC). After Aviva's takeover its general insurance chief executive, Patrick Snowball, applied the Tesco model to his ambitions: 'Look at Tesco and Asda five years ago when they decided to move into clothing. Sainsbury's didn't and look what happened . . . We want to become the Tesco of the insurance sector.'[84] It cost Aviva £1.1 billion to make its acquisition and part of the price to be paid in order to meet the £800 million cut in costs would be the loss of more than 1,700 jobs. Cost-cutting mergers affect the newly managerialized and incentivized world of the unions as well. Amicus, the GMB and the Transport and General Workers' Union (T and G) aim to merge by January 2007. The justification for the creation of such a mega-union is typically corporate: greater efficiency and administrative smooth-ness as well as the need to acquire increased investment. For Tony Woodley,[85] the T and G leader, there is an obvious model to follow: 'trade unionism, like capitalism, should know no borders.'[86] His union is therefore working closely with the US service sector union, the Service Employees International Union (SEIU). But following the methods of corporate power will end in similar results: the merger of offices and job losses in the regions.

The pressure from established and larger firms means that the clever and the genuinely innovative become vulnerable to new forms of established corporate hunger. Even that iconic British company, Lastminute.com, the online travel business, has had to concede that it lacks the global presence needed for growth. In May 2005 it accepted a £577 million takeover by Sabre Holdings, the owner of the US rival firm Travelocity. Lastminute.com itself grew through taking over its rivals but has now become part of a multi-billion-dollar conglomerate.[87] The early 2000s boom in internet businesses was a classic instance of the market 'bubble', consisting as it did of the clever, and often well connected, creating companies which were of the moment and endowed with a seemingly irresistible chic. This was a metropolitan and City moment which grew into short-lived prosperity on the basis of rumour, gossip and the refulgent allure of the fashion-ably latest craze. On 14 March 2000 Lastminute.com listed on the London Stock Exchange at 380p per share and soared to 555p within minutes as retail investors piled in. The business, which had hardly any revenues and was just nineteen months old at the time, was then valued at £835 million. Five years later the company had amassed pre-tax losses of £250 million and never regained those early share price heights. In this – as in so many other forms of e-commerce businesses – investors have wreaked revenge on the companies and withdrawn confidence, because their expectations were not met. But the expecta-tions were foolish to begin with. It is a cyclically constant truth of market capitalism that early high returns encourage the investor to expect a continuation of those returns for many years ahead. And it is an equally persistent truth that the high returns mean that capital will flow into the sector and that returns will then be reduced because of this increased competition.

The internet is still the fastest-growing medium for advertising in the UK, accounting as it does for almost 5 per cent of spending. Companies with an eye for the future, such as Tesco, adapted quickly to the new internetery. As a result the Tesco website, which was launched in 1999, is now the world's most popular online grocer with 120,000 orders a week. The story of the dotcom 'bubble' and of e-commerce generally is a familiar one: the leviathan-like power of established companies means that, as long as they can adapt and learn, they can use their market power to crush the minnows while absorbing new practices into their corporate structure. Even Tesco.com's turnover (at £307 million in 2004–5) is only a little more than 2 per cent of the company's total turnover.[88] Private equity money will still invest in e-commerce businesses, but by and large only if those businesses are defined as deriving a major percentage of their sales from the internet or from support internet services. E-commerce which trades solely or principally online is no longer an attractive investment option. With the fading away of the original avant-garde the elite corporate structure remains in place, and has been renewed by its ability to exploit new ideas in order to support power which has already consolidated itself.

Britain's biggest online businesses therefore are not innovative start-up companies but the conventional members of the FTSE 100, especially in the retail, marketing and travel business (especially airline travel). Gambling has been given a huge boost by the web. By 2005 William Hill's internet business was contributing about £52 million of annual profit, which amounted to almost a quarter of the group's total profit.[89] Many of these profits came from new gamblers who could play in the privacy of their own homes rather than having to go to a betting shop. Serious and regular gambling in Britain is for the most part a working-class habit, apart from the small numbers of the rich who are attracted to the idea of gambling in a private club like Aspinall's where they can be flattered into a display of aristocratic pretension by profligacy at baccarat and poker. The great mass of those in between have until now resisted gambling's game of chance, but the internet is neither off-puttingly grand nor touched by the shabbiness of the corner bookie shop with its slips on the floor. It is the privacy of internet gambling which makes it so appealing and so suitable a mechanism for the communication and expression of British hypocrisy's furtive pleasures.

## The Defence of the Nation

Britain's defence industry is a vast and thriving sector which has been particularly well serviced by the financial and business elites. Intimate association with governments in terms of both contracts and of personnel characterizes the industry. The respectability of the political and administrative elites dictates that they should make the usual noises about the need to enhance deterrence through arms control agreements. When it comes to nuclear weapons, the elite prides itself on 'risk management', while going through charades of consultation on some aspects of that issue. The governmental Committee on Radioactive Waste Management (CoRWM), established in 2003, wasted over a year discussing increasingly impractical ways of disposing of Britain's 470,000 $M^3$ of nuclear waste (the equivalent of five times the capacity of the interior of the Albert Hall). Eventually, it settled on the rather obvious options of either burying the waste deep underground or storing it in purpose-built facilities above ground. But before signing off some members thought that shipping the waste to Antarctica would be a neat notion while others were keen on firing the spent fuel towards the Sun. Much of the heat of the talk was generated by that facade of 'public consultation' which is so often used as an excuse for expert–elite delay or as a way of keeping the real public interest at bay. But an over-excited immersion in the H.G. Wells school of science fiction is not the real reason for the committee's wilder ideas and prevarication. Four of the committee's members are paid consultants for companies that have won contracts from the committee itself.[90]

Britain is the seventeenth-century home of modern Europe's first scientific and Newtonian revolution. The Royal Society was incorporated in 1662 when Charles II granted it a royal charter despite the puritan and parliamentarian leanings of many of its members during the years of the preceding Commonwealth.[91] The crown gave the Society its moral support rather than any money but at least the royal connection meant that the country's scientific elite could once again become respectable and associate itself with metropolitan and political power. From Newton onwards British science has needed to cultivate the power elites in order to get the money and the patronage which sustains its research. The two world wars were a particularly good opportunity to create a certain synergy between the boffin and the political elites. R.V. Jones' long and distinguished career in electronics and physics started in the Air Ministry of the 1930s and then benefited from Churchillian patronage as he moved into the world of war-time intelligence where he showed his flair in the application of original science to practical problems such as the bending of radar beams. The Cambridge mathematician Alan Turing, who also worked in White-hall during the Second World War, developed a prototype modern computer in order to speed up the decoding of communications. These were the workings of true scientific genius which came to fruition because of elite patronage and the urgency of war. But science in Britain is now touched and shaped by the two most powerful forces in the making of the power elites: the lure of money and the pull of celebrity. Lord Winston (Professor Robert Winston),[92] having been elevated by a television career as a fertility doctor, is therefore happy to advertise the benefits of milk[93] while Professor Susan Greenfield, Director of the Royal Institution, is available to give talks to City institutions.

Sometimes Britain's power elites will declare themselves to be alarmed by the dangers of biological weapons, since biological knowl-edge is advancing so rapidly and the opportunities for exploiting the biological weapons based on that knowledge grow at an equal pace. The perils are compounded by the fact that the biological materials which can be used for lethal intentions are often difficult to distinguish from the innocent forms of such material. Opportunities then arise for the ventilation of some conventionally safe disapproval of the Amer-ican government's refusal to endorse any verification arrangements which might put a degree of muscle on the 1972 International Convention which has banned biological weapons. But, by dismissing these arrangements as being both costly and ineffective, America's government at least displays a frank self-interest which contrasts with the British elite hypocrisy which profits from the defence industry while at the same time preaching about the dangers of a world destabilized by military means.[94] The early twenty-first century is the age of the political and diplomatic breakdown of those interna-tional organizations such as the European Union and the United Nations which were created in the second half of the twentieth century.[95] A balance of power – or of terror – between NATO and the Warsaw Pact had in fact been basic to the existence and comparative success of such organizations, but the collapse of one force within that balance has left one country, the USA, exposed as the sole dominant power in world affairs. In the exercise of that power, it is able to subject international organizations to a pitiless scrutiny and condemnation of their waste, fraud and bureaucracy, features which have characterized them intermittently from the beginning of their existence but which a newly energized US government can now devote more time to attacking. The logic of the political market within the international domain is the same as that of the economic market: a dominant force will always try to assert monopoly and hegemony. The US version of international order is therefore determined by the need to ensure the market access of American corporations.[96]

The British administrative and political power elites, although so much a part of this project, still find it awkward to have to confront this truth publicly, which is why it is easier to make a fuss about biological weapons than expose the subjection, through financial and business operations, of British defence interests to American ones. Alarm about biological weapons is of course one useful element in that climate of fear whose calculated uncertainties justify the war on an unspecified 'terror'. But it also deflects attention from the depth of the elite involvement in something quite as destabilizing: the provision of hardware technology and informational systems – not just to the USA but to almost any state with an open cheque book. Missile systems, tanks, helicopters and aircraft, along with their associated kit and technology, institutionalize the military complex and make it fundamental to the power elite's operation. What could typify more adequately the defence industry's ability to present itself as a part of elite respectability than the fact that Michael Portillo,[97] a former Defence Secretary, should be a non-executive director of BAE Systems, in this context a position thought quite compatible with a reputation for social liberalism? What it calls 'security' has always been at the heart of the British state's operations both at home and abroad. But security here is not the same thing as the safety of its citizens. It is the security of long-established structures of power and privilege which is really at stake here, along with the need to protect those structures from attack. As a result the authority of the business and financial elites who serve the defence sector is equivalent to the authority of the state itself, and security is the noun which covers the interests of both. Basic to these ambitions is the work of the intelligence agencies, which have a curiously client-like attitude towards the government they serve as almost semi-autonomous organizations. They therefore provide government with the information they think government wishes to obtain, as in the readiness to claim that weapons of mass destruction, fired from Iraq, could arrive on British soil in forty-five minutes. But 'security' does not only consist of MI5 and MI6. The relationships between government and private sector businesses which supply armaments and the technology of surveillance systems are more straightforwardly commercial, and they are supplemented by the private businesses which employ former army officers and intelligence officials in order to enhance the intelligence-gathering which will expand their foreign market opportunities.

An aura of the inevitable surrounds the expansion of popular psychology, along with all its manipulative assertions of the obvious, straight into the heart of the defence industry's opportunism in these markets. Psychological warfare services, known as 'psyops' to the military, was one of the great beneficiaries of the first Gulf War since it claimed responsibility for the surrender of some 90,000 troops. Appeals to subliminal fears, hopes and desires acquired a commercial currency very early in the history of modern twentieth-century psychology. Madison Avenue advertising executives, in particular, were quick to exploit the business potential of Jung's discovery that certain archetypes and symbols appealed strongly to certain kinds of human character. If the mind could, by the power of suggestion, be persuaded to associate certain chosen symbols and archetypes with certain advertised products then sales would rocket as a result of the newly asserted personal relationship between a human being and a commodity. This insight marched onwards, and with consummate ease, from the marketing of goods to the marketing of politicians in the second half of the twentieth century. It therefore seems only natural that a political communications consultancy, Strategic Communications Laboratories, should have now launched itself as the first private company to provide 'psyops' to the military. As its chief executive Nigel Oakes has pointed out in a queasy combination of frankness with hypocrisy: 'We used to be in the business of mindbending for political purposes, but now we are in the business of saving lives.'[98]

The breakdown of international order, globalized crime and the enfeebled state also lead to opportunities for Britain's Group 4 Securicor (G4S) which is now the world's second largest security company with its 340,000 staff and 120,000 customers of various kinds spread across 100 countries.[99] Providing forms of protection –

especially for companies – is a buoyant business for an organization with a £3.8 billion turnover. Global Risk, G4S's private security business, now works in Kosovo and will soon be at work in South Korea and in Afghanistan as well. The troops of G4S's armed guards offer an insight into what it must have been like to live in the era before the Peace of Westphalia (1648) concluded Europe's Thirty Years War and established the idea of the modern state with its sovereign authority inside its own boundaries, so ending the age of the mercenary army with its exclusive loyalty to the general who commanded it and to the purse that paid for it.[100] Today's expanding security business supplies the modern armed guards with their wages and, just like the great mercenary armies of the past, it needs to maintain discipline within the ranks. Wackenhut, the group's biggest US subsidiary, is threatened by the insurgents of the SEIU, who claim that the company is set to lose some $500 million in government contracts. It is fortunate therefore that company and business law is one aspect of state-run security which remains well in place since Wackenhut is now taking the union to court in order to restrain its ability to make such embarrassing claims. Meanwhile, back at home, G4S looks forward to profiting from 'justice services', an ennobling phrase used to describe electronic tags and the deportation of failed asylum seekers.

Schoolboyish glee about gadgetry can still cling to the hardware bought and used by the power elites. Q was the boffin that James Bond went to when he wanted the best and latest products for his spying kitbag, and that is the reason why the technology company QinetiQ is so called. Bond's character was the product of, and appealed to, an establishment imagination which knew that Britain in the 1950s was on the wane as a world power and which therefore sought refuge in a fantasy version of the gentleman cad of the past.[101] But no such sad escapism is detectable in the operations of the powerful and successful QinetiQ, a company which illustrates the resilience and the adaptability of the British power elites.[102] The company, which was originally part of the research arm of the Ministry of Defence (MoD), was launched as a firm in 2001 and three investment banks, Merrill Lynch, Credit Suisse First Boston, and JP Morgan, prepared a £1 billion stock market flotation of the 51 per cent of the business which is presently owned by the MoD. A time when governments with money to spare, especially that of the USA, are spending more money on their defence agencies is obviously a good time to go for a flotation. Global orders in the defence and aerospace businesses rose by 28 per cent in 2004, and QinetiQ's reported pre-tax profits in the summer of 2005 had grown from £47.6 million to £82.3 million. Its technology can have civil uses as well as military ones, as in the case of the millimetre-wave camera which was originally used to help soldiers see in the dark and is now being developed by civil airports security. But in all its operations QinetiQ shows the penetration of the financial and business elites into what was once supposed to be a government business, as well as the readiness of the erstwhile administrative elite to yield to that new potent force.

Two-thirds of QinetiQ's work comes from the MoD and just one of its contracts from that source is worth £5.5 billion. As a result of this comparatively narrow business base it is natural that the company should need its connections with the administrative elite, both past and present. Dame Pauline Neville-Jones, the former diplomat, has therefore served as the company's executive chairman and she has now been replaced by Sir John Chisholm, a former BP executive. But it is an American company, and one with significant US administration contacts, which is the second most important component within QinetiQ's corporate structure. The US private equity firm, the Carlyle Group, has sustained John Major in his new, post-prime ministerial business career, largely as a result of his friendship with George Bush senior who also works for the company. In December 2002 the group acquired another subordinate British interest when it took a 33.8 per cent holding in QinetiQ for £42 million. If the company can be floated for £1 billion that will then mean the Carlyle Group making a killing of £296 million. There have also been other US dimensions to QinetiQ's operations, for the US government is the company's second largest customer: in the summer of 2005 it acquired (for £163 million) Apogen, the company which provides information technology to the federal government and which is one of the top ten contractors for the United States Department of Homeland Security. This follows earlier acquisitions in 2004 of Westar Defense and of Aerospace, a 'systems integration' business. A company, therefore, which comprises the British government's own defence research laboratories, has become involved, and is set to become increasingly involved, in the network of US military technology which operates at a governmental level.

But that incorporation of political power into business activity, with all its consequent shifts of flowing capital, operates on British as well as on US soil. The contract to rebuild the docks which will refit nuclear-powered submarines at Devonport, Plymouth, is the largest nuclear construction project in Europe in recent times. The contract was worth an estimated £576 million at the time when it was awarded by the MoD in 1997 to DML, a company partly owned by Halliburton, the American company formerly run by the current US Vice-President Dick Cheney.[103] This was a political decision made despite all the civil service objections that the company had a chequered history in controlling costs. These fears proved to be well founded, since by 2002 the National Audit Office discovered that the costs had increased to £933 million. Perhaps when the ally calls, and especially when the ally is a business, a political and a military partner, then scruples about British public money can seem just penny-pinching. Ever since America's entry into the Second World War in December 1941 its foreign policy interests have absorbed those of Britain.[104] Which is why the business needs and the business expression of that policy leads to the prejudice in favour of an American company, despite evidence of that company's limitations.

## Private Finance Initiatives

The operation of the PFI has been the most remarkable single instance of the way in which the operations of government, and its claims to probity, neutrality and efficiency, have been undermined by the workings of the business and financial elites.[105] Pioneered by a Conservative government, and then enthusiastically adopted by New Labour, PFI involves the government entering into partnership with private enterprise at a contractual level. Instead of government bothering to build schools, hospitals and other public buildings itself, PFI is an instrument which allows privately owned consortia to finance these projects. The government then undertakes to pay back the money involved at appropriate rates of interest over the next twenty or thirty years. In a remarkable bargain for private business these consortia are then allowed to keep the buildings at the end of that period. The cliché of 'partnership' is then deployed to describe a relationship which is characterized by manipulative greed on the part of the consortia and either a supine innocence born out of ignorance or a conniving attitude bred out of self-interest on the part of officials and politicians.

The Property Services Agency had been the body which ran, bought and sold government buildings while also being answerable to ministers. After its privatization in 1994 it became the very profitable

Building and Property Group, and its success led to the idea that PFI could be extended not just to the construction of new buildings but also to the ownership and management of existing ones. 'Prime Project', the programme launched by the government in 1998, therefore proposed to sell all Britain's social service buildings to the Trillium consortium (now part of Land Securities). The power of connection and friendship was well illustrated in that proposal since the American investment bank Goldman Sachs formed part of the Trillium consortium. Gavyn Davies,[106] then the chairman of the board of governors of the BBC, was a former partner of the bank and his wife Sue Nye was a Treasury adviser to Gordon Brown. The sale to Trillium brought £315 million to the government which, duly emboldened, then prepared to sell the hundreds of buildings owned and run by the Inland Revenue and the Customs and Excise.

A coterie group organized the sale and included two officials with a notable track record in such matters. Sir Nicholas Montagu,[107] chairman of the Inland Revenue, had been a key and enthusiastic advocate of the setting up of Railtrack in his previous job at the Department of Transport and Steve Robson had argued for the same policy from his berth at the Treasury. Even while Britain's railway system was showing the effects, through deaths and injury, of the botched rail privatization two of its leading architects were not only still in place but advancing towards another mess. A smart banker is always a necessary figure in these British elite games; the chairman of Customs and Excise, Richard Broadbent, had worked for Schroders in a previous incarnation. In August 2000 therefore the announcement was made that the buildings would be sold to Mapeley Ltd, a British company. But it emerged only much later that its parent company, Mapeley UK Co. Ltd, was registered in the tax haven of the British Virgin Islands from where it was then moved to Bermuda, where the US tax authorities are not allowed access to company accounts. Mapeley Holding Co. Ltd, also based in Bermuda, owns 85 per cent of that company's shares and that holding company in turn is owned in part by Soros Real Estate Investors CV, a company formed in Holland and behind whom stands the figure of that eminent financier George Soros. It then emerged that it was Mapeley Steps Ltd, based in Bermuda, which received most of the rents paid by the Inland Revenue and the Customs for the buildings they had once owned. Both organizations had sold their buildings to a company in a tax haven.

In 2001 the company started to complain about its rate of return on the contracts. Were the contracts to collapse the public assets and the buildings once owned by the Revenue and Customs would have then become the property of Mapeley's bankers. PFI – a system which is designed to transfer risk from the public to the private sector – had now exposed two government organizations to very high risk. The company therefore received a formal assurance from the government that it would receive the extra money needed to save it. But even after that guarantee it remained the case that it was the impact of market conditions on the stock and the property markets which determined the future of what were once government-owned buildings.

The episode and its failures and confusions show in some instances a failure to keep control of the transactions. Sir Nicholas Montagu, under questioning by a parliamentary sub-committee, said that he thought the buildings sold would revert to the government in the event of Mapeley collapsing as a company, a surprising ignorance on the part of a chairman of the Inland Revenue, since the contractual obligations were quite clearly owed to the banks. But he was still able to walk away from the episode, displaying as he did that elite self-esteem which can cover up most of its tracks. Coming up to his retirement, he declared himself ready and available for further adventures: 'If a university would take me on as its vice-chancellor for three or four years or if there were a big charity that thought I had something to offer, I'd be very happy to do that.'[108]

Elite survival often requires that kind of adroit management of expectations. But the cause of that survival is also helped by the fact that government has now become more complicated as civil servants work side by side with private sector personnel engaged on contracts. The result is a complicated structure of organizations whose membership can overlap with each other. This creates a confused blurring of the boundaries between public and private, and that obscurity brings its own forms of career opportunity for the business and financial elites. Peter Gershon,[109] former managing director of the struggling Marconi defence and electronics company, was a natural choice, given the Alice in Wonderland quality of such appointments, to report to government on the reforms required by that central mystery – the machinery of British government. He recommended the establishment of a new Office of Government Commerce and, by happy coincidence, he became chairman of that body. At the same time the Treasury decided that a new 'private sector-led body' was needed to improve investment from private sources in the UK's public services. This organization (Partnerships UK or PUK) was one of those 'task forces' created in the late 1990s in order to replace the much-abused quangos. But, stuffed full of businessmen, they turned out to be quangos by any other name and smelling quite as strongly of corporate odour. Although privatized in 2001, PUK retained its public sector interests and it was its representatives who helped both to negotiate Mapeley's orginal contract and then the subsequent bailout a few months later.

## Hedging One's Bets

The readiness of the Revenue and of Customs and Excise to accept the tax avoidance games of the international business world passed without much attention despite the investigative energy of the late Paul Foot. But the takeover of another British institution, Manchester United Football Club, by the American businessman Malcolm Glazer, and its subsequent delisting as a public company, was a different matter.[110] By the early twenty-first century football had become Britain's major entertainment industry, for the business success traded on an obsessive interest in the stars' off-pitch activities as well as on their performances on the field. This was a blend of cabaret and old-style music hall with prime-time TV soap performances. In the traditional manner of old-style British group loyalty, the idea that a football club somehow 'belonged' to its fans was an important part of the enthusiasm. That was a hangover from the days when the receipts at the gates paid the team's wages and constituted a fairly transparent transfer of money. But the means that secured the glory of some forms of celebrity football also turned the game into a pawn in the anonymous world of finance and all the deliciously winding ways of its financial instruments. The entertainment attractions of individual footballers – even when (as in the case of David Beckham) they were overvalued players – led to television money and corporate sponsorship. Once some of the clubs became public limited companies they were vulnerable to takeovers. Michael Glazer simply benefited from a process of commercialization which had been authorized by Manchester United itself when it decided to become a plc, as did those shareholders (J.P. McManus and John Magnier) who decided to sell their shares in order give Glazier the controlling interest he needed in order to delist the company. The new owner first borrowed money in order to buy the club for £540 million and then, when he had enough shares to delist the company from the Stock Exchange, transferred the debt to the club. As a result, a club with average annual profits of £27 million became one saddled with £540 million of debt.

The Glazer move exposed the impotent sentimentality of sporting spectators in the face of the march of capital power on to the pitch. Silvio Berlusconi had achieved just such a coup when he bought Milan in 1986 and the Russian financial oligarch Roman Abramovich completed a similar process when he bought Chelsea in 2003. But Glazer's case was different since he had taken out loans in order to finance the takeover. The £790 million needed to buy the necessary 75 per cent of shares in order to take the club private was only one-third cash and shares; £275 million was raised by issuing preference shares to City funds and £265 million was borrowed, mostly from the US investment bank JP Morgan. That sum was secured against the club's assets, most notably the stadium itself at Old Trafford. Manchester United, therefore, by being delisted and becoming part of a private fiefdom, was not just parting company from the idea of the public limited company, it was also now entirely separate from the European business model followed by football clubs such as Barcelona, Real Madrid and Bayern Munich, in which the society is a non-profit-making organization and is answerable to the members who elect a president to run the club's affairs. The Glazer move, though so much condemned, was simply the latest application of the principle of capital and of that financial reality which had long been in charge of British football. Manchester United was already a vehicle for rich men to make money, including the club's players, none of whom had any emotional attachment to the club. This was a hot market run by cold calculation in the interests of all parties, buyers as well as sellers.

The Glazer takeover was partly financed by hedge fund managers.[111] And it is the stylish, intelligent, rapacity of the hedge funds which has made them the latest and coolest embodiment of City success. These are highly opportunistic investment companies that keep their assets offshore, are lightly regulated and earn their title because they are meant to hedge their bets. They can also borrow, using their leverage in order to push up their profits. They are highly incentivized, taking in commission, for instance, 2 per cent of the funds under management as well as up to 20 per cent or more of profits over and beyond a certain rate of return (if the chosen investments perform well). And since earnings are a function of the percentage, and because these are people who have billions of pounds under their management, there are some top hedge fund managers who receive an annual partnership share in excess of £10 million as their income. Most do not operate geographically within the City, being the products of a deregulated world of financial services whose princes of capital do not need to be tied within the old confines. Their usual habitat is Mayfair where, therefore, new ways of making money can be pursued behind the walls of the houses built for those eighteenth-century aristocrats who in their own time benefited from the capital expansiveness of the London money markets. This is a district where novel forms of alert acquisitiveness have always mingled with old associations.[112] The names of surrounding squares and streets – Eaton and Grosvenor, Eccleston and Belgrave, Kinnerton, Chester, Churton and Halkin – recall the rural origins of the estate developers who first of all urged, and then benefited from, fashionable London society's decision to move west. Perhaps there was a fugitive moment of arcadian nostalgia that surrounded the naming of those areas, but it was the investment in London land and property, along with involvement in London finance, politics and fashion, which governed the lives of those who lived in the houses built by the Grosvenor estate. The same ritual bowing to the remote locality while getting stuck into serious, local, money-making was true also of the original Portland estate in Marylebone and the naming of its development areas – Harley and Wimpole, Holles, Welbeck and Vere. A few hedge fund managers may plough their wealth back into English land, but behind these facades today, as in the eighteenth century, the financial elites are making their money out of money itself.

For one of these hedge fund managers, the young, driven and clever Hugh Hendry, his work 'is about emotional intelligence'[113] and his own new fund will be called Eclatica, with the second 'e' spelled backwards in a modish attempt at originality. Bucking the market trend and being agreeably and naughtily counter-suggestible is a quality prized among the hedge funds which see themselves as original thinkers going against the mainstream. That is partly why they do not operate within the City walls and, in a further spin on the spirit of the times, Hendry's new firm will make its pitch for originality by moving away from Mayfair to Notting Hill. 'We are,' he says, 'remote by design . . . I model myself as a private investor rather than an institutional investor.' This remoteness means that the hedge funds are seen as unaccountable, short-term and opaque but the fact that their managers do not need any PR to bolster them is a sign of genuine power. Representatives of the CBI and of the IoD will still appear on time in order to do their dutiful little interviews as if the post-war world, in which their views mattered, remained in place. But those organizations represent hardly anyone except their own officials any longer. Business balance sheets certainly show that power can come from publicity. Large and successful companies which are associated with the personalities of those who lead them – as in the case of Richard Branson at Virgin – require that the leader should maintain his public profile. But hedge fund managers do not need to make themselves available for interview nor need they indulge in any corporate stunts in order to carry on making their money. They operate in a world which is detached from the public and whose inhabitants are more or less insulated from any public display of envy. Their right to exist is unquestioned and even, to all intents and purposes, unquestionable while Britain's allegedly disrespectful and uncontrollable media retain a disciplined silence about the hedge funds and the offshore financial economy in which they operate.

The rise of the hedge funds to public notice occurred in 1992 when George Soros' hedge fund bet heavily against the pound and profited at the expense of tax-payers as the Major government squandered billions in a futile attempt at keeping sterling within the ERM. Suddenly hedge fund managers became the people to watch and it was an adroit calculation on Peter Mandelson's part to introduce Tony Blair to a few representatives of that world during the opposition years of the mid-1990s.[114] Labour's new leader required instruction about what mattered most in the financial culture of the newly burgeoning British economy. These funds now manage about £543 billion, which is just 3–4 per cent of the entire global equity market. But their real power comes from their readiness to force the pace for change as well as sometimes to block changes, as in the case of the two hedge funds (TCI and Atticus) who revolted over the Deutsche Börse bid for the London Stock Exchange, a move which led to the Börse chief executive, Werner Seifert, being forced out. This contrasts with the more passive approach of the more traditional fund institutions. Having gained a taste for activism in one direction, some hedge fund managers see the attractions of political games.[115] Michael Brown, who runs a hedge fund called Fifth Avenue Partner, which is based in Mayfair, has given £2 million to the Liberal Democrat Party (a

213

donation which subsequently came under investigation from the Electoral Commission), while Paul Marshall of Marshall Wace, which has some £10 billion under management, has given £1 million to the LibDem think tank, the Centre for Reform. Such are the latest amusements which have become available to the financial elite. A think tank, and perhaps especially a minority party's think tank, is hardly a serious political instrument. But it may be an agreeable vanity present to oneself – something to set by the side of the house in Cornwall (now a favoured financial elite location for the country home) and the one in Chester Square.

Because of the kind of financial instruments which are now available, hedge funds can operate without any transparency. They prefer, for example, to trade in contracts for difference (CFDs), and are therefore able to avoid stamp duty. But the real advantage is that CFDs carry no disclosure obligations, and a company which wants to acquire an interest in a business secretively can therefore use a hedge fund's services in order to achieve that end. But that dislike of disclosure does not just exist among the hedge funds themselves. Investment banks earn fees as a result of dealing with hedge funds, and will arrange the meetings between their corporate clients and hedge fund managers in the knowledge that what the funds really want is the kind of inside information which is basic to their business. An economy like that of Britain, which now trades to such an extent on debt and borrowing, has become extremely exposed to the activities of hedge funds as they move in to replace the traditional banks in the business of managing and structuring loans.[116] As a result of changes in loan documentation, banks now have more freedom to get rid of a debt which has become troublesome. Moreover, loan agreements no longer need the borrower's consent in order to sell the loan on. The old relationships of clubby bankers and its agreements which were the basis of gentlemanly capitalism have broken down. Some of the new debtholders may indeed have an interest in forcing a company into insolvency, and loans bought secretly by a company's competitors mean that they can gain access to secret information available only to creditors. Hedge funds can also build a blocking stake by making only a small investment in debt quite far down the structure of capital in a business. Even that small investment will give them a powerful influence over a company and they can profit from its distress if that suits the hedge fund's purposes. The immense fragmentation of European law means that the companies which are restructuring their debts and dealing with different creditors are a tremendous market opportunity for the hedge funds. When, for example, the travel company My Travel restructured in 2004 there were seventy-five different institutions that held the debt at the end of the process. But it is exactly that degree of confusion and fragmentation which suits the hedge funds' purposes as they search for the information, the opportunities and the deals that may lie within the occlusion of an often indecent obscurity.

## The Spoils of Victory

Guiltlessly rapacious and mentally pugnacious, Britain's financial and business elites at least display the virtue of candour about their ultimate goals: the making of money for themselves and the need to sustain that never-ending forward push of capital which must always find new worlds to conquer and colonize. The frankness of that avowal can also be more public than ever before since the City has won all the necessary battles for command and control. It now absorbs and directs the aims of all the other power elites and thereby makes those elites subordinate to its own interests. But the elites of finance and of business also know, as did their predecessors in the same game, that secrecy still has to be maintained and confidentiality cultivated when it is a question of the techniques to be adopted, the information required and the strategies pursued as they travel on the way to achieving their final goals. Both the short-term ambushes and the longer-term campaigns require a calculating intelligence, cool nerves and the ability to maintain an enigmatic facade about intentions. In order to realize those intentions, every tradition and every established association, whether enjoyed between individuals or between institutions, has to be subordinated to the unyielding lucidity of market logic. The merchant bank of Cazenove, brokers to the Queen, was an institution whose reputation rivalled that of the City itself and in 2004 it was providing advice to forty-three of the companies in the FTSE 100. But at the end of that same year it announced a merger with the US banking group JP Morgan, as a result of which twelve months later it was advising only thirty-eight such companies.[117] As a corporate broker, Cazenove's job was to represent the interests of its client companies on the stock market, finding out the views of investors and reporting back. But clients such as Marks and Spencer, a company it had represented for over twenty years, made a judgement that the merger with the US bank meant that Cazenove was no longer an independent adviser, and therefore they left.

It is this absence of cloying sentiment and freedom from irritable conscience which gives the City its particular flavour, and which also explains the quality of its supremacy. A particular temperament has now created the dominant circumstances of an age which it can truly call its own and in whose pleasures it can therefore exult. And the spectacle of the indulgence which accompanies the trappings of power exudes a quality which is both old and new. Britons nostalgic for empire need only visit the City bars on a Thursday night to see the modern-day successors of Clive of India at play. As the drink begins to speak and the flesh turns even pinker, the historical imagination can easily reveal to the mind's eye the eighteenth-century quality of the scene once it has stripped these torsos of their Jermyn Street shirts and then dressed them in the appropriate military tunics. For just like the army of the East India Company this is a grand band of robbers who rejoice in wresting advantage from a world which lies supine beneath their conquering and mercenary feet. Clive and his men won battles because of their hard work and talent, qualities which are also evident in the successes of these latter-day warriors. The officer class certainly lends some tone to the proceedings, but both then and now there has been a reasonably ecumenical quality to the recruitment and it would not do to inquire too closely into the antecedents of some of the more successful brigands here displayed. Animal spirits acquire tangible form, and assertive voices fill the air, for the awed competitors and the bloodily beaten have long since left the scene of battle. There is no one left who would dare deny these celebrants the right to divide the spoils of victory among themselves. With the departure of the last reveller a cold City breeze shafts its way down Threadneedle Street and the eighteenth-century scene dissolves leaving in its wake the knowledge that brigandage in Britain still lives. Whether it is siphoning off the profits in pension schemes through management fees, landing the unwary with vertiginous insurance liabilities, or just betting on the idiocy of humanity, the City of London is the most achingly modern and the most frighteningly efficient imperial institution left out there, roaming in the wild and seeking whom it may devour.

# Conclusion: How Did
# They Get Away with It?

This book has described how and why the social grouping known as the power elites, existing and multiplying in their various political, professional, financial and business forms, were able to increase their authority by stages during the late twentieth century so that they have now grown to constitute the highly effective and seemingly permanent governing class of early twenty-first-century Britain. This has been a period of elite consolidation for which there is no parallel in the country's history. As a result, the many different kinds of power which historically in Britain have existed in a scattered and diffuse form have now been allowed to organize themselves in a far more concentrated way than was the case in the past. In looking at this process, evident connections have emerged between the different kinds of power which are available to those who wish to exercise command and enforce allegiance. For Britain's power elites illustrate the truth that when it comes to the means by which human kind is governed and influenced: 'Everything is connected to everything else.'[1]

## The Pyramid of Power

In the case of British power the connections combine to form the shape of a pyramid. A broad base consists of a Parliament which is both decayed and decadent, an executive layer of government which is both haughty and incompetent and a professional class which has been subverted by a managerialism which is bland in tone but potent in its effects. The personnel who pursue their power careers along this base line are, as we have seen, interconnected in terms of ambitions entertained, verbiage mouthed and interests pursued. They can still inflict their will on their own particular worlds in order to pursue their own advantage, get their jobs and enjoy the power which has been allocated to them. But those decisions, choices and ambitions are subject to a mightier constraining force and none of these characters are as free as they think. For above this base and rising to an eminent apex of influence and power stand the business and financial elites whose power now extends in a way which seems so obvious and so matter-of-fact that it is no longer seen as the remarkable and novel thing it truly is.

Around this pyramid, the fluttering forms of broadcasters, journalists, writers and commentators of various stripe are detectable as the intelligentsia's collective mind swoops down on its occasional forays in order to inspect this carcase of a country.[2] Noises varying between the holy, self-indulgent glee of liberal sanctimony and the tribal triumphalism of conservative group-thought emerge from these coroners' inquests. But since this intelligentsia is itself so deeply implicated in the degradation its ability to understand and judge, as well as its inclination to do so, is affected and compromised. For a largely visual and celebrity culture has dictated a tyrannous alternative. When it comes to a communication with power at any level in Britain today you can either see or be seen, and a decision in favour of being seen and of therefore being part of the story of connection and influence obscures many an illuminating view, closes down some of the best avenues of investigation and offers too many of the comforting associations that power will offer both its votaries and its critics. Rather like the police force, therefore, the dominant concern of this class is to keep the peace and maintain order.

Plots, stratagems and campaigns were clearly necessary in order to effect these power changes. But this was not a conventional conspiracy involving desperadoes getting ready to close down the airports and declaring the formation of a provisional government at a hastily convened press conference. No formal coup d'état of any kind was necessary in order to institute these new power arrangements which both reflected and created such profound changes in British life and British thought. Tanks were not observed in the streets at dawn, broadcasting channels were able to maintain their usual levels of soothing service and there was, above all, no run on the pound sterling. As so often in the history of Britain's shifts of power, therefore, a certain discretion has been observed along with much continuity of form and appearance. There have been episodic moments of baffled intuition that something extraordinary has taken place, but no feats of detection have followed those fugitive deliverances. Sermons preaching the need for serious scrutiny have been delivered without appreciating that a mocking tone is often the best, and sometimes the only, way of taking the wind out of the pompously puffed-up sails of the power elites as they pursue their inexorable advance.[3] Overwhelmingly, however, this takeover has been effected with remarkably little fuss. A revolution will often happen because of tendencies, mental habits and opportunities which have been around for a very long time in a country's history[4] – which is why a successful and long-lasting regime change can then acquire the deep roots that make it difficult to dislodge. So it has proved in the case of the power elites' tightening grip on Britain. They built on predispositions while finding themselves in the time and the place that suited their ideal purpose. But the fact that this change has the appearance of a smooth evolution with no obvious blood on the streets should not blind us to the reality. Poll tax riots have come and gone as have the occasional disturbances in Bristol, Birmingham and Liverpool. But none of these street-corner insurrections, in all their pathos of the impotent, has been permitted to slow down the onward march of an awesome hegemony. Britain has allowed its power elites to effect a transformation which amounts to the degradation of an entire country.

## A Very British Coup

Now that the corpse has been discovered, its bleeding wounds displayed and the miscreants fingered, there is just one question left. Why were the power elites allowed to get away with it? A native national scepticism about reformist change and the sheer inertia of the country's political and social arrangements have in the past made Britain highly resistant to the activist thrusts demanded by revolutionary transformation. But the inertia which rejects an obvious challenge can turn into an unquestioning passivity which then becomes vulnerable to an insidious takeover, and it is the passivity of Britain in its relationship to the power elites' gliding slide into authority which is the most striking truth about the country today. When it comes to power in Britain, most of the arrangements have been top-down rather than bottom-up. The kind of revolution which observes and reinforces that truth thus ends up being a very British coup and one which can therefore be incorporated within the popular mentality. Any dissent from what has happened then becomes merely the expression of the individual voice rather than the manifesto of a collective organization, since there are no powerful groupings left to act as a counterpoise to the power elites. The Independent Labour Party, the trade unions and the nonconformist Churches were among the very few power institutions of British history which came from the people themselves, were run by them as autonomous organizations and owed nothing to patronage dispensed from above. Of these three institutions, the first has disappeared completely, the second is run by leaders who have become part of the technocratic consensus, while the third has degenerated into the sweet futility of songs of praise.

Charm, that very English disease, has also played its part in the acceptance by Britain of what has been done to it. The power elites always and everywhere act on behalf of themselves, for self-interest is the first and only law of their being. But the seductive tones and pleasing techniques adopted by some individual group members can deflect attention from the reality of the elite's collective crassness, brutality and selfishness. The patronage which authority has at its disposal means that the power elites can usually rely on finding some useful agents in order to advance their cause and so make their purposes appear gracious and pleasing to the sensibility while also being accepted as, nonetheless, inevitable. There have always been cultured British voices ready to celebrate the smooth order of an implacable power before then delighting to find their place within the dispensation which has honoured them.

A certain aesthetic appeal can also play its part when power truths deign to don a mask of beauty. This is the moment when power elitism is subsumed within the dancing delights pursued by the elites of fashion, style and society. That moment is sometimes so prolonged that it can then cover the transfer of assets from one generation to another. The sons and daughters of the power elites, although benefiting from their parents' and their ancestors' rapacity, can seem to sweeten the bitter pill that power forces us to swallow so that we may become amnesiacs and forget what has happened to us and to Britain. These children of power sometimes seem to be endowed not just with a trust fund but also with an unearned grace of being, a quality which justifies, after the deed, all the sordid means that got them and their families to where they are now.

Sir Alfred Beit, for example, was not only the heir to a baronetcy but also to the magnificent art collection built up by his father, Sir Otto Beit, the South African millionaire.[5] A Rubens, a Goya as well as the only Vermeer in private hands, were among the Old Masters that hung on his walls, all paid for by diamonds hacked out of South African soil by blacks toiling in the Beit mines. Sir Alfred's life, and that of his wife Madeleine (née Mitford), was quite impeccably that of a member of the colonial and British elite, for both belonged to the last, true, imperial generation. After marrying in 1939 the couple honeymooned in Southern Rhodesia where Sir Alfred had substantial business interests. When they returned home they started to make the necessary alterations to the house they had bought in Kensington Park Gardens so that the rectangular dining room could be turned into an oval form which would be the perfect setting for their pictures. Periods of post-war colonial luxury then followed in Cape Town, Johannesburg and, finally, Ireland. Sir Alfred had seen an advertisement for Russborough in *Country Life* and it was that Palladian mansion outside Dublin which then became the couple's home and also that of their pictures. They were a cultivated, childless couple and Lady Beit delighted in reading both Proust and Thomas Mann in the original. While the mist engulfed the house and the Irish rain poured down she would read aloud to her husband. They had the sporting instincts of their class as well: Sir Alfred was a fine shot and Lady Beit hunted with the Killing Kildares.[6]

Apart from a period as a young Conservative MP before Sir Alfred lost his seat in 1945, neither of the Beits ever did anything very much and concentrated on being sociable, filling their great house at Christmas with guests and hiring a plane to bring friends to the Dublin Horse Show. A life of such idle beauty is bound to evoke ambiguous feelings – an astonishment that so prelapsarian a life without labour should be possible, mingling with the recollection of all the blood, sweat and toil that must have been expended in order to make sure that the pictures adorned Beit walls and no one else's. Some such confused colonial sentiment and resentment must have been the inspiration behind the three, wonderfully futile, Irish robberies which, in 1974, 1986 and 2001, removed from Russborough a series of extremely famous paintings which could never have been sold without their provenance being known. For the point about the Beits was that they could have lived anywhere in the world in circumstances of equal splendour. Ireland was incidental to their pleasure. There was a marvellous innocence about the ignorance of life which led them to set themselves up quite so openly to a raid by IRA gangsters. The riches inherited from past dominion meant that they could assert, albeit elegantly, their extra-territoriality, and it is that same detachment which makes the true alpha-starred power elites also rather enviable. These are lords of being and in our dreams we, too, would like to be able to afford that display of independence. In charitable moments, we might also understand why the power elites further down the scale of social mutability ape and imitate in the way that they do. Offering, therefore, sometimes a soft-headedly resigned acquiescence as well as the resentment which is a duty, we are not as straightforward in our dismissal of all the power elites as we should be. The constraints they have imposed on us have slipped on too easily. But there is another reason why they have been allowed to get away with it – and it has to do with language.

## The Elite Deception

'Elite' is a word which has been hijacked and reused to strategic effect.[7] The original, literal, meaning describes those who are, or have been, 'elected' or chosen. That passive condition or past state also communicates the idea of a done deal which all elites are keen to impress on us, something which has been sorted and has the air of finality about it. This, it is suggested, is an arrangement which has been made on our behalf and the contract, along with the choices made, are no longer open to revision. Even as a word, therefore, an 'elite' is hardly an innocent little thing. Far from being a neutral description it is part of the power game that it seeks to describe and authorize. The word – like the people it describes – is something of a deception. Anyone who investigates any elite at all closely is likely to end up disenchanted or, at least, disabused. But when the disillusion sets in the various authorities we have on this matter may rush in to tell us that there is no point now in trying to change the state of affairs represented by the elites. On this view, the elites have become a fact of social life rather than what they were to begin with, an invention. Yet the closer we get back to the original meaning, along with its strong suggestion of a deal and a choice, then the more vulnerable any elite will appear. After all, they, or people like them, were not always there inside this grouping. So something must have happened to get them there. And once we see that the elites are where they find themselves because of an act of will, then things became clearer as well as disturbing. Because at this point, if we push hard enough, we get close to a sense of human equality. Dress anybody in a Savile Row suit or a Fortuny gown, make sure that they spend some years in Russborough or its equivalent, and then they too will end up being able to enunciate the conventional phrases at dinner about the mystery of Vermeer's brushwork, Rembrandt's understanding of character, the convoluted beauty of Proust's syntax and Mann's understanding of society.

The elites, as described in this book, exist only because they have been allowed to get away with a power grab. For their plausibility and continued existence actually require strenuous efforts both to infiltrate the circle of power in the first place and then to hang on in there for dear life. This is the reality beneath the aura of invincibility and assurance which elites have to project in order to conceal the tough-minded truths of their existence. Seeing them struggling, asserting and conniving at power leads to the conclusion that what has been done and chosen might well then be undone by somebody else's act of choice, and that somebody else might be us. But this unsettling suggestion is then obscured by the other, hijacking, meaning of the word 'elite' – the one which insists that elite, far from meaning just 'the chosen ones', also means 'the best'. This idea confuses matters, as it is meant to do. An unnecessary complication is often a fraudster's best friend because it may throw the suspicious off the scent. After all, an elite commodity – whether it is a hotel suite, a car or a case of wine – is just the best of its particular kind. Who could possibly quarrel with the idea of the right of the best to exist? Considerations of refinement, good taste and right judgement now come into play and have their uses as literary propaganda as well. Artistic excellence is surely the result of a finely discriminating elite mind because that is the best kind of mind available, if you want a powerful mental machine to discard the dross and then create the best. Dismissal of the elite, in these circumstances, would then appear crass, ungracious and a sign of stupidity. British confusions about the power elites have therefore been created by the way in which this second layer of meaning has been allowed to overlay and obscure the first. It has been to the advantage of the power elites to encourage this obscurity so that they can then be seen as the meritorious best rather than a group of chancers who just got lucky.

Literature, happily, can still trip up the elites. Humour, irony and cynicism are powerful – and distinctively British – weapons when it comes to the business of exposing the deceptions and demolishing the pretensions maintained by the practitioners of power. English literature from Dickens through Wodehouse to Anthony Powell has discovered some of its best sardonic effects when it has turned an illusionless eye on those who play the power game of status. It was an authentic touch of subversive genius on Dickens' part to turn Mr Pickwick into an innocent, exactly the opposite therefore of what one might expect of a man recently retired from the City. Pickwick's journey around the England of the 1830s performs a whole series of similar somersaults with expectations as Dickens teases the codes of social worlds which from high to low pretend to be different but whose social rituals are really just an endless mimicking of each other. In that great set piece of the comic novel, the ball at Rochester in chapter 2 of *Pickwick Papers*, Dickens describes how: 'the aristocracy of the place – the Bulders, and Clubbers, and Snipes – were thus preserving their dignity at the upper end of the room, the other classes of society were imitating their example in other parts of it. The less aristocratic officers of the Ninety-seventh devoted themselves to the families of the less important functionaries from the Dock-yard. The solicitors' wives, and the wine-merchant's wife, headed another grade, (the brewer's wife visited the Bulders); and Mrs Tomlinson, the post-office keeper, seemed by mutual consent to have been chosen the leader of the trade party.'[8] The social groups are shown to be similar in their equivalent and silly hierarchies while also revealing in authentic Dickens style the wildness of England, with its individualizing profusion of characters.

British power's neo-Gothic quirkiness, too, has never failed in its ability to produce satirical material. The diaries of Guy Liddell, MI5's director of counter-espionage during the Second World War, describe the comic chaos of repeatedly bungled secrecy while Britain was supposed to be stretching every fibre of its being in what looked like being its final, rather than its finest, hour.[9] Churchill's speech on that theme was probably meant to prepare the British for defeat. Never surrendering meant, in these circumstances, going down fighting to the sound of a final *Liebestod* of British independence. Appropriately enough, given Churchill's own quixotically flirtatious attitude towards the prospect of death ever since he was a young man, he almost did die in 1941. The indiscretion of Churchill's intimate Brendan Bracken meant that it was a German news agency which was first with the news that the Prime Minister had crossed the Atlantic to visit Roosevelt on his yacht in August 1941. But with the agency spending so much time trying to ensure that the Italian manager of Claridge's should be sacked on the presumption that his nationality made him a fascist, perhaps the resources simply were not there to protect the intelligence and the Prime Minister. Meanwhile Duff Cooper, later an ambassador to Paris, is found to be 'feeling very bad' because his wife, Lady Diana, was being threatened with prosecution since she had accepted a free sack of stale bread for her pigs. At which point the comic effect rather dies away, as Cooper starts on a power elite rant described by Liddell: 'Duff has a tremendous feeling about the superiority of the British race and about our system of government . . . He thinks the old school tie is one of the finest institutions that we have got and that widespread education is a mistake. His argument is that people in this country have far more freedom and better conditions than in any other country in the world and that therefore there is much to be said for the existing regime.'

The undoubted fact that individual members of the power elites can be absurd is calculated to provoke, therefore, an absurdist response. Dickens became the novelist most loved by the British because he tickled the national instinct for the fancifully bizarre.[10] He also, however, confirmed them in the idea that the games of social power are both important as a source of comedy and also somehow irrelevant given the essentially humane geniality of the national style. His novels document individual cases of cruelty and suffering endured by those who have no power at the hands of those who can call the shots. But they also show how, once apprised of wrong and suffering, the key of generosity and decency will unlock the human heart and wellsprings of goodness will be touched. Applied to Britain today, and given what we now know of the power elites' method of proceeding, this seems an optimistic prescription. A novel is not a political or an ideological statement, but it does offer clues to social attitudes. In the satirical glories of English letters there is both an observation of the follies of power and a confession of an inability to do anything about that power except laugh at it. Passivity here is all, a conclusion which helps the elite maintain its authority. In which case the commentator is rather like, in Malcolm Muggeridge's description of his role, the pianist in a brothel.[11] The tunes, the words and the jokes can be good ones and they are surely worth a momentary attention, sometimes as an agreeable background noise while the main business is being pursued and sometimes as a happy distraction in the intervals afforded by that same urgent activity. But it simply would not do to pretend that the entertainment so jauntily proffered by the pianist might actually change the management of the organization, its purpose and its methods of service delivery. The business does, after all, supply you with a stool to perch on and, quite often, provides you as well with the material for the song. Signing the contract did imply an acceptance of the legitimacy of the services provided by those who pay the pianist.

This book has described and commented on the outcrops of satirical material which have emerged from its main subject: the degradation of a country at the hands of its newly emerged governing order. Given the depth and solidity of that new order, the sophistication of its practised ease in the deflection of criticism and its confidence in its capacity to shape the future as well as its right to control the present, perhaps a certain gallows humour is allowable and inevitable. But the idea that Britain is a nobler place than its governors think of it as being is a persistent and resolute one in the life and the literature of these islands. For the elites in their citadels this amounts to so much news from nowhere. But at the level of genius both Milton in the seventeenth century and Blake in the eighteenth century gave voice to the high and generous theme of British liberty. It is often the anonymous many who have the best intuitions about the crookedness of power and its superficial grasp of what really endures in Britain, because in this desperate business there are no expert witnesses with a specialized knowledge, and the common experience of subjection to the power elites is something which can bind the many.

When Kipling's soldier, in 'The Return',[12] comes back home to London after fighting in the Boer War he finds a city getting ready for the vulgarly plutocratic display of Edwardian England. The contrast the poet describes between the sanctimonious rhetoric of war and the lives that are expendable because of that rhetoric is much the same just over a century after the end of the Boer War, as are the embittering consequences of that contrast. But there is still an intuition which can grasp the truth beneath the surface, even a surface as polished, pitiless and remorseless as the one presented to us by our power elites. After all, the more concentrated and extreme a form of power becomes then the more vigorously it digs, eventually, its own grave. Which is why Kipling's truth about England is also a truth about the four different national peoples governed today by the power elites:

> If England was what England seems,
> An' not the England of our dreams,
> But only putty, brass an' paint,
> 'Ow quick we'd drop 'er! But she ain't!

# Notes and References

## Chapter 1    Elite Power: Idea and Reality

1 The grand theorist of the elites is the Italian economist and sociologist Vilfredo
  Pareto (1848–1923) who, in his *Trattato di sociologia generale* (1916) outlined
  the social function and purpose of modern elites as the leaders of their societies
  and as the consolidators of their own power. S.E. Finer (Selec. and ed.), *Vilfredo
  Pareto: Sociological Writings*, trans. D. Mirfin (London: Pall Mall Press, 1966),
  provides an introduction.

2 For an account of this reformist agenda, and its relation to the self-interest of the
  'thinking' classes, see Maurice Cowling, *Mill and Liberalism* (Cambridge:
  Cambridge University Press, 1963).

3 On Marx himself, see Francis Wheen, *Karl Marx: A Life* (New York: Norton,
  1999). The most commanding synthesis of Marxism as a body of thought in its
  period of greatest success is to be found in Leszek Kolakowski, *Main Currents of
  Marxism: Its Origins, Growth and Dissolution*, vol. 2, *The Golden Age*
  (Oxford: Oxford University Press, 1978).

4 On the cultural basis in European thought of fascist movements, see Richard
  Griffiths, *An Intelligent Person's Guide to Fascism* (London: Duckworth,
  2000).

5 For the political uses of these myths, see Richard Hofstadter, *Anti-Intellectualism in American Life* (New York: Knopf, 1963) and *The Paranoid Style in
  American Politics* (New York: Knopf, 1965).

6 See E.H.H. Green, *The Crisis of Conservatism: The Politics, Economics and
  Ideology of the British Conservative Party, 1880–1914* (London: Routledge,
  1995).

7 Stanley Baldwin (1867–1947) (1st Earl Baldwin of Bewdley and Viscount
  Corvedale of Corvedale). Prime Minister 1923–4, 1924–9, 1935–7. J.R.R.
  Tolkien (1892–1973). Professor of Anglo-Saxon (1925–45), Merton Professor
  of English Language and Literature (1945–59), University of Oxford; inventor
  of *The Hobbit, or, There and Back Again* (London: George Allen & Unwin,
  1937) and elaborator of the mythic account of *The Lord of the Rings* (London:
  George Allen & Unwin, 1954–5).

8 On the development of the Bolshevik theory of the party, see Leonard Schapiro,
  *1917: The Russian Revolutions and the Origins of Present-Day Communism*
  (London: Maurice Temple Smith, 1984), pp. 21–34.

9 An accessible survey is to be found in Gwendolyn Leick, *Mesopotamia: The
  Invention of the City* (London: Allen Lane, 2001).

10 For which, see Richard Southern, *Western Society and the Church in the Middle*

227

*Ages* (London: Penguin, 1970) esp. pp. 36–41 ('The rise and limits of clerical supremacy').

11 John Julius Norwich, *Byzantium: The Apogee* (London: Penguin Viking, 1991), chronicles to superb effect the story of the Byzantine empire during its period of greatest success from c. 800 AD to the disaster of the battle of Manzikert (1071 AD).

12 Quentin Skinner, *The Foundations of Modern Political Thought*, vol. 1, *The Renaissance* (Cambridge: Cambridge University Press, 1978) describes (pp. 3–12) the rise of independent city governments in northern Italy with their characteristic ideal of liberty from the early twelfth century onwards and shows ('The survival of Republican values' pp. 139–89) the vitality of republican political thought during the age of princely forms of government which dominated the European political order from the mid-fifteenth century onwards.

13 On Niccolò Machiavelli (1469–1527), one of the best modern guides in English is Quentin Skinner, *Machiavelli* (Oxford: Oxford University Press, 1981). But see also an earlier classic, Federico Chabod, *Machiavelli and the Renaissance* (New York: Harper & Row, 1965). Gisele Bock, Quentin Skinner & Maurizio Viroli (eds.), *Machiavelli and Republicanism* (Cambridge: Cambridge University Press, 1990) place the Florentine within his historical context. J.G.A. Pocock, *The Machiavellian Moment: Florentine Political Thought and the Atlantic Republican Tradition* (Princeton, NJ: Princeton University Press, 1975) provides the sweep of a transatlantic dimension.

14 For Carlyle, see the exemplary biographical study by Simon Heffer, *Moral Desperado: A Life of Thomas Carlyle* (London: Weidenfeld & Nicolson, 1995).

15 For a polished account of these elite hierarchies, their merits and their defects, see Noel Annan, *Our Age: Portrait of a Generation* (London: Weidenfeld & Nicolson, 1990).

16 George Orwell (Eric Blair) (1903–50). See the discussion of Orwell in Maurice Cowling, *Religion and Public Doctrine in Modern England*, vol. 3, *Accommodations* (Cambridge: Cambridge University Press, 2001), pp. 527–36: 'Orwell believed that . . . he was living in an age of unfixed opinions which it was his business to fix, p. 534.

17 See Sir Robert Filmer (c. 1588–1653), whose major work *Patriarcha* (1680) was published posthumously. In this and other writings, Filmer advanced the view that Adam was the first king and that Charles I ruled by virtue of his direct descent from Adam, nonsense of a highly influential kind.

18 See George Walden, *The New Elites: Making a Career in the Masses* (London: Allen Lane, 2000).

19 *Source*: Inland Revenue and Office for National Statistics (ONS), published 22 December 2004. See www.statistics.gov.uk.

20 One of the key texts of that civilization, and an attempt at providing it with its own genealogy of 'seriousness', was F.R. Leavis (1895–1978), *The Great Tradition: George Eliot, Henry James, Joseph Conrad* (London: Chatto & Windus, 1948).

21 For that process, see Frank Giles, *The Locust Years: The Story of the Fourth French Republic 1946–58* (London: Secker & Warburg, 1991), esp. pp. 10, 304, 379.

22 For the propagandists, see Maurice Cranston, *Philosophers and Pamphleteers: Political Theorists of the Enlightenment* (Oxford: Oxford University Press, 1985).

## Chapter 2     The Political Elites: Strategies for Survival

1 For a genially self-congratulatory account of this very British arm of government, see Nicholas Henderson, *The Private Office: A Personal View of Five Foreign Secretaries and of Government from the Inside* (London, Weidenfeld & Nicolson, 1983).

2 Paul Addison, *The Road to 1945: British Politics and the Second World War* (London: Cape, 1975), interprets the experience of war domestically as a mental preparation for the sweeping victory of executive managerialism in the general election of 1945. Paul Addison, *Now The War is Over: A Social History of Britain, 1945–51* (London: Jonathan Cape, 1985), continues the theme, as does Peter Hennessy, *Never Again: Britain, 1945–51* (London: Jonathan Cape, 1992).

3 Moisey Ostrogorsky (1854–1919), Russian (and Belorussian) historian and political scientist, was the first to detect and to describe this phenomenon in detail. His *Democracy and the Organization of Political Parties*, translated by F. Clarke (London: Macmillan, 1902), 2 vols., suggests that in a mass democracy such parties degenerate pathologically and necessarily into the condition of a bureaucratic oligarchy.

4 Rt Hon. Tony Blair (1953–) MP (Lab.) Sedgefield. Prime Minister 1997–. David Cameron (1966–) MP (Con.) Witney (2001–). Leader of the Conservative Party (2005–)

5 See, however, Maurice Cowling, *The Impact of Labour 1920–24: The Beginning of Modern British Politics* (Cambridge: Cambridge University Press, 1971), for a vigorous assertion of the author's view that politics is always a plot at the top, that the Westminster political elites remained in control despite their fear of instability from below, and that they persuaded the electorate to say what the elites wanted to hear.

6 Richard Pares, *King George III and the Politicians* (Oxford: Clarendon Press, 1953), discusses how the politics of the age revolved around the fact that: 'the bishoprics, the deaneries, the prebends, and the Crown livings were awarded by the Government; the higher posts in the regular army, the whole of the navy, the revenue offices, the colonial governorships, the political or civil services – in short, nearly everything that a gentleman could accept, had to be obtained from the Government' p. 7. See esp. the account of 'Amateurs and professionals in government' pp. 1–30.

7 One of the best surveys of this particularly neurotic political elite is to be found in Jonathan Parry, *The Rise and Fall of Liberal Government in Victorian Britain* (New Haven and London: Yale University Press, 1993). See esp. his account in chapter 10 'Liberalism exuberant, 1868–85' pp. 227–46 of how the Liberal Party, eager for a high moral tone on the cheap: 'believed that only it could make working-men feel respected members of the community, yet integrate them into a political system dominated by a solid, civilised and civilising phalanx of public-spirited landowners, "expert" intellectuals and leading provincial merchants. This cross-class propertied and wise elite was capable, they thought, of operating a rational and ethical politics designed to uphold the rule of law, to promote moral values and to provide low-cost efficiency' p. 227.

8 Paul Atterbury and Clive Wainwright (eds.), *Pugin: A Gothic Passion* (London and New Haven: Yale University Press, 1994), discuss the melancholic obsessive (A.W.N. Pugin, 1812–52) who designed the building.

9 Rt Hon. Tony Benn (1925–) MP (Lab.) Bristol SE 1950–60, 1963–83; Chesterfield 1984–2001. Secretary of State for Energy, 1975–9. Rt Hon. J. Enoch Powell

(1912–98) MP (Con.) Wolverhampton SW 1950–74; (Ulster Unionist) Down South 1974–83, 1983–7. Minister of Health 1960–3. Tam Dalyell (1932–) MP (Lab.) West Lothian 1962–83; Linlithgow 1983–2005.

10 Bee Wilson, *The Hive: The Story of the Honeybee and Us* (London: John Murray, 2004), shows with flair and insight how the bee and the hive have influenced ideas about human conduct and social organization.

11 Peter Oborne, *The Rise of Political Lying* (London: Free Press, 2005), discusses with documentary detail the contemporary scene, and maintains that a qualitative shift in mendacity has occurred.

12 See Brian Brivati and Richard Cockett (eds.), *Anatomy of Decline: The Political Journalism of Peter Jenkins* (London: Cassell, 1995).

13 Rt Hon. Roy Jenkins (1920–2003) MP (Baron Jenkins of Hillhead 1987) MP (Lab.) Central Southwark 1948–50; Stechford, Birmingham 1950–76; (SDP) Glasgow, Hillhead 1982–7. Home Secretary 1965–7, 1974–6. Chancellor of the Exchequer 1967–70.

14 Rt Hon. Alan Clark (1928–99) MP (Con.) Plymouth, Sutton 1974–92; Kensington and Chelsea (1997–9). Minister of State, Ministry of Defence 1989–92.

15 Rt Hon Kenneth Clarke (1940–) MP (Con.) Rushcliffe, 1970–. Home Secretary 1992–3; Chancellor of the Exchequer 1993–7.

16 For a presentation of self-loving proceduralism masquerading as history, see Patrick Cormack (with an introduction by George Thomas, Viscount Tonypandy), *Westminster: Palace and Parliament* (London: Frederick Warne, 1981).

17 The best recent account of Restoration politics stresses the darkness of this cynicism. See Tim Harris, *Restoration: Charles II and his Kingdoms, 1660–85* (London: Allen Lane, 2005). John Milton's drama, *Samson Agonistes* (1671) gives tragic and poetic voice to the national condition of the time, seeing Samson in captivity and 'eyeless in Gaza at the mill with slaves' as the symbol of a degraded land.

18 Samuel Butler's poem *Hudibras* (1663) enjoyed great popular success because of its mockery of the high-flown rhetoric which had typified the Commonwealth's theological politics. For Butler (c. 1613–80), see Blandford Parker, *The Triumph of Augustan Poetics: English Literary Culture from Butler to Johnson* (Cambridge: Cambridge University Press, 1998).

19 The pioneering advocate of market economics was F.A. von Hayek (1899–1902). Professor of Economic Science, University of London 1931–50; of Social and Moral Science, University of Chicago 1951–62; of Economics, University of Freiburg 1962–9. See especially his *The Road to Serfdom* (London: Routledge & Kegan Paul, 1944) and *The Constitution of Liberty* (London: Routledge & Kegan Paul, 1960).

20 George Canning (1770–1827). Foreign Secretary 1807–9, 1822–7; Prime Minister April–August 1827.

21 Quoted in Charles Petrie, *George Canning* (London: Eyre & Spottiswoode, 1930), p. 29.

22 Thomas à Beckett (c. 1118–70). Chancellor of England 1155–62. Thomas Cromwell (c. 1485–1540). Lord Privy Seal 1536–40. John Prescott (1938–) Deputy Prime Minister 1997–.

23 Sir Anthony Nutting, 3rd Bt (1920–99) MP (Con.) Melton 1945–56. Minister of State, Foreign Office, 1954–6. For a hostile view of Nutting and the circumstances surrounding his resignation, see Robert Rhodes James, *Anthony Eden* (London: Weidenfeld & Nicolson, 1986) pp. 570–1, 614–15. Sir Edward Boyle, 3rd Bt (1923–81) (Baron Boyle of Handsworth, 1970) MP (Con.) Handsworth, Birmingham 1950–70. Financial secretary to the Treasury 1959–62; Ministry of Education 1962–4.

24  Sir Ian Gilmour, 3rd Bt (1931–) (Baron Gilmour of Craigmillar 1992) MP (Con.) Norfolk Central 1962–74; Chesham and Amersham 1974–92. Lord Privy Seal 1979–81.
25  Sir Edward Heath KG (1916–2005) MP (Con.) Bexley 1950–74; Bexley and Sidcup 1974–83; Old Bexley and Sidcup 1983–2001. Prime Minister 1970–4.
26  Rt Hon. Denis Healey (1917–) (Baron Healey of Riddlesden 1992) MP (Lab.) Leeds South East 1952–5; Leeds East 1955–92. Chancellor of the Exchequer 1974–9.
27  Among the most dazzling members of the new political and technocratic elite was John Freeman (1915–) MP (Lab.) Watford, 1945–55, whose career progress included a range of achievements none of which satisfied him and which, successively, he abandoned: Parliamentary Secretary, Ministry of Supply 1947–51 (resigned); Assistant Editor, *New Statesman* 1951–8, Deputy Editor 1958–60, Editor 1961–3; British High Commissioner in India 1965–8; British Ambassador in Washington 1969–71; Chairman, London Weekend Television Ltd, 1971–84. Churchill is said to have wept at the sight of the young Freeman addressing the House of Commons (in 1945) as a Labour MP while wearing the uniform of an officer commissioned in the Rifle Brigade, seeing it as a demonstration of the passing of the old order and the inevitable ascent of the newly ordered Britain. But Freeman's apparent disillusion with the pickings available in the world made by 1945 mirrored a wider, intelligentsia, disenchantment (see Anthony Howard, 'We are the masters now', in Philip French and Michael Sissons, *The Age of Austerity* (London: Hodder & Stoughton, 1963).
28  For Thomas Babington Macaulay (1800–59), his reforms of Indian law, administration and education as a member of the Supreme Council governing India (1834–8), along with the substantial private fortune he was able to amass while working in the sub-continent and which made him independently rich, see John Clive, *Thomas Babington Macaulay* (London: Secker & Warburg, 1973), pp. 289–478.
29  James Mill (1773–1836), historian and political economist, who was appointed an assistant to the Chief Examiner of Correspondence, British East India Company in 1819. Author of *History of British India* (3 vols. 1818). See Duncan Forbes, 'James Mill and India', *Cambridge Journal*, 5 1951–2. His son, John Stuart Mill (1806–73) also joined (1823) the Examiner's Office at India House, the London headquarters of the East India Company, becoming head of that office from 1856 until the Company's dissolution in 1858. Life on an early retirement pension produced his essay *On Liberty* (1859).
30  Rt Hon. Gordon Brown (1951–) MP (Lab.) Dunfermline East 1983–. Chancellor of the Exchequer 1997–.
31  Rt Hon Jack Straw (1946–) MP (Lab.) Blackburn 1979–. Political Adviser, Secretary of State for Social Service 1974–6; Special Adviser, Secretary of State for the Environment 1976–7; Home Secretary 1997–2001; Secretary of State for Foreign and Commonwealth Affairs 2001–.
32  Bernard Donoughue (1934–) (Baron Donoughue of Ashton 1983). Senior Policy Adviser to the Prime Minister 1974–9.
33  Michael Levy (1944–) (Baron Levy of Mill Hill 1997). Chairman of M and G Records 1992–7 and personal envoy of the Prime Minister to the Middle East 1999–. Involved in a wide range of charitable work in the areas of welfare and education.
34  The best recent account is Keith Kyle, *Suez* (London: Weidenfeld & Nicolson, 1991.
35  For which, see John P. Mackintosh, *The British Cabinet* 3rd edn (London:

Stevens & Sons, 1977). See also Peter Hennessy, *Cabinet* (Oxford: Blackwell, 1986).

36 See, for example, Anthony Sampson, *Anatomy of Britain* (London: Hodder Stoughton, 1962), the first in a series of august explorations ending in the baffled tone of *Who Runs this Place? The Anatomy of Britain in the Twenty-First Century* (London: John Murray, 2004).

37 For both the origins of the Hapsburg monarchy and its survival, see R.J.W. Evans, *The Making of the Hapsburg Monarchy, 1550–1700: An Interpretation* (Oxford: Clarendon Press, 1979). For the study of a crisis year in the monarchy's history, see L.B. Namier, *1848: The Revolution of the Intellectuals* (Oxford: Oxford University Press, 1948), a celebrated demolition job which regards the anti-Hapsburg rebellions as largely the result of agitation by bourgeois hunters for office who used the language of nationalism in order to advance their self-interest at the expense of the dynastic regimes. R.J.W. Evans and Hartmutt Pogge von Strandmann (eds.), *The Revolutions in Europe, 1848–49: From Reform to Reaction* (Oxford: Oxford University Press, 2000) revisit the debate on 1848 and the question of how the empire survived the challenge to its authority.

38 On this period of Whitehall reconstruction, see John Grigg, *Lloyd George: War Leader 1916–18* (London, Allen Lane, 2002), pp. 11–18, 393–400.

39 Bob Marshall-Andrews (1944–) MP (Lab.) Medway 1997–.

40 Diane Abbott (1953–) MP (Lab.) Hackney North and Stoke Newington 1987–.

41 John Morley, *The Life of William Ewart Gladstone*, 3 vols. (London: Macmillan, 1903). Roy Jenkins, *Asquith* (London: Collins, 1964); *Churchill* (London: Macmillan, 2001), *A Life at the Centre* (London: Macmillan, 1991). *'Chips': The Diaries of Sir Henry Channon*, ed. Robert Rhodes James (London: Weidenfeld & Nicolson, 1967). Alan Clark, *Diaries* (London: Weidenfeld & Nicolson, 1993).

42 Rt Hon. Kenneth Baker (1934–) (Baron Baker of Dorking 1997) supplies an example of the unintended hilarity of political autobiographies, in *The Turbulent Years: My Life in Politics* (London: Faber, 1993).

43 Edward du Cann (1924–) MP (Con.) Taunton 1956–87; Director of Lonrho 1972–9; Chairman, Lonrho plc 1984–91; Chairman, Keyser Ullman Holdings Ltd. 1970–5. Chairman of the Conservative Party 1965–7 and of 1922 Committee 1972–84. Notable opponent to Ted Heath and a significant figure within the 'Milk Street Mafia' – the group of high-ranking Conservative Party members who met at the Keyser Ullman offices in London's Milk Street in 1979 to discuss the Conservative leadership. At one point du Cann was touted as a potential leadership candidate, but ultimately gave his support to Thatcher.

44 Sir John Hoskyns (1927–). Director General, Institute of Directors 1984–9;. Director ICI plc 1982–4 and of Ferranti International plc 1986–94. Head of the Prime Minister's Policy Unit, 1979–82 and author of *Just in Time: Inside the Thatcher Revolution* (London: Aurum Press, 2000), one of the sharpest accounts of the internal politics of the government between 1979 and 1982.

45 Edward Bridges (1892–1969) (1st Baron Bridges of Headley 1957). Secretary to the Cabinet 1938–45; Secretary to the Cabinet, Permanent Secretary to the Treasury and Head of the Home Civil Service 1945–56. Burke (Frederick St John) Trend (1914–87) (Baron Trend of Greenwich 1974). Secretary to the Cabinet 1962–75. William Armstrong (1915–80) (Baron Armstrong of Sanderstead 1975). Permanent Secretary to the Treasury 1962–8; Head of the Home Civil Service 1968–74; Chairman of Midland Bank 1975.

46 Robin Butler (1938–) (Baron Butler of Brockwell 1998). Secretary to the Cabinet and Head of the Home Civil Service 1988–98.

47  Onora O'Neill (1941–) (Baroness O'Neill of Bengrave 1998), daughter of the late Sir Con O'Neill (1912–88), pro-European Union diplomat. Principal of Newnham College, Cambridge 1992 –. See her Reith Lectures, *A Question of Trust* (Cambridge: Cambridge University Press, 2002).

48  Rt Hon. Michael Heseltine (1933–) (Baron Heseltine of Thenford 2001) MP (Con.) Henley 1974–2001. President of the Board of Trade 1992–5; Deputy Prime Minister 1995–7.

49  Rt Hon. John Prescott (1938–) MP (Lab.) Kingston upon Hull East 1970–83; Hull East 1983–97; Kingston upon Hull East 1997–. Deputy Prime Minister 1997–.

50  For a characteristically romantic study of English constitutionalism, see J. Enoch Powell (with Keith Wallis), *The House of Lords in the Middle Ages: A History of the English House of Lords to 1540* (London: Weidenfeld & Nicolson, 1968).

51  Sir John Robert Seeley (1834–95) appointed (1869) to the Regius Chair of Modern History at Cambridge by Prime Minister Gladstone. See esp. his *The Life and Times of Stein, or, Germany and Prussia in the Napoleonic Age* (Cambridge: Cambridge University Press, 3 vols., 1878) for an expression of his belief in a patriotic and a disciplined state. The point of the study of English history, in Seeley's case, was that it would strengthen the national morale – something that, in a typically elite way, he feared was on the slide.

52  G.M. Trevelyan (1876–1962). Regius Professor of Modern History, Cambridge (1927–40) and Master of Trinity College, Cambridge (1940–51). See especially his *English Social History* (London: Longmans, Green & Co., 1944) and *History of England* (London: Longmans, Green & Co., 1926), which were both best-selling narratives advocating England as a liberal success story marked by the smoothness of an evolutionary and peaceful process.

53  For Arthur Bryant (1899–1985), and his effusions, see *The Fire and the Rose* (London: Collins, 1965) and *The Mediaeval Foundation* (London: Collins, 1966). See Andrew Roberts, *Eminent Churchillians* (London: Weidenfeld & Nicolson, 1994) for a study of the patriot as supporter of appeasement in the 1930s.

54  For Arnold Bennett (1867–1931) see especially *Clayhanger* (London: Methuen, 1910).

55  C.P. Snow (1905–80) (Baron Snow 1964). *Corridors of Power* (London: Macmillan, 1964) is the most celebrated of his novel-sequence of eleven volumes under the general title, *Strangers and Brothers*.

56  For the novels of Maurice Edelman (1911–75), see esp. *The Minister* (London: Hamish Hamilton, 1961).

57  Stanley Baldwin (1867–1947) (Lord Baldwin of Bewdley). Prime Minister 1923–4, 1924–9, 1935–7.

58  Neville Chamberlain (1869–1940). Prime Minister 1937–40.

59  For Alfred and his court, along with a dazzling demonstration of how the Common Law of England, far from being the sudden invention of the reign of Henry II (1154–1189), was already evolving in the reign of Alfred in the late ninth century, see Patrick Wormald, *The Making of English Law: King Alfred to the Twelfth Century*, vol. 1 *Legislation and Its Limits* (Oxford: Blackwell, 1999).

60  On Whitehall Palace (which was destroyed by a fire in 1698), see Simon Thurley, *The Lost Palace of Whitehall* (London: Royal Institute of British Architects, 1998): catalogue of an exhibition held at the RIBA Heinz Gallery, 10 September – 24 October 1998. See also the Adamson work on the Tudor and Stuart Courts cited in n. 62.

61  Rt Hon. Peter Mandelson (1953–) MP (Lab.) Hartlepool 1992. Labour Director of Communications 1985–90; Minister Without Portfolio (Millennium Dome)

1997; Secretary for Trade 1998 (resigned December 1998); Secretary for Northern Ireland 1999 (resigned January 2001); EU Trade Commissioner 2004–. Charles (Charlie) Falconer, QC (1951–) (Baron Falconer 1997). Lord Chancellor 2003–. Rt Hon Cecil Parkinson (1931–) (Baron Parkinson of Carnforth 1992) MP (Con.) Enfield West 1970–4; Hertfordshire South 1974–83; Hertsmere 1983–92. Secretary of State for Energy 1987–9, Secretary of State for Transport 1989–90. Rt Hon Sir John Major (1943–) KG MP (Con.) Huntingdonshire 1979–83; Huntingdon 1983–2001. Prime Minister 1990–7. On the similar importance of the favourite in earlier courts, see J.H. Elliott and L.W.B. Brockliss, *The World of the Favourite* (New Haven and London: New Haven & Yale University Press, 1999).

62 John Adamson, 'The making of the ancien-regime court 1500–1700' and 'The Tudor and Stuart courts 1509–1714' in J. Adamson (ed.), *The Princely Courts of Europe: Ritual, Politics and Culture Under the Ancien Regime 1500–1700* (London: Weidenfeld & Nicolson, 1999), pp. 7–41, 95–117, supply an elegant and lucid account of the court as an institution which was influential in both cultural and political terms. The importance of gestures in earlier, princely, courts went beyond the rituals of *politesse* since they signified the coded way in which power was expressed and communicated: 'The study of this repertory of gesture, however, is still in its infancy. An entire art-historical industry has grown up devoted to the iconography of images, to decoding the meaning and associations of visual symbols . . . On the other hand . . . relatively little attention has been paid by historians to the iconography of gesture: to understanding the symbolism of formalized actions, and to analysing the relation between ceremonial objects and places and their ritual use' pp. 27–8. The forms of ritual may change but the concern with precedence and the meaning of gesture which is seen in princely courts and among men in tights survives in the democratic courts populated by suited persons.

63 Alan Milburn MP (1958–) (Lab.) Darlington 1992–. Chancellor of the Duchy of Lancaster 2004–.

64 Rt Hon. Peter Hain (1950) MP (Lab.) Neath 1991–. Secretary of State for Wales 2002–; Leader of the House of Commons 2003–5; Secretary of State for Northern Ireland 2005–.

65 Rt Hon. Margaret Beckett (1943–) MP (Lab.) Lincoln 1974–9; Derby South (1983–). Secretary of State for the Environment 2001–.

66 Rt Hon. Alan Johnson (1950–) MP (Lab.) Kingston upon Hull West and Hessle 1997–. Secretary of State for Work and Pensions 2004–, for Trade and Industry 2005–.

67 See Perry Miller, *The New England Mind: The 17th Century* (Cambridge, Mass.: Harvard University Press, 1954).

68 Charles Wright Mills (1916–62). Professor, University of Columbia 1945–62. Among Mills' works see especially, *White Collar: The American Middle Class* (New York: Oxford University Press, 1953), *The Power Elite* (New York: Oxford University Press, 1956), *The Causes of World War III* (London: Secker & Warburg, 1959), *The Sociological Imagination* (New York: Oxford University Press, 1959), *Listen Yankee: The Revolution in Cuba* (London: Secker & Warburg, 1960) as well as *Power, Politics and People: The Collected Essays of C. Wright Mills* edited and with an introduction by Irving Louis Horowitz (New York: Oxford University Press, 1963). J.E.T. Eldridge, *C. Wright Mills* (London and New York: Tavistock Publications, 1983) provides an excellent introduction.

69 Diarmaid McCulloch, *The Later Reformation in England, 1547–1603* (Basingstoke: Macmillan, 1990) discusses the admixture of theology and politics in the creation of England's Reformation state.

70 For a study of the excitedly journalistic moral campaign Gladstone launched against the Turkish empire and which helped him get back into office, see Richard Shannon, *Gladstone and the Bulgarian Agitation, 1876* (London and New York: Nelson, 1963). By far the best biography of Gladstone is that by Richard Shannon, *Gladstone: Heroic Minister, 1865–98* (London: Allen Lane, 1999).

71 Isaiah Berlin, *Mr Churchill in 1940* (London: John Murray, 1940) helped to set the tone for these exercises in gratification.

72 For this theme, see P.F. Clarke, *Lancashire and the New Liberalism* (London: Cambridge University Press, 1971). But the intellectual arguments in favour of state intervention and welfarism had already been rehearsed by T. H. Green (1836–82), Whyte's Professor of Moral Philosophy at Oxford 1878–82. See his *Lectures on the Principles of Political Obligation* which were first published posthumously in the three volumes of his collected works (1885–8) and which are now available in *Thomas Hill Green: Lectures on the Principles of Political Obligation and other Writings* (Cambridge: Cambridge University Press, 1986).

73 See K. O. Morgan, *Labour in Power 1945–51* (Oxford: Clarendon Press, 1984) for an account of this process.

74 On this theme, see Patrick McDevitt, *May the Best Man Win: Sport, Masculinity, and Nationalism in Great Britain and the Empire, 1880–1935* (London: Palgrave Macmillan, 2005)

75 See Henry Pelling, *A Short History of the Labour Party*, 3rd edn (London: Macmillan, St Martin's Press, 1968).

76 Herbert Stanley Morrison (1888–1965) (Baron Morrison of Lambeth 1959) MP (Lab.) S Hackney 1923–4, 1929–31, 1935–45; East Lewisham 1945–52; South Lewisham 1951–9. Lord President of the Council and Deputy Prime Minister 1945–51.

77 Aneurin Bevan (1897–1960) MP (Labour) Ebbw Vale 1929–60. Minister of Health and Housing 1945–51; Minister of Labour January–April 1951.

78 Estelle Morris (1952–) (Baroness Morris of Yardley 2005) MP (Lab.) Birmingham, Yardley 1992–2005. Secretary of State for Education 2001–2.

79 Rt. Hon. Charles Morris (1926–) MP (Lab.) Manchester, Openshaw 1963–83; Government Assistant Whip 1966–7; Deputy Chief Whip 1969–70.

80 Rt Hon. Alfred Morris (1928–) (Baron Morris of Manchester 1997) MP (Lab.) Manchester Wythenshawe 1964–97. Minister for the Disabled, Department of Health and Social Security 1974–9.

81 Hilary Armstrong (1945–) MP (Lab.) Durham North West 1987–. Government Chief Whip 2001–.

82 Rt. Hon. Ernest Armstrong (1915–96). MP (Lab.) Durham North West 1964–87. Assistant Government Whip 1967–9; Lord Commissioner, HM Treasury 1969–70; Parliamentary Under-Secretary of State, Department of Education and Science 1974–5; Department of the Environment, 1975–9.

83 See Noel Annan, *Our Age* (London: Weidenfeld & Nicolson, 1990), p. 372, for the remark of John Carswell, a Treasury official, on the economist Lord Robbins: 'I never encountered anyone except Otto Clarke of the Treasury who was more confident that he was right.'

84 Ann Cryer (1939–) MP (Lab.) Keighley 1997–.

85 John Cryer (1964–) MP (Lab.) Hornchurch 1997–.

86 Hilary Benn (1953–) MP (Lab.) Leeds Central 1999–.

87 Gwyneth Dunwoody (1930) MP (Lab.) Exeter 1966–70; Crewe 1974–83; Crewe and Nantwich 1983–.

88 For an argument in favour of the proposition that Wales is a participatory democracy see, however, David Smith, *A People and a Proletariat: Essays in the*

235

*History of Wales, 1780–1980* (London: Pluto Press, 1980). See also Hywel Francis and David Smith, *The Fed, A History of the South Wales Miners in the Twentieth Century* (London: Lawrence & Wishart, 1980).

89 On Peel, the best biography (2 vols.) remains Norman Gash, *Mr Secretary Peel* (London: Longman, 1961) and *Sir Robert Peel: The Life of Sir Robert Peel after 1830* (London: Longman, 1972).

90 For a study of these years, see Rt Hon. Nigel Lawson (1932–) (Baron Lawson of Blaby 1992) MP (Con.) Blaby 1974–92. Chancellor of the Exchequer 1983–9. His book, *The View from No. 11: Memoirs of a Tory Radical* (London: Bantam Press, 1992) is a work which surpasses any of the biographies and autobiographies produced by the inner prime ministerial circle of those years.

91 See Robert Rhodes James, *Churchill, A Study in Failure, 1900–39* (London: Weidenfeld & Nicolson, 1970), pp. 338–9 and *Anthony Eden* (London: Weidenfeld & Nicolson, 1986), p. 261. The motion of 29 January 1942 was lost by 1/464.

92 Nicholas Soames (1948–) MP (Con.) Crawley 1983–97; Mid-Sussex 1997 –. Minister of State for the Armed Forces, Ministry of Defence 1994–7.

93 Dominic Grieve (1956–) MP (Con.) Beaconsfield 1997–.

94 Shaun Woodward (1958–) MP (Con.) Witney 1997–9; (Lab.) Witney 1999–2001; MP (Lab.) St Helens South 2001–. Parliamentary Under-Secretary, Northern Ireland Office 2005–.

95 John Horam; (1939–) MP (Lab.) Gateshead West 1970–81; (SDP) Gateshead West 1981–3; (Con.) Orpington 1992–.

96 Charles Clarke (1950) MP (Lab.) Norwich South 1997–. President, National Union of Students 1975–7; Secretary of State for Education 2002–5; Home Secretary 2005–.

97 Rt Hon. Harold Wilson (1916–95) (Baron Wilson of Rievaulx 1983) MP (Lab.) Ormskirk 1945–50; Huyton 1950–83. Prime Minister 1964–70, 1974–6. Anthony Crosland (1918–77) MP (Lab.) S Gloucestershire 1950–5; Grimsby 1959–77. Secretary of State for the Environment 1974–6; Foreign Secretary 1976–7; Author of the influential *Future of Socialism* (London: Jonathan Cape, 1956), which argued for a combination of personal liberty and state regulation of the economy along with an occasional dash of hedonism characteristic of the author's own emancipated manner. Richard (Dick) Crossman (1907–74) MP (Lab.) Coventry East 1945–74. Secretary of State for Health and Social Security 1968–70. See his *Plato Today* (London: Unwin, 1937) as well as his posthumously published *Diaries of a Cabinet Minister* (London: Hamish Hamilton and Jonathan Cape, 1975, 1976, 1977), the first examples of the diary of a political insider being published so close to the period being described. Note the view of a one-time Labour activist A.L. Rowse: 'Dick Crossman was always giving trouble, no sense of direction or loyalty, no sense . . . Dick took an opportunity in the smoking-room of the Commons to beard Attlee, "Mr Attlee, I think the new foreign policy statement of the party was very good." Dick told the story himself. "And, do you know, he never said anything at all. I thought he hadn't heard me. So I said again. 'Mr Attlee, you know, I thought the party's new statement of its foreign policy very good.' And all he said to me was: 'Did you?'" ' (Richard Ollard (ed.), *The Diaries of A.L. Rowse* (London: Allen Lane, 2003), p. 397.) Hugh Gaitskell (1906–63) MP (Lab.) Leeds South (1945–63). Chancellor of the Exchequer 1950–1; Leader of the Labour Party 1955–63.

98 Rt Hon. R.A. Butler (1902–82) (Baron Butler of Saffron Walden 1964. MP (Con.) Saffron Walden 1929–65. Home Secretary 1956–62. Rt Hon. Harold Macmillan (1894–1986) (1st Earl of Stockton) Prime Minister 1957–63. Rt Hon. Douglas Hurd (1930–) (Baron Hurd of Westwell 1997) MP (Con.) Mid-

Oxfordshire 1974–83; Witney 1983–97. Home Secretary 1985–9; Foreign Secretary 1989–95. Rt Hon. Christopher Patten (1944–) (Baron Patten of Barnes 2005) MP (Con.) Bath 1979–92. Chairman of the Conservative Party 1990–2; Governor of Hong Kong 1992–7.

99 Correlli Barnett, *The Audit of War: The Illusion and Reality of Britain as a Great Nation* (London: Macmillan, 1986), pp. 38–51, discusses the schizophrenia involved in the mental assumptions behind the 'illusion of limitless possibility', despite the fact that Britain was broke in 1945.

100 For Thomas Starkey, see G.R. Elton, *Reform and Renewal: Thomas Cromwell and the Common Weal* (Cambridge: Cambridge University Press, 1973), pp. 46–55, 138–9.

101 R.H. Tawney (1880–1962). Professor of Economic History, London School of Economics (1931–49). See esp. his three central works, *The Acquisitive Society* (London: G. Bell & Sons, 1921), *Equality* (London: George Allen & Unwin, 1931) and *Religion and the Rise of Capitalism* (Harmondsworth: Pelican, 1926).

102 Harold Laski (1893–1950). Lecturer, then Professor, London School of Economics. Chairman of the Labour Party (1945) and an apologist for the secular state in a torrent of publications among which *A Grammar of Politics* (London: George Allen & Unwin, 1925), *Reflections on the Revolution of Our Time* (London: George Allen & Unwin, 1943) and *Liberty in the Modern State* (London: George Allen & Unwin, 1948), typify his neo-religious faith in the future.

103 H.G. Wells (1866–1946). Novelist, journalist and popular historian. *A Modern Utopia* (London: Odhams, 1905) expresses his belief in social progress while *Mind at the End of Its Tether* (London: Heinemann, 1945) shows his abandonment of that position and his conviction that nature was going to destroy humanity.

104 Michael Oakeshott (1901–90). Professor of Political Science, London School of Economics 1951–69. See his *Rationalism in Politics and other Essays* (London: Methuen, 1962) for his hostility to the 1945 world of central planning as well as for an example of his prose style, which was regarded by some as beautifully sinuous and by others as an exercise in self-indulgent tortuousness.

105 F.A. von Hayek (1899–1992).

106 Isaiah Berlin (1909–98). OM (1971) Kt (1957). Chichele Professor of Social and Political Theory, Oxford 1957–67. A much garlanded savant, conversationalist and essayist who was the most important of the English Cold War intellectuals and who, in that respect, enjoyed a very good war in the 1950s and 1960s. *Two Concepts of Liberty* (Oxford: Oxford University Press, 1948) is the essay which made Berlin's reputation as the high priest of liberal democracy and noisy foe of totalitarianism. Subsequent statements such as *Historical Inevitability* (London, New York: Oxford University Press, 1954) and *Vico and Herder* (Oxford: Oxford University Press, 1976) were polemical restatements of that same theme, although they were presented as works of serious history.

107 John Gray's journey started with the academic triumphalism of *Hayek on Liberty* (Oxford: Blackwell, 1984) and has come to rest in the disillusion of *False Dawn: The Delusions of Global Capitalism* (London: Granta Books, 1998).

108 Paul Johnson's career has shifted from the position advanced in *The Suez War* (foreword by Aneurin Bevan) (London: MacGibbon & Kee, 1957) towards the isolationism embraced in *The Offshore Islanders* (London: Weidenfeld & Nicolson, 1972), which has proved to be a persistent theme and ended in the chastisement of *Intellectuals* (London: Weidenfeld & Nicolson, 1988).

109 See Anthony Giddens, *The Third Way: The Renewal of Social Democracy* (Cambridge: Polity Press, 1998).

110 Andrei Cherny, *The Next Deal: The Future of Public Life in the Information Age* (New York: Basic Books, 2000).

111 Alan Milburn, speech to the Social Market Foundation, 8 December 2004.

112 Will Hutton, *The State We're In* (London: Jonathan Cape, 1995).

113 Rt Hon. John Biffen (1930–) (Baron Biffen of Tanat 1997) MP (Con.) Oswestry, 1961–83; Shropshire North 1983–97. Leader of the House of Commons 1982–7; Lord Privy Seal 1983–7.

114 Rt Hon. Sir Keith Joseph (1918–94) 2nd Bt (Baron Joseph of Portsoken in the City of London 1987) MP (Con.) Leeds North East 1956–87. Secretary of State for Industry 1979–81; Secretary of State for Education and Science 1981–6.

115 The Hon. William Waldegrave (1946–) (Baron Waldegrave of North Hill 1999). MP (Con.) Bristol West 1979–97. See his *The Binding of Leviathan: Conservatism and the Future* (London: Hamish Hamilton, 1978).

116 John Bolton (1948–) Assistant Secretary, US State Department, 1989–93; President, National Policy Forum, Washington, 1995–6; Senior Vice-President, American Enterprise Institute, Washington, 1997–; Under Secretary of State for Arms Control and International Security 2001–5 and is now (2005–) US Ambassador to the United Nations. Richard Perle (1943–), Assistant Secretary, Defense Department 1981–7; Resident Fellow, American Enterprise Institute, Washington 1987–; Chairman, Defense Policy Board Advisory Committee 2001–3. Paul Wolfowitz (1943–). Deputy Assistant Secretary, Defense Department 1977–80; switches from the Democratic to Republican Party 1981; Director of Policy Planning, State Department 1981–2; Assistant Secretary, State Department 1983–6; US Ambassador to Indonesia 1986–9; Under-Secretary, Defense Department 1989–93; Dean, Paul H. Nitze School of Advanced International Studies, Johns Hopkins University 1993–2001; Deputy Secretary, Defense Department 2001–5; President, the World Bank 2005–.

117 David Willetts (1956–) MP (Con.) Havant 1992–. Paymaster-General 1996.

118 Chris Pond (1952–) MP (Lab.) Gravesham 1997–. Parliamentary Under Secretary, Department of Work and Pensions 2003–.

119 Institute for Fiscal Studies Director, 1991–2002, Andrew Dilnot; 2002 – Robert Chote.

120 See Anthony Powell, *Journals 1982–6* (London: Heinemann, 1995), p. 141 for an account of dinner at Number 10, Downing Street on Wednesday 27 March 1985: 'The talk at this Downing Street dinner . . . ranged over East Germany, to the condition of Young People in this country, topics on which I am not outstandingly hot. Mrs T did however, please me by saying that everything from which we are now suffering is *all* discussed in the plainest terms in Dostoevsky's *The Possessed* (as I prefer *The Devils*); a fact I have been preaching for decades. I wonder when, how, she got round to this. Did she read the novel . . . or was that pointed out to her by someone? I fear probably the latter' (emphasis in the original).

121 Rt Hon. Sir Alastair Goodlad (1943) MP (Con.) Northwich 1974–83; Eddisbury 1983–99. Government Chief Whip 1995–7; High Commissioner to Australia 2000–05.

122 Rt Hon Sir John Nott (1932–) MP (Con.) Cornwall, St Ives 1966–83. Secretary of State for Defence 1981–3, Chairman and chief executive, Lazard Brothers and Co. Ltd, 1985–90.

123 Members indicated with an asterisk (*) in endnotes 123–127 left the House of Commons at the 2005 general election. In the Parliament that was elected at the general election of 2001 and that sat until 2005 the Directorate consisted of fifty-

eight members of whom eleven (asterisked*) left the House of Commons at the general election of 2005. This grouping consisted of: Tony Baldry (Con.) Banbury; Gregory Barker (Con.) Bexhill and Battle; Stuart Bell (Lab.) Middlesbrough; Henry Bellingham (Con.) Norfolk North West; David Burnside* (Ulster Unionist) South Antrim; John Butterfill (Con.) Bournemouth West; David Cameron (Con.) Witney; Christopher Chope (Con.) Christchurch; Kenneth Clarke (Con.) Rushcliffe; Jack Cunningham* (Lab.) Copeland; Quentin Davies (Con.) Grantham and Stamford; Jeffrey Donaldson (UUP) Lagan Valley; Stephen Dorrell (Con.) Charnwood; Alan Duncan (Con.) Rutland and Melton; Michael Fallon (Con.) Sevenoaks; Frank Field (Lab.) Birkenhead; Howard Flight* (Con.) Arundel and South Downs; Cheryl Gillan (Con.) Chesham and Amersham; John Greenway (Con.) Ryedale; John Selwyn Gummer (Con.) Suffolk Coastal; David Heathcoat-Amory (Con.) Wells; Doug Henderson (Lab.) Newcastle-upon-Tyne North; George Howarth (Lab.) Knowsley North and Sefton East; Gerald Howarth (Con.) Aldershot; Michael Jack (Con.) Fylde; Robert Jackson* (Con.) Wantage (crossed the floor to join the Parliamentary Labour Party: January, 2005); Paul Keetch (Lib. Dem.) Aldershot; Peter Lilley (Con.) Hitchin and Harpenden; John Maples (Con.) Stratford on Avon; Michael Mates (Con.) Hampshire East; Francis Maude (Con.) Horsham; Brian Mawhinney* (Con.) Cambridgeshire North West; Andrew Mitchell (Con.) Sutton Coldfield; Lewis Moonie* (Con.) Kirkcaldy; Archie Norman* (Con.) Tunbridge Wells; Stephen O'Brien (Con.) Eddisbury; Richard Page* (Con.) Hertfordshire South West; Michael Portillo* (Con.) Kensington and Chelsea; John Randall (Con.) Uxbridge; John Redwood (Con.) Wokingham; Geoffrey Robinson (Lab.) Coventry North West; Chris Smith* (Lab.) Islington and Finsbury; Nicholas Soames (Con.) Mid Sussex; Michael Spicer (Con.) Worcestershire West; Bob Spink (Con.) Castle Point; John Stanley (Con.) Tonbridge and Malling; Hugo Swire (Con.) Devon East; Robert Syms (Con.) Poole; Peter Tapsell (Con.) Louth and Horncastle; Ian Taylor (Con.) Esher and Walton; John Thurso (Lib. Dem.) Caithness, Sutherland and Easter Ross; David Tredinnick (Con.) Bosworth; Andrew Tyrie (Con.) Chichester; David Willetts (Con.) Havant; Brian Wilson* (Lab.) Cunninghame North; Nicholas Winterton (Con.) Macclesfield; Tim Yeo (Con.) Suffolk South; George Young (Con.) Hampshire North West. Of the forty-seven members of the original Directorate who were re-elected at the general election of 2005, two (David Cameron (Con.) Witney and Bob Spink (Con.) Castle Point) had ceased to be counted among the Directorate in terms of their declared business interests by November 2005. See *Register of Members' Interests as at 1 November 2005* (London, The Stationery Office Ltd., 2005) which updates the earlier *Register of Members' Interests as at 28 January 2005* (ibid).

The twenty-two additional members of the Directorate who sit in the House of Commons elected in 2005 comprise two groups: a) MPs who were re-elected in 2005, had not been members of the Directorate when they sat in the preceding Parliament but have now acquired new, declared, business interests on a significant scale and b) MPs elected for the first time in 2005 and who have declared such interests in the register published in November 2005.

**a) The first grouping includes:** David Blunkett (Lab.) Sheffield, Brightside; Stephen Byers (Lab.) Tyneside North; David Curry (Con.) Skipton and Ripon; Oliver Letwin (Con.) Dorset West; David Ruffley (Con.) Bury St Edmunds; Robert Walter (Con.) Dorset North; Derek Wyatt (Lab.) Sittingbourne and Sheppey.

**b) The second group includes:** Brian Binley (Con.) Northampton South; Philip Dunne (Con.) Ludlow; Lynne Featherstone (Lib. Dem.) Hornsey and Wood

Green; John Hemming (Lib. Dem.) Birmigham, Yardley; Jeremy Hunt (Con.) Surrey South West; Nick Hurd (Con.) Ruislip-Northwood; Mark Lancaster (Con.) Milton Keynes North East; William McCrea (DUP) Antrim South; Brooks Newmark (Con.) Braintree; John Penrose (Con.) Weston-Super-Mare; Mark Pritchard (Con.) The Wrekin; Malcolm Rifkind (Con.) Kensington and Chelsea (returning after losing his seat in 1997); Grant Shapps (Con.) Welwyn Hatfield; Graham Stuart (Con.) Beverley and Holderness; Rob Wilson (Con.) Reading East.

In the current Parliament elected in 2005 the Directorate consists therefore of sixty-seven members, nine more than the fifty-eight who sat in the last Parliament.

The following nine MPs who sat in the Parliament elected in 2001, although not directors, held shareholdings whose significance made them allied to the Directorate and they continued to declare such shareholding interests after their re-election to the House of Commons in 2005: John Barrett (Lib. Dem.) Edinburgh West; Barbara Follett (Lab.) Stevenage; Philip Hammond (Con.) Runnymede and Weybridge; Charles Hendry (Con.) Wealden; Tim Loughton (Con.) East Worthing and Shoreham; Fiona Mactaggart (Lab.) Slough; George Osborne (Con.) Tatton; Richard Shepherd (Con.) Aldridge-Brownhills (later declared a remunerated directorship in the register of 1 November 2005); John Baron (Con.) Billericay (declared a directorial interest which, however, was unremunerated). MPs elected in 2005 and whose scale of shareholding interests also represents a close relationship to the Directorial class include: Adam Afriyie (Con.) Windsor; Peter Bone (Con.) Wellingborough; Susan Kramer (Lib. Dem.) Richmond Park.

124 The twenty-one MPs with continuing professional careers and who sat in the Parliament elected in 2001 were: Paul Beresford (Con.) Mole Valley, Dental Surgeon; William Cash (Con.) Stone ,Solicitor; Denzil Davies* (Lab.) Llanelli Barrister; Andrew Dismore (Lab.) Hendon, Solicitors' consultancy; Jonathan Djanoogly (Con.) Huntingdon, Solicitor; Michael J. Foster (Lab.) Hastings and Rye, Solicitors' consultancy; Edward Garnier (Con.) Harborough, Barrister; Dominic Grieve (Con.) Beaconsfield, Barrister; Douglas Hogg (Con.) Sleaford and North Hykeham, Barrister; Greg Knight (Con.) East Yorkshire, Solicitor; Mark Lazarowicz (Lab.) Edinburgh North and Leith, Member, Faculty of Advocates, Edward Leigh (Con.) Gainsborough, Barrister; Elfyn Llwyd (Plaid Cymru) Meirionnydd Nant Conwy, Barrister; Humphrey Malins (Con.) Woking, Solicitor; Robert (Bob) Marshall-Andrews (Lab.) Medway, Barrister; Andrew Murrison (Con.) Westbury, Surgeon; Richard Ottaway (Con.) Croydon South, Solicitor; Mark Simmonds (Con.) Boston and Skegness, Chartered Surveyor; Anthony Steen (Con.) Totnes, Barrister; Howard Stoate (Lab.) Dartford, Medical Practitioner; Nigel Waterson (Con.) Eastbourne, Solicitors' consultancy.

After the 2005 election this group was joined by seven newly elected MPs to constitute the new grouping of twenty-seven members with continuing professional interests: David Burrowes (Con.) Enfield, Southgate, Solicitor; Geoffrey Cox (Con.) Torridge and Devon West, Barrister; Christopher Fraser (Con.) Norfolk South West, Management Consultant; Mark Harper (Con.) Forest of Dean, Chartered Accountant; David Jones (Con.) Clwyd West, Solicitor; Alasdair Mcdonnell (SDLP) Belfast South, Medical Practitioner; Andrew Slaughter (Lab.) Ealing, Acton and Shepherd's Bush, Barrister.

125 The landed interest was represented in the last Parliament by ten members: Tim Boswell (Con.) Daventry; James Clappison (Con.) Hertsemere; Geoffrey Clifton Brown (Con.) Cotswold; Michael Lord (Con.) Suffolk Central and Ipswich

North; Michael Mates (Con.) Hampshire East; Robert Smith (Lib. Dem.) West Aberdeenshire and Kincardine; Gavin Strang (Lab.) Edinburgh East and Musselburgh; Robert Walter (Con.) Dorset North; Shaun Woodward (Lab.) St Helens South; Roger Williams (Lib. Dem.) Brecon and Radnorshire. After the 2005 election this grouping increased to fourteen having been joined by, among newly elected members, the following: Richard Benyon (Con.) Newbury; Robert Goodwill (Con.) Scarborough; Paul Rowen (Lib. Dem.) Rochdale and, among re-elected members, by: Desmond Swayne (Con.) New Forest West.

126 Those members with continuing Lloyds syndicate interests were: Jonathan Djanoogly (Con.) Huntingdon; David Tredinnick (Con.) Bosworth and Peter Viggers (Con.) Gosport.

127 The MPs with significant income from journalism were: Diane Abbott (Lab.) Hackney North and Stoke Newington; Robin Cook (Lab.) Livingston (died August 2005); George Galloway (Lab.) Glasgow Kelvin (re-elected to the House of Commons in 2005 as the Respect member for Bethnal Green and Bow); William Hague (Con.) Richmond, Yorkshire; Boris Johnson (Con.) Henley; Michael Portillo* (Con.) Kensington and Chelsea and Ann Widdecombe (Con.) Maidstone and The Weald. Michael Gove (Con.) Surrey Heath joined this grouping at the 2005 general election.

128 On this issue see the investigation of Tesco's links with government in http:// archive.corporatewatch.org/profiles/tesco/tesco3.htm: 'Tesco was also a £12 million sponsor of the Millenium Dome. It was reported in the *Observer* (26 July 1997) at the time that lobbying firm LLM (Lawson Lucas Mendelsohn) – involved in a campaign on behalf of Tesco to block plans for a tax on shopping centre car parks – had "suggested that a £12 million Tesco donation to the Millenium Dome was part of a quid pro quo deal" – giving its support to a government project in order to endear itself to New Labour. The paper went on to say that there is no suggestion that Tesco made the Dome donation to help it get its way over the car park tax issue. But the plan to impose the tax was dropped from the White Paper on transport and the terms of the exemption were exactly as LLM's Ben Lucas had suggested. *The Sunday Times* (12 July 1998) said that the estimated cost to Tesco of the car park tax would have been £40 million.'

129 For the assimilationist mind at work in Scotland see J.G.A. Pocock, *Virtue, Commerce and History: Essays on Political Thought and History, Chiefly in the Eighteenth Century* (Cambridge: Cambridge University Press, 1985) and especially pp. 230–53 ('From the Financial Revolution to the Scottish Enlightenment') for a characteristically stimulating account of how the provincial elites of Edinburgh after the Act of Union (1707) – legal, land-owning, mercantile, academic and clerical – were 'dedicated to the furtherance of sociability, conversation, and moral and economic improvement'. The emphasis on the last became distinctively Scottish 'because in Scotland there was no Tory landed interest, but only Jacobites, Highlanders, Borderers and a past remembered as more barbarous than it probably had been . . .' In these circumstances, '. . . the Whig belief that conversation and commerce go together merged with a perception of economic improvement as immediately superimposed upon feudal, agnatic, and hunter-warrior states of society.' The dangerous evidence of the Highland rebellion of 1745 served to quicken this perception among enlightened Scottish circles and led to a confrontation with the 'heavily armoured Calvinism' which now seemed to be part of the country's independent past rather than of its British future. Moreover, this 'rapid advent of an enlightened morality merged with a Scottish tradition of study in the Roman civil law' which was 'itself turning . . . towards the analysis of jurisprudence in terms of manners, moral, and sociability' (p. 238).

Bruce Lenman, *Integration, Enlightenment and Industrialisation: Scotland 1746–1832* (London: Edward Arnold, 1981) adds a cultural dimension to this story of elite assimilation, particularly in 'Growth, Enlightenment and Integration 1760–1775', pp. 29–55. The success enjoyed by Scottish artists and architects such as Robert Adam illustrated how, 'It was vitally important for the careers of many ambitious Scots in the eighteenth century that various forms of classicism constituted an international cultural vocabulary immediately accessible to, and therefore saleable to, the ruling classes of what contemporaries called the polite nations.'

130 On the survival of Jacobitism as a serious force intellectually as well as a threat militarily see J.C.D. Clark, *English Society 1688–1832: Ideology, Social Structure and Political Practice during the Ancien Regime* (Cambridge: Cambridge University Press, 1985, pp. 119–98.

131 Rt Hon. John Morris, QC KG (1931–) (Baron Morris of Aberavon 2003) MP (Lab.) Aberavon 1959–2001. Deputy General Secretary, Farmers' Union of Wales 1956–8; Secretary of State for Wales, 1974–9; Attorney-General 1997–9.

132 For a celebratory version of this mythology's conservative aspects at its most dewy-eyed, see *The Collected Works of Samuel Taylor Coleridge*, general editor: Kathleen Coburn, vol. X, *On the Constitution of Church and State* (1829) ed. John Colmer (London: Routledge & Kegan Paul, 1976) and esp. p. 67 for the evidence of Coleridge's panic attack at the thought of '. . . the true historical feeling, the immortal life of an historical nation, generation linked to generation by faith, freedom, heraldry, and ancestral fame, languishing, and giving place to the superstitions of wealth, and newspaper reputation.' England would then fall victim to, 'Talents without genius: a swarm of clever, well-informed men: an anarchy of minds, a despotism of maxims.' To this terror may be added the danger of, 'Despotism of finance in government . . . of presumption, temerity and hardness of heart, in political economy.' Cheerfulness breaks in however at the recollection (p. 19) that, 'a Constitution is an idea arising out of the idea of a state; and because our whole history from Alfred onward demonstrates the continued influence of such an idea, or ultimate aim, on the minds of our forefathers . . . we speak . . . of the idea itself, as actually existing . . . in the minds and consciences of the persons, whose duties it prescribes, and whose rights it determines.' Coleridge here combines the influence of cloudy German philosophy with some warm sentiment about the life-giving rootedness of English society. Hegel, as it were, has met Heidi and decided that they should both settle in Ambridge.

133 Quoted in William Donaldson, *Brewer's Rogues, Villains and Eccentrics: An A–Z of Roguish Britons Through the Ages* (London: Cassell, 2002) p. 561. Andrew Roberts, *Salisbury: Victorian Titan* (London: Weidenfeld & Nicolson, 1999) is the authoritative modern biography of the Prime Minister.

# Chapter 3    The Professional Elites: A Collective Aberration?

1 The New Elizabethanism of the 1950s, having been given a kick-start by the coronation of Elizabeth II in 1953, produced a crop of romantic explorations of this theme. For an example among historical works see A.L. Rowse, *The Expansion of Elizabethan England* (London: Macmillan, 1955) and the author's enthused description (p.1) of the expansion of 'the most taut and vigorous national society in Europe' to a point at which it 'became increasingly identified with the central movement in the history of the modern world'.

2 Correlli Barnett, *The Lost Victory: British Dreams, British Realities, 1945–50*

(London: Macmillan, 1955) discusses the post-war failure to modernize British industry in the light of the cultural attitudes of the British governing elite. See esp. pp. 123–51, 'The Brave New World and the Cruel Real World'.

3  For an influential explanation which reflects the circumstances of the early Thatcherite period, see Martin Wiener, *English Culture and the Decline of the Industrial Spirit 1850–1980* (Cambridge: Cambridge University Press, 1981).

4  V.H. Galbraith, *Kings and Chroniclers: Essays in English Mediaeval History* (London: Hambledon Press, 1982) describes the milieu. See esp. pp. 78–112, 'The Literacy of the Mediaeval English Kings'. For an account of the institutional workings, see H.G. Richardson and G.O. Sayles, *The Governance of Mediaeval England from the Conquest to Magna Carta* (Edinburgh: Edinburgh University Press, 1964) and esp. pp. 240–50, 'The Household and the Exchequer' and pp. 265–84, 'Statecraft and learning'.

5  G.R. Elton, *The Tudor Revolution in Government* (Cambridge: Cambridge University Press, 1953) remains a classic account of the bureaucratic drama. But see also 'English national self-consciousness and the Parliament in the 16th century', in his *Studies in Tudor and Stuart Politics and Government*, vol. 4 (Cambridge: Cambridge University Press, 1992), pp. 131–43, 'The English people early acquired a high degree of national self-consciousness,' (p. 139) and the fact that 'Parliament was in fact a part of the king's Parliament' (p. 139) was related to that development. 'The primary concern of Parliament . . . the reason for which it was called and the work demanded of it by monarch and nation alike – was not political but legislative: it authorised taxation and it made laws' (p. 140).

6  A.N. Wilson, *The Victorians* (London: Hutchinson, 2002) provides a magisterial survey of the age and its central figures.

7  Roy Lewis and Angus Maude MP, *Professional People* (London: Phoenix House, 1952), describes the now lost world of professional self-esteem.

8  The use of high street analogies also shows the consumerist origins of this new form of power. See John Carvel, 'Minister hails Debenham's model for NHS healthcare "boutiques"', *Guardian*, 13 October 2005, for an account of how Sue Slipman, director of the Foundation Trust Network, has urged the application of what she terms a 'Debenham's model of healthcare' across the NHS. 'A Debenham's department store is made up of a collection of branded boutiques, providing shoppers with convenient access to a full range of popular labels. That, she said, is what NHS general hospitals may look like soon.'

9  The Austrian-born American management consultant, Peter Drucker, is the founder of the modern, largely dismal science of management. *The New Society* (New York: Harper & Row, 1950), *The Practice of Management* (New York: Harper & Row, 1954) and *Managing in Turbulent Times* (New York: Harper & Row 1980) showed the originality of Drucker's genius. However, the libraries of management textbooks produced by his imitators have been a study in corporate plod and leaden prose. For a welcome note of realism about the ambiguous relationship between aims and consequences in business and economics, see Steven Levitt and Stephen Dubner, *Freakonomics* (London: Allen Lane, 2005).

10  On the rise of the 'civilian general', whose battles are exclusively fought within the Whitehall machinery of government, see the criticisms of Colonel Tim Collins quoted in Lewis Smith, 'Colonel attacks "civilian soldier" generals who have never fought', *The Times*, 12 October 2005: 'One particular little red, fat general has never been in a fight in a playground. He's a civilian soldier in the true sense of never letting anything happen.' Collins 'was also critical of the financial management of the Army and said that centralisation of services such as recruitment had damaged efficiency. When he took over the Royal Irish he

was 250 men short of a full complement and had been told that there was no one willing to join up. He took over recruitment and within weeks he had had enough, having discovered that recruits were being turned away for "bizarre reasons such as having too many tattoos".'

11 Quoted in Libby Purves, 'You simply can't trust IT', *The Times*, 8 March 2005.

12 See also Jonathan Carr-Brown, 'NHS chaos exposed by new e-mails', *Sunday Times*, 13 November 2005 for a description of the technical problems and administrative delays experienced in introducing the government's IT programme for the booking of NHS hospital appointments by GPs.

13 Quoted in Matthew Parris, 'Ting! The Treasury cash register goes. Another £50m down the drain', *The Times*, 5 March 2005.

14 See Simon Jenkins, 'Where are the missing billions?', *Evening Standard*, 17 March 2005.

15 Elizabeth Judge and Sam Coates, 'Government in ID card talks with firms before Bill passed', *The Times*, 30 May 2005.

16 For further information, see Andrew Gilligan, 'Don't blink, the £5.5bn ID scheme won't work', *Evening Standard*, 23 May 2005.

17 For an account of British intelligence's scandals and intermittent comic effects, see Tom Bower, *The Perfect English Spy: Sir Dick White and the Secret War 1935–90* (London: Heinemann, 1995).

18 Peter Wright, *Spycatcher: The Candid Autobiography of a Senior Intelligence Officer* (New York: Viking Press, 1967).

19 Heather Brooke, 'The four hundred laws that shackle your right to know', *The Times (Law)*, 24 May 2005. See also Sean O'Neill and Jill Sherman, 'Government's secrecy culture blocks freedom of information', *The Times*, 30 September 2005.

20 Quoted in Gabriel Rozenberg, 'Blunders added up for UK's leading statistician', *The Times (Business)*, 5 August 2005.

21 Quoted in *The Times (Business)*, 5 August 2005.

22 Andrew Turnbull (Baron Turnbull of Enfield 2005) (1945–) Principal Private Secretary to the Prime Minister 1988–92; HM Treasury 1992–4; Permanent Secretary, Department of the Environment 1994–7; Department of the Environment, Transport and Regions 1997–8; Permanent Secretary, HM Treasury 1998–2002 and Secretary of the Cabinet and Head of the Home Civil Service, 2002–5.

23 For these claims, see Peter Riddell, 'The veteran servant who can stop being totally civil', *The Times*, 29 July 2005.

24 See *Private Eye*, 2–15 September 2005.

25 John Birt (1944–) (Baron Birt of Liverpool 2000) Controller of Features and Current Affairs London Weekend Television 1977–81; Deputy Director General BBC 1987–92; Director General BBC 1992–2000; Personal adviser to Tony Blair 2001–5. Joins the venture capital firm Terra Firma, 2005.

26 See the account in Steve Hewlett, 'Blue skies thinker with the eye of an accountant', *Guardian*, 4 July 2005.

27 Sue Cameron, 'Political threats to Whitehall have come to a head', *Financial Times*, 10 October 2005.

28 For these and other figures involved, see Paul Waugh, 'Not one Whitehall job axed in Labour purge', *Evening Standard*, 5 August 2005.

29 London School of Economics report, sponsored by the Sutton Trust. See Tony Halpin, 'Demise of grammar schools leaves poor facing uphill struggle', *The Times*, 25 April 2005, p. 6. See also the report by the ONS in *Population Trends* (2005), analysing people aged 36–45 years in 2001 who were living with their parents in 1971. Nearly 60 per cent of these men and 42 per cent of women with a parent in a professional or managerial job were themselves professionals or

managers. Only 27 per cent of men and 22 per cent of women whose parents were part-skilled or unskilled rose to the top two social classes. Only 15 per cent of men who were part-skilled or unskilled had had a parent in the professional or managerial class. Richard Ford and Karl Mansfield, 'Why class is permanent, even in this golden age of equality', *The Times*, 30 September 2005 discuss the findings.

30 See the report on the findings of a Warwick University study of 48,281 students in Roger Dobson and Geraldine Hackett, 'Higher school fees equal lower degrees for boys', *Sunday Times*, 10 July 2005.

31 Quoted in Dobson and Hackett, 'Higher school fees'.

32 Professor Sir Howard Newby (1947–). Professor of Sociology, University of Essex 1983–8; Vice-Chancellor University of Southampton 1994–2001; Chief Executive, Higher Education Funding Council 2001–.

33 Reported in Tony Halpin, 'Closure of key subjects is "not a crisis"', *The Times*, 29 June 2005.

34 Robert Mendick, 'Parents on Blair's turf turn against city academy', *Evening Standard*, 9 March 2005, gives details of the present, and of some proposed, academies.

35 Tony Halpin, 'Labour's star academy on the wane as secondary failures rise', *The Times*, 17 May 2005.

36 Matthew Taylor and Rebecca Smithers, 'New academy schools fuel education row', *Guardian*, 5 September 2005.

37 Alan Ryan, 'Fading ivy', *Financial Times Magazine*, 4 June 2005. On this theme, see Jennifer Washburn, *University, Inc.: The Corporate Corruption of American Higher Education* (New York: Basic Books, 2005).

38 On the idea of a 'society of orders', see Pierre Goubert, *The Ancien Régime: French Society 1600–1750* (London: Weidenfeld & Nicolson, 1969) and esp. pp. 153–92, 'The nobility: in search of a definition' and 'Types of noblemen'.

39 R.W. Southern, *Scholastic Humanism and the Unification of Europe*, vol. 1 (Oxford: Blackwell, 1995), pp. 237–63, describes the background to the development of canon law in eleventh and twelfth-century Europe.

40 William Doyle, *The Old European Order, 1660–1800* (Oxford: Oxford University Press, 1978), pp. 73–95, 'Ruling orders', describes the variety of privileges enjoyed by the nobility 'although social precedence, sword bearing, coats of arms, and special standing at law were universal' (p. 74) and 'the essence of being noble was to be recognised as such'.

41 For an historical dimension to the connection in England between aristocracy and land-ownership, see K.B. McFarlane, *The Nobility of Later Mediaeval England* (Oxford: Clarendon Press, 1973), pp. 41–60, 'The nobility and the land'.

42 For a brilliant synthesis, infused with the author's commitment to patriotic socialism, see Georges Lefebvre, *The French Revolution: From its Origins to 1793* (London: Routledge & Kegan Paul, 1962).

43 For the theocratic details, see Jean Calvin, 'Civil government', in *Institutes of Christian Religion*, ed. J.T. McNeill, 2 vols. (London: SCM Press, 1961), vol. 2, pp. 1485–1521.

44 Russell Meiggs, *The Athenian Empire* (Oxford: Clarendon Press, 1972), describes how Athens 'made it her policy to select and honour individual friends of Athens in the cities and to use their services' p. 215. See 'The instruments of empire', pp. 205–19, and 'Imperial jurisdiction', pp. 220–33.

45 See David Ibbetson and Andrew Lewis, 'The Roman Law tradition', in A.D.E. Lewis and D.J. Ibbetson, (eds.), *The Roman Law Tradition* (Cambridge: Cambridge University Press, 1994), pp. 1–14, for an account of how the ancient

Roman legal texts as interpreted in the sixteenth–eighteenth centuries came to form 'the base of an elaborate system of Natural law, an idealised system to which national laws might aspire' (p. 4). '– the practical dominance of reasoning by deducation and analogy was so deeply embedded that it was easily detachable from its roots in the writings of the Roman jurists' (p. 6). But in England from the late thirteenth century to the sixteenth century 'legal history is largely the story of the development of remedies based on indigenous procedures' and on 'a strongly held ideological commitment to the insularity of the Common law and its separation from the Civil (Roman) law, which was seen to be at the base of continental systems' (p. 6). The authors contrast the diagnostic expertise of Roman law with the Common law of England and Wales as a legal system which 'is essentially indistinct from custom and practice, and where the nearest approach to a lawyer is the tribal elder who is perceived as remembering and articulating this custom' (p. 11).

46  For the political importance of patronage networks and of personal relation-ships based on obligation and loyalty in the history of ancient Rome see Matthias Gelzer, *The Roman Nobility* (Oxford: Blackwell, 1969), English translation by Robin Seager of Gelzer's *Die Nobilität der Romischen Republik* (1912) and *Die Nobilität der Kaizerzeit* (1915): 'The entire Roman people, both the ruling circle and the mass of voters whom they ruled, was, as a society, permeated by multifarious relationships based on fides and on personal connections . . . These relationships determined the distribution of political power' (p. 139). For Gelzer's description of the workings of 'political friend-ship', see pp. 101–10.

47  As a guide to some long-standing features of conduct at the Bar of England and Wales, see Henry Cecil, *Brief to Counsel* (London: Michael Joseph, 1958) and esp. p. 50 ('Choosing a master'), p. 128 ('The leading question') and, invaluably, p. 142 ('What do you do when you know your client is guilty').

48  See J.H. Baker, *The Common Law Tradition: Lawyers, Books and the Law* (London: Hambledon Press, 2000), pp. 107–15 ('Case-law in England and continental Europe'), for a protest against the oversimplification of the contrast between the English lawyer who works from decided cases and the continental lawyer who works from codes and doctrinal literature.

49  For an account of how this idea of the common law shaped English politics in a profound way, see J.G.A. Pocock, *The Ancient Constitution and the Feudal Law: A Study in English Historical Thought in the Seventeenth Century* (Cam-bridge: Cambridge University Press, 1957) and esp. pp. 30–55 ('The common-law mind: custom and the immemorial').

50  For F.W. Maitland (1850–1906), see his *Selected Historical Essays* (selected by Helen M. Cam) (Cambridge: Cambridge University Press, 1957), pp. 122–34, 'English law, 1307–1600', and pp. 97–121, 'History of English Law'. 'Somehow or another, England, after a fashion all her own, had stumbled into a scheme for the reconciliation of permanence with progress' (p. 134). For Lord Denning (Alfred Thompson Denning, 1899–1999), see his remarks on the correct under-standing of, and praise for, the doctrine of precedent, in *The Discipline of Law* (London: Butterworths, 1979).

51  Although the total number of barristers over the past thirty years has increased from some 3,400 to about 11,500.

52  Frances Gibb, 'Rich QCs should be made to share says Lord Falconer', *The Times*, 21 July 2005, and 'Courts face crisis as barristers fight back over pay cuts', *The Times*, 19 September 2005.

53  The ten highest-paid barristers paid by the criminal defence service in 2004–5 were:

|  | £ |
|---|---|
| 1. James Sturman, QC | 1,180,000 |
| 2. Simon Bourne-Arton, QC | 902,000 |
| 3. Kalyani Kaul | 766,000 |
| 4. Gilbert Gray, QC | 755,000 |
| 5. Balbir Singh | 750,000 |
| 6. Peter Griffiths, QC | 690,000 |
| 7. Trevor Burke, QC | 683,000 |
| 8. Thomas Derbyshire | 668,000 |
| 9. George Carter-Stephenson | 653,000 |
| 10. David Spens, QC | 639,000 |

The top ten sets of barristers' chambers, by present turnover, in 2004–5 were:

|  | million |
|---|---|
| 1. Brick Court Chambers | 32 m |
| 2. Essex Court Chambers | 31 m |
| 3. One Essex Court | 27.3 m |
| 4. Fountain Court Chambers | 27 m |
| 5. Blackstone Chambers | 24.3 m |
| 6. 3–4 South Square | 23.5 m |
| 7. Wilberforce Chambers | 22.2 m |
| 8. 20 Essex Street | 22.0 m |
| 9. Maitland Chambers | 21.8 m |
| 10. No5 Chambers | 21.6 m |

*Source*: *The Lawyer*. See *The Times* (*Law*), 11 October 2005, p. 6.

At these levels of earnings we find ourselves among the practitioners of the Commercial Bar where the pickings are the juiciest, life is at its most voluptuous and the legal minds, among those who have decided to arrive at an accommodation with the power realities of the financial and business elites, are much the sharpest. Jonathan Sumption, QC, can therefore afford in every sense the luxurious proposition that: 'There's not much law in this job. It's obvious what the law is once you've worked out the facts. But being a barrister is so much fun.' Lord Grabiner, QC, also a Commercial silk, advised both Robert Maxwell and Rupert Murdoch in their various legal disputes. Having represented Murdoch against the trade unions after the decision of the proprietor of *The Times* to move the newspaper to Wapping he is well qualified to offer a comparison: 'Murdoch is astute, very clever and always listens to my advice, whereas Maxwell always argued, thinking he was as good a lawyer as a businessman. But, although he was extremely overbearing, I liked Robert. He sacked me then rehired me. It was a good lesson. No one has ever really fazed me since.' In more recent times, Lord Grabiner admits that he has: 'enjoyed working with the entrepreneur Philip Green', and finds that 'being a barrister is fantastic.' See *The Times* (*Law*), 11 October 2005.

54 Claire Dyer, 'James Sturman QC. First lawyer to get £1m plus in legal aid fees', *Guardian*, 15 September 2005.

55 See Baker, *The Common Law Tradition*, pp. 3–28 ('The third university of England').

56 Private interview.

57 For Austin, see W.E. Rumble, *The Thought of John Austin: Jurisprudence, Colonial Reform and the British Constitution* (London: Athlone Press, 1985).

58 Quoted in W.E. Rumble 'John Austin', *Oxford Dictionary of National Biography*, vol. 2 (Oxford: Oxford University Press, 2004). For Robinson, see *The*

*Diary of Henry Crabb Robinson: An Abridgement,* ed. with an introduction by Derek Hudson (London: Oxford University Press, 1967).

59 Noted in Lance Price, *The Spin Doctor's Diary: Inside Number 10 with New Labour* (London: Hodder & Stoughton, 2005).

60 For the law code of Hammurabi, ruler of the first (Amorite) dynasty of Babylon (reigned c. 1792–50 BC), see Gwendolyn Leick, *Mesopotamia: The Invention of the City* (London: Allen Lane, 2001), pp. 151, 186, 300n. 173.

61 I have relied on the facts and figures given in the best recent analysis of the Law Lords as an institutional group, Maxwell Barrett, *The Law Lords: An Account of the Workings of Britain's Highest Judicial Body and the Men who Preside over It* (London: Macmillan, 2001).

62 Barrett, *The Law Lords,* p. 31.

63 Anthony Lloyd (1929–) (Baron Lloyd of Berwick, 1993). Judge of the High Court of Justice, Queen's Bench Division (QBD) 1978–84; Lord Justice of Appeal 1984–93; Lord of Appeal in Ordinary 1993–9.

64 Personal information.

65 Barrett, *The Law Lords,* pp. 33–5.

66 Leonard Hoffman (1934–) (Baron Hoffman of Chedworth, 1995). Advocate of the Supreme Court of South Africa 1958–60; Judge of the High Court of Justice, Chancery Division 1985–92; Lord Justice of Appeal 1992–5; Lord of Appeal in Ordinary 1995–.

67 Richard Scott (1934–) (Baron Scott of Foscote 2000). Judge of the High Court of Justice, Chancery Division 1983–91; Lord Justice of Appeal 1991–4; Vice-Chancellor of the Chancery Division of the High Court 1994–2000; Lord of Appeal in Ordinary 2000–.

68 Johan Steyn (1932–) (Baron Steyn of Swafield, 1995). Senior Counsel of the Supreme Court of South Africa 1970; Judge of the High Court of Justice, QBD 1985–91; Lord Justice of Appeal 1992–5; Lord of Appeal in Ordinary 1995–.

69 Barrett, *The Law Lords,* pp. 158–73, provides a detailed account of the Judicial Committee of the Privy Council.

70 Note, however, the decision of the National Westminster Bank to appoint Robert Alexander, QC (1936–2005) (Lord Alexander of Weedon) as its chairman (1989–99) when the bank was going through a difficult period in the late 1980s.

71 According to Lord Devlin's son, Tim Devlin.

72 Gordon Slynn (1930–) (Baron Slynn of Hadley, 1992). Judge of the High Court of Justice, QBD 1976–81; Advocate General 1981–8; Judge 1988–92, European High Court of Justice, Luxembourg; Lord of Appeal in Ordinary 1992–2002.

73 Robert Goff (1926–) (Baron Goff of Chievely 1986). Judge of the High Court of Justice, QBD 1975–82; Lord Justice of Appeal, 1982–6; Lord of Appeal in Ordinary 1986–98.

74 James Mackay (1927–) (Baron Mackay of Clashfern 1979). Lord Advocate of Scotland 1979–84; Lord of Appeal in Ordinary 1985–7; Lord Chancellor of Great Britain 1987–97.

75 Barrett, *The Law Lords,* pp. 14–16.

76 Noted in Barrett, *The Law Lords,* p. 24.

77 See, for example, the career of William Allen Jowitt (1885–1957) (Earl Jowitt of Stevenage), who was the Liberal MP for Hartlepool (1922–4) and was then returned to the House of Commons to serve as the Liberal MP for Preston in the general election of 1929. Within a week of his election, however, he resigned from the Liberal Party and, having stood successfully as the Labour candidate at the resulting by-election in Preston, became Attorney-General in the Labour administration led by Ramsay MacDonald. Jowitt continued in that post on the

formation of the National Government in August 1931 but then lost his seat in the general election of later that year and was forced out of the Labour Party because of his support for that government. In 1936, he was readmitted to the Labour Party and in 1939, at a by-election, was elected the MP for Ashton under Lyme. He served as Solicitor-General (1940–2) in the war-time coalition and then became the Labour government's Lord Chancellor (1945–51), taking the title of Baron Jowitt of Stevenage. He was raised within the peerage to a viscountcy in 1947 and created an earl in 1951.

78 Similar self-serving statements can be found in Quintin Hogg, Lord Hailsham of St Marylebone, *The Dilemma of Democracy: Diagnosis and Prescription* (London: Collins, 1978). Within a year the dilemma had resolved itself and Lord Hailsham was back on the woolsack.

79 Michael Havers (1923–92) (Baron Havers of St Edmundsbury, 1987). MP (Con.) Wimbledon, 1970–87; Attorney General 1979–87; Lord Chancellor 1987 (Retired due to ill health, 1987).

80 Personal recollection.

81 See Bob Sherwood, 'Falconer to unveil plans for big legal shake-up', *Financial Times*, 21 March 2005, and Frances Gibb, 'Hiring a lawyer "will be as easy as buying beans"', *The Times*, 18 October 2005.

82 Frances Gibb and Greg Hurst, 'Lawyers wait for verdict on how they judge themselves', *The Times*, 21 March 2005.

83 Frances Gibb, interview with Ken Macdonald, QC, 'Fancy a job with the new-look CPS? Join the queue', *The Times* (*Law*), 24 May 2005.

84 On the new career of the retired Lord Chief Justice of England and Wales, Lord Woolf, as a mediator, see Frances Gibb, 'Lord Woolf courts new clients in a third career', *The Times*, 4 October 2005.

85 As pointed out eloquently by Joshua Rozenberg, in 'A short step to vigilantism', *Daily Telegraph*, 1 September 2005.

86 Lewis Smith, Andrew Norfolk and Dominic Kennedy give an account of the case in 'The doomed miners – and flying solicitors', *The Times*, 29 June 2005. See also Andrew Norfolk's article in *The Times*, 11 November 2005, about the NUM and the sick miners, for an account of a related case in which the Yorkshire-based firm of solicitors, Raleys, advised the miners involved to allow the union to fund their legal claims, handled by Raleys, in return for paying part of their eventual compensation to the union. But under the Coal Health Scheme it is the government, and not the union, which pays the legal bills for successful claims and ultimately the NUM did not have to pay legal costs in any of the 28,000 cases handled by Raleys. Costs for the scheme, originally estimated at £1 billion, have now risen to an estimated £8 billion and solicitors' fees to date amount to £665 million. Raleys have been paid £53 million of public money for their legal work on the cases which have been settled. The Law Society announced (6 July 2005) that it would investigate more than thirty firms of solicitors who have pursued claims for compensation under the Coal Health Scheme.

87 Edmund Burke (1729–97). Irish author and Whig politician who, in his *Reflections on the Revolution in France* (1790), launched a polemical attack on the events of 1789 in Paris and romanticized the European order displaced by those events. For an example of his fundamentally aesthetic view of the world see *A Philosophical Enquiry into the Origin of Our Ideas of the Sublime and Beautiful* (1757).

88 Private interview.

89 For these firms' figures on revenue and salaries, see Bob Sherwood, 'Lawyers

earning £1m on the increase', *Financial Times*, 15 June 2005.

90 Clare Dyer, 'Lawyers threaten strike over low pay', *Guardian*, 6 June 2005. See also Frances Gibb, 'Rich QCs should be made to share, says Lord Falconer, *The Times*, 21 July 2005.

91 Joshua Rozenberg, interview with Murray Rosen, QC, 'Calling time at the Bar', *Daily Telegraph*, 16 June 2005.

92 Harry Woolf (1933–)(Lord Woolf of Barnes, 1992). Judge of the High Court of Justice, QBD 1979–85; Lord Justice of Appeal, 1986–92; Lord of Appeal in Ordinary, 1992–6; Master of the Rolls, 1996–2000; Lord Chief Justice, 2000–5 (retired).

93 Quoted in Joshua Rozenberg, 'A reform to rival Magna Carta', *Daily Telegraph*, 22 September 2005.

94 Judges on this course also had to undergo a personality test in order to assess their suitability as managers. Lord Phillips of Worth Matravers, Master of the Rolls, was moved to remark afterwards: 'It's very exciting. Everyone is very enthusiastic.' See 'Lawdiary', *The Times (Law)*, 8 March 2005.

95 See, in this instance, the judges' campaign to protect their pensions in the light of the Inland Revenue's enforcement of the new ruling (from April 2006) which imposes a life-time limit of £1.5 million on the tax relief allowed on pension benefits, after which a tax of 25 per cent on top of income tax will be imposed. The 107 High Court judges (on £155,404 a year) and the 37 Court of Appeal judges (on £175,671 a year) will have built up in the majority of cases substantial personal pension funds during their preceding, high-earning, years at the Bar. Since judges' pensions are governed by the provisions of statute law they are unable to opt out of the new tax requirements. The Judicial Pensions Bill proposed by the government will, however, exempt them from these controls and therefore maintain their effective extra-territorial status beyond the legal provisions which apply to their fellow citizens in questions of taxation. See Frances Gibb, 'Judges threaten to resign over pensions losses', *The Times*, 6 October 2005.

96 For these figures, produced by the Sutton Trust, see Frances Gibb, 'Elite education still rules the law', *The Times*, 24 May 2005. The independent Commission for Judicial Appointments has noted how, in the process of appointment of recorders in the Midland Circuit in 2004–5, 'male, Oxbridge educated barristers fared disproportionately well' and that candidates known to the senior judiciary seemed 'to be at an advantage' while some senior judges had 'attempted to overturn some of the interview panels' conclusions'. See *The Times*, 20 October 2005.

97 Quoted by David Pannick, QC, 'Britain is losing its dignity with this Whitehall farce', *The Times (Law)*, 8 March 2005.

98 David Mellor (1949–) MP (Con.) Putney 1979–97 Chief Secretary to the Treasury 1990–2; Secretary of State for National Heritage 1992 (resigned).

99 Private interview.

100 Peter Goldsmith (1950–) (Lord Goldsmith of Allerton 1999) Attorney General 2001–.

101 For an account of the implications of Lord Goldsmith's visit to Washington in February 2003 where 'senior US officials and lawyers in the run-up to the Iraq war . . . sought to persuade him that the conflict would be legal even without a second United Nations resolution', see Guy Dinmore and Christopher Adams, 'Goldsmith "persuaded" by US over Iraq', *Financial Times*, 21 March 2005. Philippe Sands, *Lawless World: America and the Making and Breaking of Global Rules* (London: Allen Lane, 2005) provides an account of the legal advice used in order to justify the US and UK military intervention in

Iraq.

102 A random sample of 1,006 adults aged 18+ interviewed by telephone between 12 and 14 August 2005. See Tania Branigan, 'Britons would trade civil liberties for security', *Guardian*, 22 August 2005.

103 Michael Howard (1941–) MP (Con.) Folkestone and Hythe 1983–; Secretary of State for Employment 1990–2; Secretary of State for the Environment 1992–3; Home Secretary 1993–7; Conservative Party leader 2003–5.

104 For Lord Bingham's remarks, see Clare Dyer, 'Law lord hits back at politicians after attacks on judges', *Guardian*, 15 September 2005.

105 For the uneasy coexistence of the English rose and the British bulldog within the national self-understanding and the long history of elite fascination with the idea of an imminent social breakdown, see Geoffrey Pearson, *Hooligan: A History of Respectable Fears* (London: Macmillan, 1983). For a more recent example of the same governing class nerviness within No. 10 see Philip Webster and Frances Gibb, 'Blair takes on the judges to dispense more swift justice', *The Times*, 12 October 2005: 'Signalling a big expansion of what he called summary justice through on-the-spot fines and anti-social behaviour orders, he [the Prime Minister] said "You cannot do it by the rules of the game that we have at the moment. You just can't." Referring to the anti-social behaviour of youths Mr Blair claimed that: "Half of them end up getting off at the end of it".'

106 See Paul Peppis, *Literature. Politics and the English Avant-Garde: Nation and Empire, 1901–1918* (Cambridge: Cambridge University Press, 2000). For an example of the combination of a militaristic ideology with a neo-classical aesthetic in the life and work of a representative figure, see T.E. Hulme (1883–1917), *Speculations: Essays on Humanism and the Philosophy of Art*, ed. Herbert Read (London: Kegan Paul, 1936).

107 A stimulating deconstruction of the sickness of this bourgeois view of crime and criminals is supplied in the novels of Jake Arnott. See *True Crime* (London: Sceptre, 1999), *He Kills Coppers* (London: Sceptre, 2001) and *The Long Firm* (London: Sceptre, 1999).

108 Robert (Bob) Boothby (1900–86) (Lord Boothby of Buchan and Rattray Head 1958) MP (Con.) for East Aberdeenshire (1924–58). Following the publication of a story in the *Sunday Mirror* in 1964 with photographs, concerning his friendship with Ronald Kray, he said he had met him three times to discuss 'business proposals'.

109 Thomas Edward Neil (Tom) Driberg (1995) (1905–76) (Baron Bradwell 1975) MP (Independent) Maldon (1942–5). (Lab.) Barking (1959–74). Journalist and politician on the left of the Labour Party. His candid autobiography, *Ruling Passions*, published posthumously (London: Jonathan Cape, 1977) documents his playful eroticism.

110 For these penal statistics, see Jonathan Aitken, 'What I now know about our prisons', *Guardian*, 21 June 2005. See also Jonathan Aitken, *Porridge and Passion* (London: Continuum, 2005).

111 The police force, like any power elite grouping, has been assiduous at manipulating the system of pay. See Ed Harris, 'Sir Ian's fury at sick police on full wages', *Evening Standard*, 30 September 2005, for a report on the approximately 2,000 officers of the Metropolitan Police (7 per cent of the total strength of 30,604 officers) who were receiving full pay in 2005 while working on 'restricted duties' following long-term illness or depression. 1.2 million sick days are taken each year by the police forces of England and Wales, 247,000 of which are taken in London. Each police officer takes on average 9.3 sick days off per year.

112 For details of the most recent exercise in 'rationalization', involving on this

occasion mergers between the different police forces, see 'Big is beautiful', *Economist*, 24 September 2005. A conventional justification for these large units is, naturally enough, their supposed increased effectiveness in waging war on terror.

113 For a sardonic account of this incident, Mark Steyn, 'Thames Valley Police Living in Neverland', *Daily Telegraph*, 14 June 2005.

114 Described in Max Hastings, 'The police can't be exempted from disciplines we all face', *Guardian*, 10 September 2005.

115 Sir Ian Blair (1953–). Deputy to the Chief Constable, Thames Valley Police 1997; Chief Constable, Surrey Police 1998; Deputy Commissioner, Metropolitan Police 2000–5; Commissioner, Metropolitan Police 2005–.

116 BBC interview, quoted by Rod Liddle, 'Slippery of the Yard', *Sunday Times*, 25 September 2005.

117 For this remark and the quotations that follow, see Sir Ian's interview with Vikram Dodd, 'The top policeman branded too PC rides storm of criticism', *Guardian*, 2 July 2005.

118 Reported in *Private Eye*, 2–15 September 2005.

119 See Alan Macfarlane, *Witchcraft in Tudor and Stuart England: A Regional and Comparative Study* (London: Routledge & Kegan Paul, 1970). Keith Thomas, *Religion and the Decline of Magic: Studies in Popular Beliefs in Sixteenth and Seventeenth Century England* (London: Weidenfeld & Nicolson, 1971) remains the pioneering study of the subject.

## Chapter 4 The Financial and Business Elites: Dividing the Spoils

1 For an account of a recent such ceremony, see *The Times*, 21 March 2005, p. 13. On the theme of England as 'Druid country', see Neal Ascherson, *Games with Shadows* (London: Radius, 1988), pp. 90–3.

2 S. Yassukovich, Letters page, *Spectator*, 12 March 2005.

3 *International Financial Markets in the UK*, International Financial Services, www.ifsl.org.uk. 1,094,000 people were employed in UK financial services in September 2004, up 4,000 from 2003.

The UK (with $353 billion) was exceeded only by the USA as an exporter of commercial invisibles (trade in services and income) in 2003. Net exports of the UK financial sector were £19.03 billion in 2004, 9 per cent up on the £17.48 billion recorded in 2003. The insurance industry was the largest single contributor, with net exports totalling £6.4 billion.

For the City of London, see http://www.cityoflondon.gov.uk/Corporation/media_centre/keyfacts.htm. The City records an average of $753 billion foreign exchange turnover each day (31 per cent of the global share). It has 44 per cent of the global foreign equity market and 70 per cent of all eurobonds are traded in London. It is also the world's leading market for international insurance and UK worldwide premium income reached £153 billion in 2003.

£2,713 billion total assets were under management in the UK in 2003 and 20 per cent of international bank lending was arranged in the UK. £1,406 billion pension fund assets were under management, making this the third largest centre in the world for such activity. (In 2003, there were 287 foreign banks in London and 351 foreign companies were listed on the London Stock Exchange.)

4 For the connections between the most powerful figures in British business, see *The Power 100*, *The Times*, 8 November 2005 (www.timesonline.co.uk/power100).

5 The classic history of the institution is in J.H. Clapman, *The Bank of England: A History*, 2 vols. (Cambridge: Cambridge University Press, 1944). It is now supplemented by David Kynaston, *The City of London*, vol. 1: *A World of its Own, 1815–90*; vol. 2: *Golden Years, 1890–1914* (London: Chatto & Windus, 1994, 1996).

   On the architectural achievement of Sir John Soane (1753–1837), see David Watkin, *Sir John Soane: Enlightenment Thought and The Royal Academy Lectures* (Cambridge: Cambridge University Press, 1996).

6 For an account of the subterranean river Fleet which forms a natural boundary between the City and Westminster and which was bricked over from Fleet Street to the Thames in 1765, see Peter Ackroyd, *London: The Biography* (London: Chatto & Windus, 2000) pp. 555–8.

7 Average gross weekly earnings for full-time employees in Great Britain in 2000 were highest in a central band of England running roughly from Warwickshire in the South Midlands to Hampshire and West Sussex. Within this geographic band gross earnings in the City of London were the highest at £765 per week, followed by Bracknell Forest Unitary Authority at £559 per week. *Source*: 'Average gross weekly earnings: by area, April 2000', *Social Trends*, 31, www.statistics.gov.uk.

8 On the increased popularity of cosmetic surgery, and especially liposuction, among male City workers see *The Times*, 7 November 2005. The number of procedures carried out on men by members of the British Association of Aesthetic Plastic Surgeons rose by 64 per cent between 2003 and 2004, from 822 to 1,348.

9 Julie Bindel, 'The high price of robbing the rich', *Guardian Weekend*, 17 September 2005.

10 Hugh Brogan, *The Penguin History of the United States of America* (London: Penguin, 1983), pp. 386–417.

11 Theodore Zeldin, *France 1848–1945*, vol. 1, *Ambition, Love and Politics* (Oxford: Oxford University Press, 1973), pp. 53–62, describes the consequential growth in financial speculation.

12 Marjolein't Hart, 'The United Provinces 1579–1806', in Richard Bonney (ed.), *The Rise of the Fiscal State in Europe, 1200–1815* (Oxford: Oxford University Press, 1999) pp. 309–25, analyses the Dutch fiscal achievement. Geoffrey Parker, *The Army of Flanders and the Spanish Road 1567–1659* (Cambridge: Cambridge University Press, 1972), pp. 127–38 ('The Army of Flanders and Logistics') and pp. 127–38 ('Financial Resources') demonstrates the gravity of the Spanish military and financial difficulties especially since, 'Without constant financial support, the expensive army mobilized to repress the rebellion was liable to fall into revolt itself', p. 138.

13 Gary Duncan, 'Hurricane pushes UK trade deficit to record', *The Times*, 12 October 2005.

14 François Mitterrand (1916–96). Minister of Justice 1956–7; Leader of the French Socialist Party 1971–81; First Socialist President of the Fifth Republic, France 1981–95.

15 Silvio Berlusconi (1936–). Prime Minister of Italy 2001–. Founder of a major Italian conglomerate, controlling some 45 per cent of television output and with interests in advertising, publishing and cinema. Also owns AC Milan football club. Elected Prime Minister as leader of the centre-right coalition, Casa della Libertà (House of Freedom).

16 Robert Maxwell (1923–91) MP (Lab.) Buckingham 1964–70; acquired British Printing Corporation 1981, renamed Maxwell Communications Corporation; acquired Mirror Group Newspapers 1984; falls overboard in mysterious circumstances from his luxury yacht, 5 November 1991; revelation of his

personal plundering of the assets of the Mirror Group Pension Fund follows death.

17 Sir Michael Richardson (1925–2003). Partner, Cazenove and Co. 1970–80; Managing Director,1981–90, Vice-Chairman 1990–5, N.M. Rothschild and Sons Ltd.; Chairman, Smith New Court plc 1990–5.

18 Personal information.

19 J.H. Plumb, *The Commercialisation of Leisure in Eighteenth-Century England* (Reading: University of Reading Press, 1973) describes the origins of sport as a business.

20 Niall Ferguson, *The Cash Nexus: Money and Power in the Modern World, 1700–2000* (London: Allen Lane, 2001), pp. 116–17, 158–61.

21 J.R. Jones, *The Revolution of 1688 in England* (London: Weidenfeld & Nicolson, 1972) pp. 288–310. Jonathan I. Israel (ed.), *The Anglo-Dutch Moment: Essays on the Glorious Revolution and its World Impact* (Cambridge: Cambridge University Press, 1991), supplies a synoptic survey.

22 Ferguson, *The Cash Nexus*, p. 113 and Fernard Braudel, *Civilization and Capitalism*, vol. 2, *The Wheels of Commerce* (London: Collins, 1982). English translation of *Les Jeux d'Échange* (Paris: Librairie Armand Colin, 1979) pp. 390–5.

23 William Cobbett, *Rural Rides* (London: Oxford University Press, 1830) p. 53 (quoted in Ferguson, *The Cash Nexus*, p. 200). The best account of William Cobbett (1768–1835) and his brand of reactionary rural radicalism is to be found in Richard Ingrams, *The Life and Adventures of William Cobbett* (London: Harper Collins, 2005).

24 Sir Lewis Namier, *The Structure of Politics at the Accession of George III* (London: Macmillan, 1957), pp 1–61 discusses 'Why men went into parliament'. See also John Brewer, *The Sinews of Power: War, Money and the English State, 1688–1783* (London: Random House, 1989).

25 J. K. Galbraith, *The Great Crash: 1929* (London: Hamish Hamilton, 1972) illustrates the role of speculation in one economic collapse.

26 Rebecca Knight, 'Regulator admits snags in consumer controls', *Financial Times*, 31 May 2005.

27 Patience Wheatcroft, 'FSA in need of more scalps', *The Times (Business)*, 8 October 2005.

28 Neil Hume, 'PM's attack angers City watchdog', *Guardian*, 6 June 2005; Patience Wheatcroft, 'Business editor's commentary', *The Times (Business)*, 7 June 2005.

29 Bob Sherwood, 'Long arm of the US regulator', *Financial Times*, 10 March 2005.

30 See Nick Kochan and Bob Whittington, *Bankrupt! The BCCI Fraud*, (London: Gollancz, 1991) and Peter Truell and Larry Gurwin, *False Profits: The Inside Story of the World's Most Corrupt Financial Empire* (Boston: Houghton Mifflin, 1992). For the collapse of the BCCI case see Rory Cellan Jones, 'The End of an Epic', *http://news.bbc.co.uk/1/hi/business/4401210.stm* and Guardian Unlimited's timeline of the BCCI case, *http://www.guardian.co.uk/bcci/story/0,14169,1607458,00.html*.

31 For a measured statement of the case, see Samuel Brittan, *Capitalism with a Human Face* (Aldershot: Edward Elgar, 1995). For a more excitable interpretation of the democratic consequences of liberal capitalism, see Francis Fukuyama, *The End of History and the Last Man* (London: Hamish Hamilton, 1992), esp. pp. 39–51: 'there is a fundamental process at work that dictates a common evolutionary pattern for *all* human societies – in short, something like a Universal History of mankind in the direction of liberal democracy' (p. 48).

32  The Institute for Economic Affairs (IEA) is an independent body funded by donations from individuals and various organizations. See *www.iea.org.uk*.

33  Rt Hon. Peter Walker (1932–) (Lord Walker of Worcester) 1992. Secretary of State for Energy, 1983–7; Secretary of State for Wales, 1987–90.

34  Christopher Robin Haskins (1937) (Baron Haskins of Skidby 1998). Chairman of Northern Foods 1986–2002; Chairman Better Regulation Task Force 1997–2003; Member, New Deal Task Force 1997–2001.

35  David Alec Gwyn Simon (1939–) (Baron Simon of Highbury 1997). Chairman of BP 1995–7; Director Bank of England 1995–7; Minister of State Treasury and Department of Trade and Industry 1997–9.

36  Geoffrey Robinson (1938–) MP (Lab.) Coventry North West (1976–). Chief Executive Jaguar Cars 1973–5. Chairman TransTec plc 1986–97. Paymaster-General 1997–8.

37  For some characteristic examples of the fruits of office see the post-cabinet careers of the following: Rt. Hon. David Young (1932–) (Lord Young of Graffham 1984) Secretary of State for Employment 1985–7, for Trade and Industry 1987–9; Chairman, Cable and Wireless 1990–5; Director, Saloman Inc. 1990–4. Rt Hon. John Wakeham (1932–) (Lord Wakeham of Maldon). Secretary of State for Energy 1989–92; Leader of the House of Lords, 1992–4; Chair Press Complaints Commission 1995–2001, Royal Commission on Lords Reform, 1999; and Lord Walker of Worcester, Non-Executive Director, British Gas, 1990–6.

38  Personal information.

39  Alexa Baracaia, 'Drinks are on me . . . all £36,000-worth of them', *Evening Standard*, 30 September 2005.

40  Personal information.

41  For the following salaries, see Natasha Courtenay-Smith, 'What Britain earns', *Independent*, 5 October 2005.

42  Ross Lydall and Keith Dovkants, 'The growing cost of Ken's secret army', *Evening Standard*, 30 September 2005.

43  Robert Peston, 'Crozier's fat cheque should have been in the mail', *Sunday Telegraph*, 22 May 2005.

44  Ben Webster, 'Trains still late but "fat controllers" get bonus of up to £250,000', *The Times*, 13 May 2005. Andrew Clark, 'Network Rail off regulatory track with board bonuses', *Guardian*, 13 May 2005, p. 19. Paul Cheston, '£13m fine for rail disaster', *Evening Standard*, 7 October 2005.

45  *Private Eye*, Issue 1133, 27 May–9 June 2005.

46  Clive Hollick (1945–) (Lord Hollick of Notting Hill 1991). Director, Logica plc 1987–91; Chairman, Meridian Broadcasting Ltd. 1992–6; Chief Executive, United News and Media plc (now United Business Media) 1996–2005.

47  Jane Martinson, 'Hollick refuses to hand back £250,000 despite investor vote', *Guardian*, 13 May 2005, Patience Wheatcroft, 'Little reason to hand over a bonus', *The Times (Business)*.

48  Alan Cane, 'Why progress requires ambition and risk', *Financial Times*, 11 March 2005.

49  Richard Wray, 'Marconi dealt fatal blow as BT shuts it out of 21st century' *Guardian*, 29 April 2005.

50  Frank Portnoy, 'A serious question for all the overpaid bankers', *Financial Times*, 4 August 2005.

51  The Hay Group, 'Home Truths: Pay and Property in the UK', *www.haygroup.-co.uk*.

52  Jill Sherman, 'South East rejects call for massive increase in new homes', *The Times*, 4 June 2005.

53 Quoted in Patience Wheatcroft, 'Agencies need greater focus', *The Times (Business)*, 11 August 2005.

54 Patience Wheatcroft, *The Times (Business)*, 8 October 2005, 'Sir Digby's warning that the West has only five years of competitive edge left to master the Chinese challenge is as chilling as it is timely'. See also, conventionally, Adair Turner, *Just Capital: The Liberal Economy* (London: Macmillan, 2001), 'If China catches up to half of US GDP per capita in the next fifty years it will by then be an economy three times larger than America's simply because its population will be six times bigger'.

55 Mure Dickie, 'China's merchant adventurers set off in search of global conquests', *Financial Times*, 16 March 2005, p. 8. Richard McGregor and Raphael Minder, 'China to lead exports by 2010, says OECD', *Financial Times*, 17 September 2005.

56 Nic Hopkins, 'Fund seeks gate to Indian riches', *The Times (Business)*, 16 May 2005, p. 43. Catherine Philp, 'Rising middle class drives consumer revolution', *The Times (Business)*, 16 May 2005, p. 43. (See also Ram Mahesh Sivanandan, '"Pray as you go" deal for Indian mobiles', *Financial Times*, 4 June 2005

57 On this theme, see Scott Sandage, *Born Losers: A History of Failure in America* (Cambridge, Mass: Harvard University Press, 2005).

58 Quoted in James Morone, 'Good for Nothing', *London Review of Books*, 27 (10), 19 May 2005.

59 Luke Johnson (1962–). Director, Pizza Express 1992–5, 1998–9; Chairman, Pizza Express 1996–8; Director, Abacus Recruitment 1995–9, New Media SPARK 1990–2001; Chairman, Signature Restaurants Ltd. 1997–.

60 Luke Johnson, 'Goons, clowns and the rise of China', *Sunday Telegraph*, 22 May 2005.

61 Alex Singleton, 'Mandelson and EU taking the clothes off our backs', *The Business*, 21 August 2005.

62 Ambrose Evans Pritchard, 'Britain could soon be Europe's sick man again' *Daily Telegraph*, 5 September 2005.

63 David Gow, 'Books lift profits for Bertelsmann' *Guardian*, 8 September 2005.

64 Leader, 'Börse shareholder democracy triumphs', *Financial Times*, 8 March 2005

65 Lucy Kellaway, 'Good managers make sure they devalue their employees', (review of El Kersten, *The Art of Demotivation: A Visionary Guide to Transforming your Company's Least Valuable Asset* (Detroit: Despair Inc., 2005)), *Financial Times*.

66 'The end of the affair', *Economist*, 24 September 2005.

67 Personal information.

68 John Kerr (1942–) (Lord Kerr of Kinlochard, 2004). Assistant Under Secretary of State, Foreign and Commonwealth Office (FCO) 1987–90; Ambassador and UK Permanent Representative to the European Union 1990–5; Ambassador to the USA 1995–9; Permanent Under Secretary of State and Head of Diplomatic Service FCO 1997–2002.

69 Richard Wilson (1942–) (Lord Wilson of Dinton 2002). Deputy Secretary, Cabinet Office 1987–90; Deputy Secretary, HM Treasury 1990–2; Permanent Secretary, Department of Environment 1992–4; Permanent Under Secretary of State, Home Office 1994–8; Secretary of the Cabinet and Head of the Home Civil Service 1998–2002; Master of Emmanuel College, Cambridge 2002–.

70 Terence Burns (1944–) (Lord Burns of Pitshanger, 1998). Chief Economic Adviser, HM Treasury and Head of Government Economic Service 1980–91; Permanent Secretary, HM Treasury 1991–8; Non-Executive Director, Legal and General Group 1999–2001; Chairman, Abbey National plc 2002–.

71 Sir Peter Middleton (1934–). Deputy Secretary 1980–3; Permanent Secretary, HM Treasury, 1983–91; Chairman, Barclays Bank 1991–2004 (retired).

72 Charles Powell (1941–) (Lord Powell of Bayswater, 2000). HM Diplomatic Service 1963–91; Private Secretary and Adviser on Foreign Affairs and Defence to the Prime Minister; Director, Jardine Matheson Holdings 1991–2000; Director, National Westminster Bank plc 1991–2000; Director, Moet-Hennessy-Louis Vuitton 1995–; Chairman, Schindler Holdings 2003–.

73 Ewen MacAskill and David Leigh, 'Blair's special envoy to Brunei on BAE payroll', *Guardian*, 8 October 2005.

74 Dame Pauline Neville-Jones (1939–). HM Diplomatic Service 1963–96; Chairman, Joint Intelligence Committee, Cabinet Office 1993–4; Political Director and Deputy Under Secretary of State, FCO 1994–6; Senior Adviser to High Rep. for Bosnia 1996; Managing Director and Head of Global Business Strategies, NatWest Markets, 1996–8.

75 Francis Wheen, 'Return of an odd Balkans couple', *Guardian*, 24 June 1998, p. 5.

76 See Cathy Newman, 'Birt quits McKinsey amid conflict of interest concerns', *Financial Times*, 13 July 2005 and Anthony Hilton, 'Politicians and the curse of the consultants', *Evening Standard*, 28 November 2005.

77 Sir Michael Barber (1955–). Professor of Education, University of Keele 1993–5; Head of Standards and Effectiveness Unit, Department of Education and Employment 1997–2001; Head of the Prime Minister's Delivery Unit and Chief Adviser to the Prime Minister on Delivery 2001–.

78 David Leigh and Rob Evans, 'DTI fires senior civil servant after claims of abusing public money', *Guardian*, 20 October 2005.

79 *Private Eye*, Issue 1133, 27 May–9 June 2005.

80 Andrew McIntosh (1933–) (Lord McIntosh of Haringey, 1982). Deputy Leader of the Opposition 1992–7; Deputy Government Chief Whip, House of Lords, 1997–2003; Captain of the Yeomen of the Guard 1997–2003; Minister for Media and Heritage 2003–.

81 Antony Barnett, 'The big casino bosses, the Vegas trips and the ministers', *Observer*, 7 August 2005.

82 *New Scientist*, 'Drug Giants in the firing line: 27 August 2005.

83 Frances Gibb, 'Drug chiefs face trial over £100m NHS fraud', *The Times*, 12 September 2005.

84 Steve Hawkes, 'Ambitious Aviva snaps up RAC for £1.1 bn', *Evening Standard*, 9 March 2005.

85 Tony Woodley (1948–). Deputy General Secretary Transport and General Workers' Union 2002–3; General Secretary, T&G, 2003–.

86 David Hencke, 'Big three plan superunion with 2.4 million members', *Guardian*, 15 September 2005, p. 14.

87 Richard Wray, 'Lastminute agrees £577m takeover', *Guardian*, 13 May 2005, p. 23.

88 Carlos Grande, 'Online successes prove to be hard-won', *Financial Times*, 8 March 2005.

89 Kevin Done and Matthew Garrahan, 'Revolution takes wing in leisure industry', *Financial Times*, 8 March 2005.

90 Mark Henderson, 'Top adviser quits "bleeding obvious" nuclear committee', *The Times*, 3 June 2005.

91 On the early history of the Royal Society see Michael Hunter, *Science and Society in Restoration England* (Cambridge: Cambridge University Press, 1981).

92 Robert Winston (1940–) (Lord Winston of Hammersmith 1995). Professor of

Fertility Studies, University of London at the Institute of Obstetrics and Gynaecology, Royal Postgraduate Medical School 1987–. Television series: *Making Babies*, BBC 1996–7; *The Human Body*, BBC 1998; *The Secret Life of Twins*, BBC 1999, etc. Director of Pirandello, *Each in His Own Way*, Edinburgh Festival 1969.

93  On Lord Winston's lacteal adventures with St Ivel, see Sarah-Kate Templeton, 'Winston's "clever milk" campaign under fire', *Sunday Times*, 6 November 2005.

94  For an example of such a ventilated concern see Sir Michael Quinlan (Permanent Under Secretary of State, Ministry of Defence, 1988–92), 'It is crucial to enhance deterrence', *Financial Times*, 16 March 2005.

95  F.H. Hinsley, *Power and the Pursuit of Peace: Theory and Practice in the History of Relations between States* (Cambridge: Cambridge University Press, 1963), pp. 139–49, 335–67. See also Philippe Sands, *Lawless World* (London: Allen Lane, 2005), pp. 1–22.

96  On the relationship between the corporation and the state, see Joel Bakan, *The Corporation: The Pathological Pursuit of Profit and Power* (London: Constable & Robinson, 2004), pp. 139–58.

97  Michael Portillo (1953–). MP (Con.) Enfield, Southgate 1984–97, Kensington and Chelsea 1999–2005. Chief Secretary, HM Treasury 1992–4; Secretary of State for Employment 1994–5; Secretary of State for Defence 1995–7.

98  Oliver Morgan, 'Lobby firm goes to war', *Observer*, 11 September 2005.

99  Christine Seib, 'Security provider has sights locked', *The Times (Business)*, 16 May 2005.

100  On the effects of the war, see Henry Kamen, *The Iron Century: Social Change in Europe 1550–1660* (London, Weidenfeld & Nicolson, 1971) pp. 42–4, 277–8, 223–6, 424–5. The career of the war's outstanding mercenary general, Albrecht von Wallenstein (1583–1634), Herzog (duke) von Friedland, Herzog von Mecklenburg, Fürst (prince) Von Sagen, is discussed in J.V. Polišenský, *The Thirty Years War*, translated by R. Evans (London: B. T. Batsford, 1971) pp. 116–18, 120–1, 137–9, 194–15, 210–13. See Polišenský pp. 254–65 ('The Peace and its Consequences') for the judgement that the European settlements arrived at in the Peace of Westphalia (1648), '. . . inaugurated an era when this [world] history becomes effectively a unitary one involving the whole continent of Europe and the overseas dependencies of the maritime powers' p. 257.

101  Ian Fleming, *Goldfinger* (London: Jonathan Cape, 1959) provides the best example of this theme.

102  Christine Buckley, 'QinetiQ makes £163m push into US', *The Times*, 3 August 2005, p. 45 and Terry Macalister, 'Labour has £1bn defence float in its sights', *Guardian*, 28 September 2005.

103  Rich Cookson and Rob Evans, '"Unsuitable" firm won huge MoD contract', *Guardian*, 22 August 2005.

104  On the punishing impact on Britain of the loan agreement arranged between it and the USA in 1940–1, see Robert Skidelsky, *John Maynard Keynes*, vol. 3, *Fighting for Britain 1940–41* (London: Macmillan, 2001) pp. 94, 99–107, 111–14, 121–5, 126–33, 180–1, 360–71, 378, 391, 401, 403, 408, 414, 427, 428, 429.

105  This account of the PFI follows the details described by the late Paul Foot in his masterly dissection of this story in a *Private Eye* Special Supplement. Issue 1135, 24 June 2005.

106  Gavyn Davies (1950–). Chief UK Economist 1986–93; Partner, Goldman Sachs, 1988–2001; Chairman, BBC Board of Governors, 2001–4.

107  Sir Nicholas Montagu (1944–). Deputy Secretary, Department of Social Security

1990–7 (seconded to Department of Transport 1992–7); Chairman, Board of Inland Revenue 1997–2004.

108 Quoted in Foot, *Private Eye*.

109 Sir Peter Gershon (1947–). Managing Director, Marconi Electronic Systems Ltd 1994–9; Chief Operating Officer, BAE Systems 1999–2000.

110 Matt Dickinson, 'Glazer gets his prize to leave United with burning issues', *The Times Sport*, 13 May 2005, and Richard Williams 'United's new order banks on business as usual', *Guardian Sport*, 14 May 2005.

111 Patrick Hosking, 'Cheerleader for market's dynamos', *The Times (Business)*, 18 May 2005.

112 Simon Jenkins, *The Selling of Mary Davies and Other Writings* (London: John Murray, 1993).

113 James Drummond, 'On the contrary, it's Notting Hill for Mayfair', *Financial Times*, 25 July 2005.

114 Personal information.

115 George Trefgarne, 'City's whiz-kids have a political agenda', *Daily Telegraph*, 26 September 2005. See the register of donations: www.electoralcommission.-gov.uk/regulatory-issues/regdpoliticalparties.cfm?ec%7Bts%20%272006%2D13%2012%3A47%3A47%27%7D

116 Gillian Tett, 'Who owns your loan? Why Europe's businesses will face surprises if trouble hits', *Financial Times*, 29 July 2005.

117 Jill Treanor, 'Marks and Spencer and BAA dump the Queen's broker', *Guardian*, 15 October 2005.


# Conclusion:  How Did They Get Away with It?

1 A remark which has been attributed, uncertainly, to Vladimir Ilyich Lenin (1870–1924).

2 Combining depth of learning and range of reference with a cheerful and appropriate cynicism, Maurice Cowling, *Religion and Public Doctrine*, vol. 3, *Accommodations* (Cambridge: Cambridge University Press, 2001) describes how the English intelligentsia has tried to interpret both England and English religion during the past two centuries.

3 John Lloyd, *What the Media are Doing to our Politics* (London: Constable & Robinson, 2004).

4 See, for example, Albert Sorel, *Europe and the French Revolution: The Political Traditions of the Old Regime* (London: Collins, 1969), especially pp. 352–8, 'Natural Frontiers' and pp. 358–63, 'The Tradition of Conquest', English translation of *L'Europe et la Révolution Française: Les Mœurs et les Traditions Politiques* (Paris: Librairies Plon, 1885), for a panoramic account of how the French military campaigns of the 1790s, though pursued under the banner of 1789 ideology, built on a centuries-old tradition which asserted the French state's right to a policy of conquest beyond the 'natural boundaries' of the old Gaul. Sovereignty might have passed from the king to the people but the strategic aims of the armée révolutionnaire were continuous with those of Louis XIV: 'The men who now ruled . . . transferred to the people all the ideas that their predecessors had applied to the majesty of the king. They aroused in the people a lust for glory, urged them into war, and founded on their passions the power they exercised in their name' p. 352.

5 Sir Otto Beit 1st Bart (1865–1930), brother of Alfred Beit (1853–1906) who was the close friend and business partner of Cecil Rhodes (1853–1902). Sir Alfred Beit 2nd Bart (1903–94) MP (Con.) St Pancras South East 1931–45.

6 As the English art critic Philip Hamerton pointed out: 'capital is the nurse and governess of the arts, not always a very wise or judicious nurse, but an exceedingly powerful one . . . But for capital to support the fine arts, it must be abundant – there must be superfluity. The senses will first be gratified to the full before the wants of the intellect awaken.' *Thoughts about Art* (London: Macmillan, 1873) p. 125 (quoted in an excellent survey of artistic acquisitiveness, Colin Platt, *Marks of Opulence: The Why, When and Where of Western Art 1000–1900 AD* (London: HarperCollins, 2004), p. xi.

7 The English word 'elite', like the French '*élite*', is derived as a past participle (in its Old French form, *élit*) of the French verb '*élire*' (meaning 'to elect', 'to choose'). Emile Littré, *Dictionnaire de la Langue Française*, tome 3 (Jean Jacques Pauvert ed., 1956), defines it as meaning that which has been '*élu*'/chosen. He also notes how 'élite', when used in French as a substantive noun or substantive adjective, is often combined with the metaphorical use of '*fleur*' since the two words both express 'the best that exists among many individuals or objects of the same kind: "the elite of the army"; "the flower of the army". But the words carry with them something of their original meaning' (translation mine). Behind the acquired meaning of the best, therefore, there lurks the older association with an elected choice, someone's 'will', or what has been chosen/'*élu*'. Littré's example from the *Chronicles* of Jean Froissart (1333–1400/1) 11,11.15 shows the beginning of the emergence of the rhetorical use of the word as 'the best' (as opposed to the literal sense of 'the chosen') when the Constable of Scotland is described as taking 'five hundred lancers from the elite of all the best in Scotland' '*cinq cents lances à l'élite de tous les meilleurs d'Éscosse*'.

The earliest example of the use of the word 'elite' noted in the *Oxford English Dictionary*'s definition is in Byron, *Don Juan* (1823), XIII, lxxx:

> With other Countesses of Blank – but rank;
> At once the 'lie' and the 'elite' of crowds.

By 1848, the use of the word in English was well established, as can be seen in W.H. Kelly, *The History of Ten Years, 1830–40*, 2 vols. (1848); vol. 1. p. 439, 'The elite of the Russian nobility' (English translation of Louis Blanc, *Histoire de Dix Ans, 1830–40*, 2 vols., 1844–5). I am grateful to Professor Richard Griffiths for his guidance on these references.

8 This episode is discussed with a typical acuteness in P.N. Furbank, *Unholy Pleasure or The Idea of Social Class* (Oxford: Oxford University Press, 1985), pp. 132–5.

9 Guy Maynard Liddell (1892–1958). See Nigel West (ed.), *The Guy Liddell Diaries Vol. 1 1939–42* (London: Frank Cass, 2005) pp. 304–5

10 On Dickens and humour, see John Carey, *The Violent Effigy: A Study of Dickens' Imagination* (London: Faber & Faber, 1973), pp. 54–9.

11 On Muggeridge and his satirical Christian anarchy, see Richard Ingrams, *Muggeridge: The Biography* (London: HarperCollins, 1995).

12 *Rudyard Kipling's Verse: Definitive Edition* (London: Hodder & Stoughton Ltd, 1940) p. 485.

# Select Bibliography

John Adamson (ed.), *The Princely Courts of Europe: Ritual, Politics and Culture Under the Ancien Régime 1500–1750* (London: Weidenfeld & Nicolson, 1999)

Noel Annan, *Our Age: Portrait of a Generation* (London: Weidenfeld & Nicolson, 1990).

Joel Bakan, *The Corporation: The Pathological Pursuit of Profit and Power* (London: Constable & Robinson, 2004).

Correlli Barnett, *The Audit of War: The Illusion and Reality of Britain as a Great Nation* (London: Macmillan, 1986).

Maurice Cowling, *Mill and Liberalism* (Cambridge: Cambridge University Press, 1963).

Niall Ferguson, *The Cash Nexus: Money and Power in the Modern World, 1700–2000* (London: Allen Lane, 2001).

John Gray, *False Dawn: The Delusions of Global Capitalism* (London: Granta Books, 1998).

Peter Hennessy, *Whitehall* (London: Fontana Press, 1990).

John Hoskyns, *Just in Time: Inside the Thatcher Revolution* (London: Aurum Press, 2000).

Nancy Mitford (ed.), *Noblesse Oblige: An Enquiry into the Identifiable Characteristics of the English Aristocracy* (London: Hamish Hamilton, 1956).

K.O. Morgan, *Labour in Power 1945–51* (Oxford: Clarendon Press, 1984).

Geoffrey Pearson, *Hooligan: A History of Respectable Fears* (London: Macmillan, 1983).

Colin Platt, *Marks of Opulence: The Why, When and Where of Western Art 1000–1900 AD* (London: HarperCollins, 2004).

Quentin Skinner, *The Foundations of Modern Political Thought* 2 vols. (Cambridge: Cambridge University Press, 1978).

George Walden, *The New Elites: Making a Career in the Masses* (London: Allen Lane, 2000).

Alan Watkins, *The Road to Number 10: From Bonar Law to Tony Blair* (London: Duckworth, 1998).

Martin Wiener, *English Culture and the Decline of the Industrial Spirit 1850–1980* (Cambridge: Cambridge University Press, 1982).

Charles Wright Mills, *The Power Elite* (New York: Oxford University Press, 1956).

# Index

# INDEX

working-class consciousness 70, 78, 85

Worldcom 175

Wright, Braxton Bragg xii

Wright, Peter 102

Yeo, Tim 82, 239 n123

*Yes Minister* 48